SPEAKING OUT

SPEAKING OUT

*Therapists
and Patients—
How They Cure
and Cope with
Mental Illness
Today*

**by Barbara Field
Benziger**

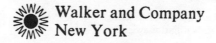 Walker and Company
New York

**Dedicated to all those
who suffer mental torment**

ACKNOWLEDGMENTS

I wish to thank Kay Kidde, editor, for her invaluable help, friendship, and support in the early stages of the book, involving countless interviews, and learning to ask more and better questions.

It is hard to find words to thank Kathy Dobkin, editor. She has worked on this book with me with endless enthusiasm, encouragement, and just plain hard work.

For my final editor at Walker, Patricia Aks, I have boundless admiration and gratitude.

I wish to thank the doctors, other professionals, and patients whose interest and cooperation made this book possible.

I thank my psychiatrist, Dr. Herbert Walker, for his guidance.

For my husband's, children's, and mother's constant caring and understanding, I am deeply grateful.

I thank Walker and Company for their perpetual faith in me, and their understanding affection.

CONTENTS

FOREWORD

In 1969 I read a fine book on the trials and experiences and recovery of a remarkable woman. She is Barbara Field Benziger who once had a considerable experience, good and poor, with psychiatrists, and with well-run and poorly run hospitals. She told vividly of the awful shock of finding herself locked up in a room with absolutely no right to telephone or write an uncensored letter to her husband. She told also of the shock of getting a psychiatrist whom she disliked instantly and who hence could not possibly help her. She later met a kind, sympathetic, and able psychiatrist who greatly helped her.

Mrs. Benziger's second book covers a wide area of what happens to many people who for a while are mentally disturbed. I am an admirer of people who have been seriously ill and are willing to tell their experiences firsthand, and I am so well aware of their value to medical students, that in the last several years I have collected some 800 books telling the experiences of people who have been hospitalized. This book is one more outstanding contribution to the area of psychiatric literature. The book can be invaluable also in teaching the relatives of an ill or recently recovered person how they can help lead him or her back to good health.

Walter C. Alvarez, M.D.

INTRODUCTION

This book grew out of my realization that some people who have received psychiatric treatment—whether within a hospital or as an outpatient—have experienced relapses, or returned to the emotional state that led them to seek help in the first place. When I wrote *The Prison of My Mind* (New York: Walker and Co., 1969), an account of my emotional illness, I had recently emerged from a year of hospital treatment and I felt fine—almost euphoric. It appeared that the seemingly endless depression, the fear, the panic that had culminated in my hospitalization were banished forever. But those same feelings returned, and again I needed therapy. Again I was faced with the search for an appropriate psychotherapy and a doctor with whom I could develop a good relationship. (My doctor, who had done so much to help me recover the first time, had died.)

It took months to find the right doctor, and in that time I learned how complex and varying the field of psychiatry is.

In such a fast-paced, impersonal age as ours countless people find themselves faced with emotional troubles. Many people attempt to find personal solutions through therapies that do not suffice; others have been hospitalized and don't know where to go next or, like myself, are thrown into panic when they feel the beginnings of the seemingly impossible—a relapse. But there are numerous competent facilities, therapeutic modes, and doctors in this country; the problem for most people is to find them.

Today a great number of books are available about psychiatric theories, but a theory is only as good as the person who practices it. When it gets down to fundamentals, two people can tell you the most about any kind of psychotherapy: the psychotherapist who practices it and the person who has been treated by that therapy. These are the people who have contributed to this book.

I have tried to cover the different aspects of psychiatry as it is practiced today, from the hospital experience and aftercare through the various outpatient psychotherapies, and the legal picture of contemporary mental health. In compiling material for this book, I interviewed staff members of public and private institutions such as the Menninger Clinic, heads of hospitals, private psychotherapists, and therapists involved in some newer concepts in psychiatry and psychology.

The first chapters in each section are adaptations of my discussions with professionals in the field and address such specific points as the length and conditions of a treatment, and the type of patients a doctor (or facility) treats. (The interviews with the doctors and professionals were transcribed from tapes and edited in narrative form with their approval.) A number of the doctors and facilities covered in the book are from the New York area, but they treat people from all over the world and are representative of the current trends in the field.

Learning how people are helped by one or another facility or therapy can finally come only from the people themselves. The second part of each section consists of my (indicated by my initials B.B.) interviews with patients and former patients, who have contributed their feelings and experiences with different therapies and facilities. These are courageous, candid accounts, and each person's story does much in the way of dispelling the myths surrounding mental illness. The names of these patients have been changed to protect their identity.

It would be terribly presumptuous of me to claim that this book covers every approach to psychotherapy and every psychiatric facility in use today; that is a much larger task than can be contained in one volume. However, I believe that the treatments discussed here are the most representative of current psychotherapies in extensive use.

I have included a special section covering the legal aspects of mental health—the rights of patients, for instance, issues for too long ignored but which are recently gaining much needed attention.

In the course of working on the present book, I have had the rare opportunity as a layperson to learn a great deal about the field of mental health. One truth I discovered is that in public hospitals as well as in some private ones, the patient has little or no choice in selecting his or her doctor. Therefore, the results of one's hospitalization can contain a certain amount of luck. In some of the overcrowded public hospitals, a patient may see a doctor once a month—or *much* less—if he or she is lucky. In reality it is only people of some financial means who can afford a psychiatrist or psychotherapist of their choice—a doctor who can treat them on an outpatient basis or in a hospital of one's own choosing. In this I have been blessed.

My personal experience as a former patient and my talks with doctors and other former patients have made it quite clear that there is a social stigma attached to emotional illness that labels a person, sometimes for life. Education is changing much of that, yet it persists even in this most liberal of times. I have felt for a long time that the negative attitude of society toward people who are suffering or who have suffered from emotional problems has acted as a deterrent to people who want help, who need help, but who are afraid to actively seek it for fear of being labeled and stigmatized. The problems inherent to finding the appropriate type of psychotherapy are only aggravated by this fear. The situation is changing, thanks in great part to concerned individuals such as the people who have contributed to this book; but much remains to be done toward establishing an enlightened social attitude about emotional illness.

I have learned, during the process of my own treatment, that my depressions are caused partly from a biochemical imbalance, partly from heredity, and partly from early environmental factors. I need both drugs and psychotherapy at times. Some people's depressions may be caused by just one of these factors, or perhaps two. Recent research in psychiatry and biochemistry has supported earlier theories that such disturbances as schizophrenia, chronic depression, and the manic-depressive disturbance have a genetic basis; that is, some people have a particular "programming" in their genes that results in a chemical imbalance in their bodies, which leads to apparent emotional disturbances. I believe also that a bad environment can certainly aggravate the problem of mental illness.

Medication is available for most biochemical disturbances, and just as a diabetic must take insulin to stay at a "normal" level, so must a manic-depressive take Lithium to balance his biochemistry. Part of finding an appropriate therapy, then, is finding a doctor who is aware of the most recent advances in psychiatric medicine and is thereby able to make a correct diagnosis. Since I have learned that one of the causes of my emotional problems is organic, I have been helped considerably in my own struggle; I hope that others will be able to benefit as I have—and as many of the people in this book have—from the modern developments in medical psychiatry.

My sincerest hope is that this book will help people from all walks of life to gain insight and understanding toward improving their personal lives; and I hope that it will aid families and friends of emotionally distressed people to understand more fully that help is available from competent, dedicated individuals. Please note that a glossary has been provided, to explain the technical terms that appear in the following discussions.

Finally, I want to thank the many doctors and professional workers in the field of psychiatry who have not only contributed to this book, but who have helped in my own and other people's search for personal well-being.

PART ONE

The Hospital
Experience

WHEN A PERSON enters a psychiatric hospital—whether voluntarily or involuntarily—he or she is in the midst of one of the most terrifying times of a person's life. He is no longer the same as the person looking for "ten easy ways to enjoy a better life"; or the person who wants to expand his horizons. The feeling is much more like being at the end of the road. Helpless. Afraid. His horizons have become so bleak or so unacceptable that for a time, anyway, it seems better to limit them to a hospital boundary then to continue life "outside."

Only a person who has been hospitalized and released can convey the real feelings of what it was like to need hospitalization and can teach another person that the hospital is not, after all, the end of the road. In a well-staffed psychiatric hospital, where the purpose of hospitalization has not been overshadowed by ineptitude and political obstacles, the chances for recovery are good. The battle is not over—it has just begun.

Numerous advances have been made in the mental health field since the first "mental hospital" was built in the early nineteenth century in this country. There are more humane facilities, advanced medications, individual psychotherapies. But I do not deny for a moment that too many of this country's institutions, which are passing off as "mental hospitals," are unfit for human beings, or that in some state hospitals a sane person could be driven mad. This is a monumental problem in our society, which is only now gaining the recognition necessary for substantive change; it is a breach of humanity and law and must be attacked both from within the field of mental health and through legal channels. (Part Seven of this book covers the legal aspects of mental health.) A thorough treatment of the situation at what I call "bad" hospitals is the subject of another book, and I have not included such hospitals in this section. For the purposes of this discussion, let's look at reports from hospitals where good things are happening.

The following four hospitals are exemplary of public and private institutions where the staff's dedication is evident and the patients' struggle for recovery are the goals. Fees cover a wide range, of course, depending upon whether the hospital is public or private.

CHAPTER ONE

The Public Closed Hospital:
A New Jersey County Hospital
Martha Allbriton

Martha Allbriton is the pseudonym for a psychiatric charge technician working on the staff of one of New Jersey's public county psychiatric hospitals, a locked facility. She attended college for two years before taking the civil service position in the hospital. Presently, she is also completing her degree in psychology and sociology.

It was primarily her personal interest in psychiatry and people that led Mrs. Allbriton into the field of mental health. Her own concern for the well-being of patients in the hospital has resulted in changes within the hospital treatment program. She is an active member of the hospital's employees organization; the organization is recognized by the county and the state as an official employees' bargaining committee, and is not associated with an outside union. Because it is an independent organization, its members have been able to use it as an agent for bringing about changes within the hospital facility itself, as well as aiding their own positions. For example, the organization raises funds to purchase facilities for the patients when state and county funds are not available, and they are able to negotiate for improvements for patients.

Mrs. Allbriton herself has taken in released patients to her own home when aftercare facilities were not available to them.

Here, Mrs. Allbriton discusses her work in the hospital and her personal work with former patients.

Martha Allbriton, Psychiatric Charge Technician

In a county hospital, we see patients who reflect all aspects of life—patients from families with emotional illness, patients from the middle and lower classes, patients who have been and who never have been hospitalized previously. Generally, people are here because they have had poor life adjustments. They were unable to get along with their families, unable to hold jobs, unable to cope with financial problems. With younger people, the problem is generally an inability to get along with their peers; with older people, the cause of their breakdowns is often a change in their lifestyles, and with women, emotional problems caused by menopause.

Often, a personal crisis will precipitate an illness in someone's life, even though that person may have been functioning perfectly all right up to that time.

The patients with whom I work are all long-term patients. They have been here sixteen, twenty, or more years. The hospital has recently introduced a federally financed rehabilitation program for both long-term (chronically ill) and short-term patients, designed to speed up the patients' release. Roughly, this is intensive therapy every day, and it includes various activities. I believe the program is equipped to take about thirty-five people at a time. It is aimed, primarily, at patients who are most likely to make it—generally in the eighteen to thirty-five age range.

We have the same problem as most public hospitals—and that is a shortage of psychotherapists. Most of the time, a doctor is on the ward for perhaps fifteen minutes to an hour—and in my ward, of a hundred twenty-four patients, it's pretty obvious that each person gets very little time with the doctor.

However, the hospital has begun a training course for its employees; we're learning more therapeutic methods in relating to the patients, how to give a sort of one-to-one therapy, and how to gain insight into a patient's problems. The main thing is to allow the patient to feel comfortable talking to us, to develop trust among the patients, and among the patients and staff. Right now, I am in such a course, with about fifteen other staff members.

When I began the training course, I was assigned to a maximum security ward for men. At first, I was actually quite afraid to go there by myself. But after the first day or two, when the patients began to respond, I became more relaxed and began to see that the patients weren't dangerous; they weren't so bad, after all. I was on that ward for about four months. They were four very enlightening months, not only about the patients, but about my own attitudes and ways of relating to patients.

The course will take about two years, and hopefully, in that time, all the hospital workers will have taken it. With the hospital staff trained in patient-staff relationships and in basic therapeutic techniques, the patients stand a far better chance of recovering more quickly.

The hospital has a workshop where patients are able to learn a new trade. Sometimes, a person has to go into another vocation after he or she is released. In these cases, it is often because their job had something to do with their breakdown. For teen-age patients, the hospital has a regular school course, affiliated with one of the local high schools.

In some ways, working as a technician in the hospital is an uphill battle. As in any type of institution, change comes about much slower than the *need* for change. Things get bogged down in the bureaucratic operations, and the whole machine is slow to turn. There is one woman here in an administrative position, who is very understanding and aggressive. She acts as a sort of go-between for us when we have a problem.

She helped us, for instance, last year, when we wanted to give the patients a Christmas party—the hospital was going to forgo such a party that year. It was a fight, but we ended up with our party.

At present, the hospital offers primarily medication treatment. There is no shock treatment here, and no insulin therapy. Occupational therapy plays a large part in the treatment process.

Most of the wards in the county hospital are locked wards; but patients can earn a privilege card for doing certain chores and, in general, for good behavior. This card gives them the freedom of the hospital grounds. In addition, there are off-ground privileges; a patient may earn the right to go to some of the neighboring towns—to shop, to go to a movie, or to enjoy some other outside activity.

We have no locked *rooms* for patients anymore. Formerly, there were Maximum Security Wards, where a patient who became overactive was locked in a room until he or she calmed down. But they are no longer locked into rooms.

Perhaps one of the biggest problems for the patients is the release time. I've found that when a short-term patient is released, he or she is elated at the prospect of being outside again. The long-term patients, though, become quite apprehensive. They're afraid of what the outside is like. Remember, some of these people have been here fifteen or more years.

The return rate here is quite high. I can't speak for official figures, but I would estimate that it is well over half of the released patients. One of the most recurrent reasons for a person returning to the hospital is the seemingly general aversion of the ex-patient to taking his medication. There seems to be a stigma attached to continuing the medication they received in the hospital. They don't understand, or don't seem to, that a lot of people take medication—people who have, and people who haven't been in a hospital.

Also, many patients return because they simply can't cope with a changed world, with a new life. Their families do not understand their needs as a recently released patient. Any of these things can trigger a person's distress and bring him or her back to the hospital. And when a person returns, he returns with symptoms similar to the ones that resulted in his first hospital stay.

The staff members here at the hospital have no contact with a patient's family during the person's stay. There is contact between family and staff in the rehabilitation program, however.

On the whole, I'd say that the younger patients, especially the short-term patients, have a much lower return rate. They seem better able to gain insights into their problems.

There is such a thing as a chronic repeater. Sometimes a person's relapse involves some deterioration of his or her personality, and in such a case, the second stay will be longer than the first.

There are some people who, without any rehabilitation or aftercare, have left the hospital after long-term stays, and never returned. For instance, one woman I worked with had been here thirteen years; she was released completely on her own, and made it with a new job and a new life. I get a card from her every year on the holidays.

Patients who've been released are now able to take advantage of a monthly outpatient program through the hospital. Also, New Jersey has a halfway house, similar in ways to New York's Fountain House. It's called Prospect House, in East Orange, and it provides job training, placement, and other services.

The rehabilitation program will include much more follow-up. This sort of thing has been needed for a long time. The hospital also has a halfway house for people who need more support in reestablishing their lives.

Working in a mental hospital, I have developed relationships with patients that are perhaps closer than some doctor-patient relationships. I see these people every day, after all. And it's impossible to be around people without taking an interest in and having compassion for them. Often, we're the only people to whom patients can turn.

About four or five years ago, for instance, I took an ex-patient into my home. She didn't come directly from the hospital; she'd been out for about a year. One of the social workers from the county agency called me and wanted to know if I would take this woman in. She had heard that I'd been interested in doing this sort of thing, helping former patients to adjust to living outside.

At first, my husband was against the idea. We have children, and he was concerned that something might happen to affect the children. The upshot was that we did agree that Mary, as I will call her, come to live with us, and she stayed for a year.

Mary was a very likable person, but sometimes she would come downstairs, maybe fifty times a day, for coffee, and she'd become quite argumentative. She would try anything to upset me, and when she thought she'd succeeded, she'd seem content and go back upstairs. That was the main problem with her, and I tried to cope with it as best I could, to react in a human way.

We were all fond of Mary, despite her periods of argumentative coffee klatches. We'd known in advance that she was a very difficult person to live with. After a year, she decided to live on her own, but she only lasted a month.

We received a call from the social worker, asking us if we'd take her in again, but we already had another person living with us.

Mary did end up holding down a job. Fortunately, her employer was very understanding, and this got her through the first period on the job.

I've had a woman living with me for almost three years now—Ann, a former alcoholic. She was also very paranoid at one time. She had been a patient in the hospital and had a relapse while she was staying with us, about a year and a half ago. It was on a weekend. I had left the house around noon and didn't get back until about seven. I called her down for dinner, but she didn't answer, so I sent my son upstairs to see if she was asleep. He knocked on the door, but she didn't answer.

I went upstairs to see what the matter was, and found her in a deep sleep. It was obvious that she'd been drinking. We called Emergency at Memorial Hospital, and they pumped her stomach. She stayed in the hospital for about a week, and was doing quite well when the hospital brought in a psychiatrist. She started telling him about her past delusions—perhaps about her alcoholic delusions, too—and she ended up in the hospital again. I've always felt that if she hadn't talked about that, she wouldn't have been sent back—but then, I'm not the doctor.

She stayed in the hospital for about six weeks that time, and then when it came time for her release, she asked if she could come back to stay with me again. I said yes, if she didn't drink again. I told her that I had no control over what she did on the outside, but that she couldn't do any drinking in the house. She did return, got a job, and has been working a year and a half.

Ann's biggest problem was that she didn't want to take her medication. I mentioned this earlier as a problem with people who return to the hospital. Ann had that stigmatization about taking her medicine. So once I told her, "Just go into the bathroom and take it. No one has to know that you're taking it or why you're taking it."

The problem of stigma, a social stain on a person who's been hospitalized, continues. A short time ago Ann told me about an experience she'd had at work. Her employer got a letter from a patient in the halfway house that is attached to the hospital. The patient was applying for a job and had given the address of the halfway house. Ann overheard people in the office talking about it, wondering where this place was. One woman finally said, "Oh, that's the funny farm—you know."

No one in Ann's office, not even her employer, knows she has been a mental patient. I doubt that she would have been hired if they had known. This incident increased her own conviction of that. The employer threw the application from the patient away. And Ann said she felt relieved. If this person had come to work where she was, she felt that her "secret" would have been exposed. It's appalling that people have to live that way—half inside a closet.

Ann has had a great deal of insight into her problems; and insights and recovery can only come through other people's understanding and support. Former mental patients are human beings who've been through a bad time, and they cannot get better unless other people understand that first.

CHAPTER *TWO*

The Private Open Hospital:
New York University Hospital
George Ginsberg, M.D.

New York University Hospital's psychiatric wing is a part of the University Hospital, a voluntary, nonprofit hospital. It is a private institution and is qualified for both Medicaid and Medicare, as well as private insurance coverage. Ten West, as the psychiatric unit is known, has an average patient population of twenty-two, and is one of the most heavily staffed such units in the metropolitan New York area. Generally, a patient will see either his own doctor or a resident doctor every day; between the staff and the patient's private doctor each person's treatment program is worked out.

Dr. Ginsberg, the psychiatrist in charge of the psychiatric unit of NYU Hospital since 1968, received his medical training at Columbia University's College of Physicians and Surgeons and took his residency training in psychiatry at New York University-Bellevue Medical Center. He was also trained in psychoanalysis at the New York Psychiatric Institute. He has published numerous articles in professional journals, is Director of Graduate Education in Psychiatry at New York University Medical School, and in addition to his duties at NYU Hospital, has a private practice in New York City.

In this chapter, adapted from my conversation with Dr. Ginsberg, he discusses the general approach to treatment at NYU Hospital, the admissions policy of the hospital, the types of patients and length of stay in

Ten West, and follow-up care for released patients. We discussed the idea of stigma and mental illness, and some of Dr. Ginsberg's observations in this area are also included.

George Ginsberg, M.D.

New York University Hospital's psychiatric unit bears no resemblance to the image of a dark, secluded hospital wing sometimes conjured at the words "psychiatric ward." The unit is open and completely voluntary; patients have the same personal and civil rights as patients in any other unit of the hospital. They can pack up and leave any time they wish. However, people are here for treatment; we indicate that we don't want them running off and that we expect their cooperation.

During the average patient's four- to five-week stay, he will live in a double room, furnished very much like a sitting room with low beds and chairs. If someone needs privacy, he will live in one of the private rooms, which are used on the basis of a patient's individual needs, as well as on the basis of economic considerations. When two patients are rooming together, we try to ensure that they are compatible.

On any given day, a patient avails himself of the numerous activities offered by our staff. None of the craft workshops are compulsory, but are organized for the people who wish to participate. As a patient is able to tolerate it, he may also participate in outings—museum visits, walks to the parks, and perhaps some shopping excursions. After a certain level of a person's improvement has been reached, it can be dull hanging around the hospital all day, and these outings are therapeutic.

We are geared toward treating a person who is in the midst of an acute crisis which can be treated over a relatively short period of time. We are not set up for long-term hospitalizations, so when a person who needs long-term care is referred to us, we will evaluate his case carefully and recommend another facility. Two general types of crises will result in a person seeking hospitalization at University Hospital: some sort of depression and/or suicide attempt, and a loss of contact with reality.

How do we get people through an acute situation? This depends upon what a person's individual needs are; determining those needs requires competent professional judgment, which will gear the treatment toward the individual problem. For example, we know that one or another family of medications is helpful for a given illness; we also know that the same illness can be helped with electric [shock] treatment. Yet, given the same illness in a milder form, perhaps neither medication nor electric treatment will be necessary. The psychiatrist must be able to determine which treatment is best for which patient at which stage of his life.

A few specific illustrations may serve to clarify my point. Let us say that a patient is admitted to the hospital because he is suffering from an acute attack of mania. Several potential treatments are possible. There is reasonable evidence to suggest that Lithium is the first choice of treatment, so we might well begin to administer Lithium shortly after the patient is admitted. However, it takes some time before the ingested Lithium reaches a therapeutic level in a person's bloodstream. One person may be able to manage during that time; but with someone else, we may have to rely temporarily on a major tranquilizer, until the appropriate Lithium level is reached.

Some people medically cannot tolerate Lithium, so in a case such as that, we would have to choose another form of treatment. Still others would have such serious side effects that Lithium could not be continued, and adjustments would have to be made. We might have to add a compound to alleviate the side effects, for instance, or we might have to alter our therapeutic strategy altogether.

Similarly, if a patient is admitted for an acute depression, potential treatment for him might range from no medication to medication such as tricyclic antidepressants, mono-amine oxidase inhibitors to electric treatment. The length of any given patient's stay may vary, too—from a few hours to a few days, to a few weeks or even months.

The decisions about any patient's treatment rest upon the doctors' professional knowledge of an individual's physiology, anatomy, biochemistry, genetics, socio-cultural history, and mental development. The psychiatrist's expertise in medicine, behavior theory, learning theory, and pharmacology, among other areas, is what he offers the patient toward a judgment on the patient's appropriate treatment.

When a patient's acute episode is over, he leaves to return to his own life, and if it is indicated, he will receive additional treatment as an outpatient, either through our clinic or through a private doctor. Basically, then, we help a person reconstitute his life so that he is able to deal with any underlying problems, either on his own or through outpatient treatment, when he leaves us.

Our admissions policy is voluntary; we receive most of our patients on a referral basis. Patients are referred for admission by our staff physicians at University Hospital, physicians from all over the metropolitan area, or they are admitted by self-referral, which includes an informal referral from friends who have been here or have heard of us. We also have a twenty-four-hour-a-day, seven-day-a-week emergency facility. If things get out of control for someone to the extent that he needs to be admitted immediately, he will be admitted through the emergency room if space is available. Most commonly, however, a patient is admitted through the more formal procedure.

The average number of patients in the psychiatric unit is about twenty-two. That number fluctuates more or less seasonally. We'll tend to get a rise in admissions over the holidays, which will taper off just after New Year's and then start to pick up again and run high until the early spring. At a time when the admission rate is at its peak, we will have to put patients on the waiting list. At that point, we have to begin making some sort of selection, and the selection is based upon what type of person we can do the most for.

Although most of our patients come from the metropolitan New York area, there is no geographical limitation in our admissions policy. It's not that uncommon in the course of a year, for instance, to admit people from Paris, Saigon, or London. One of the reasons for this is our New York location where a number of international companies have offices; it has happened that when an employee in one of these organizations has had a breakdown, the company will fly him to New York for treatment here.

Economically and socially, the patients cover a wide range of backgrounds. We have treated multimillionaires and people on welfare. Medicare and Medicaid, as well as private insurance, help offset the cost of a patient's hospitalization.

When a person comes here from a previous hospital experience, it is generally for one of two reasons: first, an individual may have been in a hospital some time ago and happens to suffer a crisis when he is in our vicinity. Second, a person may be transferred here by a doctor, via the family's request, from another hospital. Very seldom, in this type of situation, will the patient be coming from a long-term "locked" hospital. If a person's condition requires such a hospital, this is not the place for him.

I would guess that most people, if they visited University Hospital's psychiatric wing, would wonder what in the world these patients are doing in a psychiatric unit. Outwardly they look like anyone else and they don't act strangely. But someone just looking wouldn't know that this person just tried to commit suicide, or that that person is coming out of a severe depression. People's problems go much deeper than a superficial judgment can determine.

Many of our patients are charming, bright, delightful human beings who have run into trouble at a particular period in their lives. Many have had a full life before their hospitalization, and when they are released, return to it. Because most of our patients have families or someone who cares to return home to, we rarely run into problems of finding an appropriate aftercare facility for a released patient. Hopefully, by the time someone is discharged, his crisis is over and he is ready to leave. If a patient is apprehensive about returning to work, for instance, we will arrange for him to remain as an inpatient and he will go out on pass to get accustomed to the job again, with the security that he can return here evenings. Patients are not released unless they think they can cope with their outside situations. We would prefer, if anxieties about a patient's outside life persist, that he go out on pass first.

We do provide follow-up for released patients; we don't simply turn someone out into the street. We don't recommend discharge for anyone unless he has a careful plan about his future. Usually, when a patient does not have a private psychotherapist, we will introduce him to a psychiatrist outside the hospital. Before he leaves, we arrange a meeting with that doctor and the patient.

It is not at all unusual when a former patient stops back on his own, generally to say hello, to say that he's out of therapy now and to thank us. Others will also "drop in" with the same "I was in the neighborhood" guise, and I can tell that they are on the verge of a crisis. Often, they may not consciously realize it themselves; yet somehow they feel it—some part of them feels it—and that brings them here, under the guise of saying hello. This pattern has always intrigued me. When a person in this state "drops in," we'll usually get a call from him a day or two later saying he is ill. Certain illnesses are chronic, or have cycles of crisis, some of our discharged patients suffer relapses and are rehospitalized.

In theory, however, I am against rehospitalization unless absolutely necessary. I don't mean this in the sense that I support the state program of releasing thousands of hospitalized patients from public institutions indiscriminately, merely to reduce the hospital load. This sort of unfortunate practice is little more than a case of politicians playing politics, and it results in what has become known as the revolving-door syndrome, creating inflated welfare roles and making victims for unethical proprietary homes. (It does no one in society any good to reduce the state hospitals' loads from 20,000 to 7,000 if 13,000 people aren't getting any help when they need it.) However, I do believe that rehospitalization can be avoided in a large number of cases if a person has a good doctor who will see him through every day of a crisis. One's doctor must know the needs of his patient and the most effective treatment for that person.

For some people, rehospitalization is the treatment of their own choosing; for others, it isn't. They are either encouraged to return to the hospital or are put in a hospital involuntarily.

I think that one of the problems the public must tackle before the idea of emotional illness is accepted as a part of life is the stigma attached to it. In my experience, although most patients' families react quite sensibly toward the idea of emotional illness within their families, I have seen people behaving as though the patient were guilty of original sin. People's attitudes about mental disturbances vary according to their social ethnic, economic, and religious backgrounds. However, I feel that there is a general aversion in the public mind to emotional illness, and in part I think that this is based upon people's emotional responses to situations. For example, it's very difficult for most people to face the idea of mental illness because to an extent we're all emotionally ill at one time or another. Not in the sense that the newer, more radical psychiatrists would have it, but to the extent that we all have felt certain things at certain times. Who hasn't felt the abysmal depths of depression at one time or another? No one who is close to life in any sensible, sensitive way hasn't been sad or depressed or perhaps even flirted with the idea of suicide. But when you are faced with someone who has actually tried to commit suicide, you become terrified. And one of the most common reactions to that kind of fear is to separate yourself from the thing you fear: "I'm different from that person; he is crazy, I am sane . . . therefore, I could never really kill myself."

This is a sort of thing that will be with us always; perhaps it is part of the human condition. Education, legislation can change the overt problems, but people still have to learn that an individual who suffers from emotional illness is not substantively different from anyone else who has ever felt anything.

CHAPTER THREE

The Public Open Hospital:
New York Psychiatric Institute
Phillip Polatin, M.D.

Dr. Phillip Polatin, Professor Emeritus of Clinical Psychiatry, College of Physicians and Surgeons, has been associated with the New York Psychiatric Institute for more than thirty-six years. Until his retirement in 1973, he was the Clinical Director of the Institute as well as Professor of Clinical Psychiatry at the College of Physicians and Surgeons and Attending Psychiatrist at the Presbyterian Hospital. After his retirement, he became consultant for the hospital, and began treating private patients at the Atchley Pavilion of the Medical Center (Presbyterian Hospital).

Dr. Polatin's achievements in the area of psychiatry have been considerable. In 1939, he and his colleagues were the first to call attention to a type of fracture that was occurring in the vertebrae of people who had received Metrazol therapy, which has now been replaced by electroshock therapy. As a result of this finding, methods were devised to medicate patients before receiving this type of therapy in order to prevent the harmful side effects. He also devised the technique of "ambulatory insulin," with his colleagues, a method that required smaller amounts of insulin in the treatment of schizophrenia, and no longer made it necessary to have the patient in a coma. In 1949, Dr. Polatin, along with Dr. Paul Hoch discovered a new form of schizophrenia—pseudo-neurotic schizophrenia—which was a type of disturbance that was basically, at its roots, schizophrenia and amenable to treatment as such, but which was covered over by symptoms that appeared as neurotic disorders. This discovery consumed a great deal of time and work, and was later accepted throughout the world.

Dr. Polatin's published works are numerous, and they include such books as *A Guide to Treatment in Psychiatry* (Lippincott, 1966), *How Psychiatry Helps* (with his wife, E. C. Philtine: Harper & Bros., 1949), and *The Well-Adjusted Personality* (also with E. C. Philtine: Simon & Schuster, 1968). He has contributed chapters to numerous other books, and has published some 75 articles for psychiatric and other publications.

Phillip Polatin, M.D.

One of my favorite subjects, the New York Psychiatric Institute is always a pleasure to talk about. In November, 1971, we had a celebration of the Institute's 75th anniversary over a period of two days, with lectures, seminars, and excellent addresses by the Institute's director, the commissioner of the Department of Mental Hygiene, and the governor of New York, as well as many other outstanding individuals.

Many people do not know that the New York Psychiatric Institute is administered and financed by the State of New York, although in the field of research it is an integral part of the College of Physicians and Surgeons, Columbia University, and of Presbyterian Hospital, where many of the staff are stationed for particular purposes. For example, one staff member has an office in Presbyterian Hospital in charge of psychosomatic medicine; another is stationed at the Babies' Hospital, caring for child psychiatric cases; another is assigned to Vanderbilt Clinic Emergency Room to be available for the treatment of psychiatric emergencies; while still another is assigned to Community Psychiatry at the Black Building.

Since the Institute is financed by the State of New York, only residents of New York State are admitted, unless an ongoing research problem is so complex that there are not sufficient patients representing the particular condition. In that contingency, patients from other states will be interviewed and accepted if they are suitable.

I might stress that patients enter the New York Psychiatric Institute willingly and only after an extensive interview by one of the staff members. If found suitable, the patient is placed on a waiting list and, after a relatively short period of time, receives a letter indicating when to arrive for admission. This procedure applies for children, adolescents, and adults including a very limited number of older people. The charge per day, week, or month is not fixed, but is determined according to what the patient or family can afford to pay. The staff is totally unaware of what patients pay.

Medicare, but especially Medicaid, pays many of the hospital expenses for the individual patient; and all patients are voluntary.

There are approximately 200 beds at the Institute, and for the most part, they are always occupied, creating a waiting list for admissions.

Before a patient is admitted, he or she, or the family, completes an extensive questionnaire, which reveals practically all the facts in the person's case. This questionnaire is then submitted to the admitting resident of the appropriate ward, who carefully peruses the material. If, in his mind, it seems that the person is not suitable for the Institute, a letter to this effect is sent to the person or to his family. If, on the other hand, the person is considered suitable, the registrar is asked by the ward's resident to set a date for the psychiatric examination. Again, the person may be found suitable or unsuitable on the basis of this examination. If he or she is found suitable for admission, the person's name is placed on a waiting list until a bed is available; this is usually a very short wait. The patient is then assigned to one of the almost 50 residents at the Institute—each resident is under the supervision of a permanent staff member.

The Institute is set up to do research work in all fields of psychiatry, including biological, psycho-social, and genetic psychiatry, in an effort to discover the causes and treatment of disorders. At the same time, the Institute's goals have been broadened to include postgraduate teaching for the entire State hospital system.

Since moving to the Medical Center in 1929, the Institute's functions have expanded to include teaching in psychiatry to all the medical students in the College of Physicians and Surgeons.

The Institute is also directly concerned with the problems of community psychiatry, and several years ago, a department was established at the Institute called the Washington Heights Community Center. This includes not only inpatients, but community outpatients as well, and its treatment methods encompass all the social, genetic, and other factors making up a community. Caring for the 200 patients are about 40 to 50 residents, and supervising these residents are ten permanent staff members from the department of clinical psychiatry. Regarding education, the student body has grown rapidly to over 1,200 pre- and postgraduate candidates in all the mental health disciplines, all using the various facilities of the Psychiatric Institute.

The Institute is divided into several research units and departments: clinical psychiatry, communication sciences and developmental processes, biologic psychiatry, internal medicine, psychoanalysis, behavioral psychology, medical genetics, neuropathology, psychology, social sciences, and the various services (Washington Heights Community Service, Children's Service), to name only a few. There are also the brief therapy unit, the long-term therapy unit, the halfway house, and prevocational services, rehabilitation services, and other departments. In short, the Institute has an enormous variety of functions, educational as well as therapeutic.

Our faculty is not staffed by visiting members, but only by those carefully evaluated by the director of the Institute. Permanent staff appointments are made mainly through the New York State Department of Mental Hygiene and the appointees become members of the State Civil Service Administration. There are other employees of the Institute who are not civil servants, and these people are appointed by the Institute's director for special research projects.

Patients admitted to the Institute must be, as I have already mentioned, residents of the State of New York, and they must be able to speak English; however, if a patient is part of the Washington Heights Community Psychiatric Program, he may be Spanish speaking. He will either be provided with a translator or assigned to a doctor who speaks Spanish.

Patients are admitted to the Institute, otherwise, regardless of their ability to pay, their race, religion, or ethnic background. Generally, patients are in the younger age group. Very frequently, the patient has a history of emotional tension and upheaval in the family; consequently, we do conduct family therapy. Here, the family and the patient are usually treated together by the patient's therapist and by the patient's psychiatric social worker.

We find that many people are sent to us by social agencies, by friends, by former patients, and by psychiatrists, many of whom received their training through the Psychiatric Institute.

Most of the patients here suffer from some form of schizophrenia, whether mild, moderate, or severe. A few have manic-depressive and psycho-neurotic disorders. The younger age group may have personality disorders, behavior disorders, or reactions to drugs.

Many of our patients have had previous treatment before coming here. I would judge that about 30 percent have had previous therapy, while about 70 percent have never had therapy before. Those who have had previous therapy may have been in private treatment; a few have been in therapy through a clinic, either public or private; for most, their previous therapy was brief.

When a patient comes to the Psychiatric Institute, it is usually for admission as an inpatient. He may remain in the long-term therapy department for six to twelve months, or a bit longer. In the Washington Heights Community Department, his stay may be about three to five days.

The patients, when sufficiently improved, are discharged from the inpatient department to the outpatient facility or to the halfway house, where therapy is continued. A person may also become a night patient, working during the day and returning to the hospital in the evenings to receive therapy; or, he may become a day patient, remaining in the hospital during the day for treatment, and going home to his family at night. In these cases, the social worker becomes very active, helping the patient in his adjustment between the hospital and the outside world—assisting him in getting a job, in continuing school, in joining recreational facilities—at the same time that the patient is continuing his therapy with his doctor.

The main types of therapy practiced at the Institute are: analytic psychotherapy, supportive psychotherapy, protected workshop, group therapy, family therapy, drug therapy, electroshock therapy (although very rarely and only when essential). Insulin treatment was discontinued many years ago. Hypnosis, reconditioning, and behavior therapy are also a part of the therapeutic regimen, as well as social therapy. Occasionally, dreams are used in treatment, particularly in the case of those being treated in analytic psychotherapy.

We do not use the classical form of psychoanalysis, which is very intensive and extends over a long period of time. Analytic psychotherapy, which we use instead, is based on many of the same principles as psychoanalysis, including the interpretation of dreams, but requires much less time.

Patients ideally remain in therapy with the same therapist for as long as it is necessary, whether they are inpatients or outpatients, usually over the range of several weeks to a year or two. Sometimes, a resident will terminate his training or move to another facility or service, and this of course will mean that his patients must be transferred to another therapist. This is a regrettable situation but, I am afraid, unavoidable.

When therapy is completed, about 85 percent of the patients are markedly improved; they have better judgment, clearer insight into themselves, and are happier, better adjusted, and more successful in their work endeavors. Sexually, financially, maritally, socially they are very much improved. As they understand themselves better, they comprehend their inner motives and drives and their inner and outer adjustments are greatly augmented.

Families of patients are very anxious when a relative is admitted to the Institute; but it is noteworthy that when a patient is ready to leave, the family would often like him to stay a while longer with us. I don't really think that there is a stigma attached to being a patient at the Psychiatric Institute; often, patients and their families will say, quite frankly, that they feel no stigma about it. As a matter of fact, there is an organization consisting of members of patients' families who have done a great deal to cooperate with the staff in order to make patients feel more comfortable about coming here.

The most helpful approach to a patient, from a patient's view, is the appropriate combination of drug therapy and psychotherapy; this combination helps get a person through an acute crisis as well as helping him work out the more basic problems.

Should a released patient show some sign of relapse or a return of his symptoms, he may be readmitted to the Institute, but usually for a short period of time. Generally, when someone has to be readmitted, he will snap back more quickly than he did before.

We have conducted several follow-up studies on patients who have been treated at the Psychiatric Institute, and very generally, we have found that a high percent of these former patients have maintained the improvement in their lives that they made here.

Because we use a variety of therapies, we view ourselves as eclectic. But when I say a variety of therapies, I am speaking of therapies that we feel have proven out, that is, they are standard, and have withstood research and testing, including the testing of our follow-up program.

The therapies with which we do not agree are Esalen-based therapies, direct analysis, megavitamin therapy, the various encounter therapies, existential psychotherapy, various types of "brainwashing therapy," gestalt therapy, hypno-drama, psychosurgery, T-groups (training groups), structured interactional group therapy, transactional analysis, transcendental meditation, and others.

CHAPTER FOUR

The Menninger Foundation Clinic

Roy Menninger, M.D., President
J. Cotter Hirschberg, M.D.
Stephen A. Appelbaum, Ph.D.

The Menninger Clinic encompasses the Menninger Foundation's outpatient services, their adult and children's hospitals, and a number of aftercare programs. Since the Menninger Sanitarium was incorporated in 1925 by Dr. C. F. Menninger and his sons, William and Karl, the Clinic has treated over 60,000 patients—adults and children. The year 1975 was the Foundation's golden anniversary; over the past 50 years, the organization has grown from a small hospital housing thirteen patients to one of the country's leading centers for psychiatry and psychotherapy, on both an educational and clinical basis; professionals in the field of mental health who have worked there comprise approximately 7 percent of the country's mental health workers.

In addition to its own services, the Foundation and Clinic work closely with the Topeka, Kansas, public hospitals and educational facilities. Dr. Roy Menninger, oldest son of the late William Menninger, is currently the Foundation's president. Prior to his election as president, he was Director of the Department of Preventive Psychiatry.

Dr. Menninger graduated from Swarthmore College, Swarthmore, Pennsylvania, and received his medical doctorate from the Cornell University Medical College, New York City. His psychiatric residency was taken at three Boston hospitals: Boston State, Boston Psychopathic, and

Peter Bent Brigham. He served as Chief of Neuropsychiatry at an Army hospital in Salzburg, Austria.

A Fellow of the American Psychiatric Association and the American College of Physicians, Dr. Menninger is also an active member of the Group for the Advancement of Psychiatry, the American Association for the Advancement of Science, the American Medical Association, and many other national and regional organizations.

The following conversation with Dr. Menninger first appeared in the Winter 1974-1975 issue of *Menninger Perspective* (Volume 5, Number 4, pp. 22-27), and is reprinted here with permission of the Menninger Foundation.

Roy Menninger, M.D., President of the Menninger Foundation

The opening of a psychiatric clinic here in the 1920s occurred at a time when the public attitude toward mental illness was indifferent at best, and rather negative at worst. Ill people were looked upon as pariahs and treated that way: relegated to isolated buildings and forgotten. From the outset our hospital was a radical statement to the contrary: that psychiatric patients are human, that they should not be ostracized, that they could be understood, and the most radical thought of all, that they *are* treatable and *can* get better. This positive stance in a field forsaken by almost everyone has come to be a standard for psychiatric treatment now throughout the country.

The question has been asked: How could one institution accomplish all this?

I suppose it came about because of a conviction that it *could* be done. This optimistic view was reinforced by the joining of two concepts: the psychoanalytic understanding of behavior and the concept of using the milieu, the environment, as a part of the treatment process. Psychoanalytic theory had not previously been applied to the treatment of hospital patients, since most persons working in this field had treated only office patients whose illnesses were not overly severe. Here, we applied that understanding to the more seriously disturbed people who sought our help and needed hospitalization. To this was added the intentional use of the environment—enlisting the attention and help of not only the nurses but the aides, the recreational and art and music therapists, even the housekeeping staff as well as the mental health professionals. Each of these persons worked with the patient according to the understandings about his illness that psychoanalytic theory had helped to generate. From this emerged comprehensive concepts about the social environment of the patient and how it could influence his treatment in positive directions.

But there have been other notable achievements as well. An unusual aspect of our setting has been the central clinical role played by psychologists, almost from the beginning. Moreover, under the tutelage of David Rapaport and later, Gardner Murphy, the psychologists on the staff made significant contributions to the diagnostic testing process.

Indeed our impact on psychiatric education was quite a significant contribution. Stimulated by the great needs of the Veterans Administration after World War II, we began a sizeable program that distinguished itself for having a curriculum of study, a comprehensive program of instruction that differed sharply from the exclusively tutorial and rather casual approach that characterized teaching in this field for many years. Through this systematic approach to psychiatric education, it was possible to train considerably larger numbers of psychiatric residents.

My father, Dr. Will Menninger, and my uncle, Dr. Karl, played important roles in this. It was their vision, along with that of their father, Dr. C. F., that gave us that unique direction in those early years, and which shaped our pioneering programs in education and application. In the thirties, Dr. Karl's book, *The Human Mind,* popularized psychiatry by making it understandable to the layman, getting across the idea that the forces which motivate ill people are not so different from those which motivate the rest of us—that the difference was one of degree, not kind. Dr. Will was fond of remarking that the true incidence of mental illness was one in one—that we are all, at times, affected.

When Dr. Will served as chief psychiatrist for the Army during World War II, he legitimized psychiatry as a field of medicine with an important contribution toward the total care of the soldier. Moreover, he demonstrated that psychiatry had something to add to the understanding of groups, the maintenance of morale, and the nature of leadership. It was this broader relevance which helped to open the way toward an application of psychiatric knowledge to groups and organizations and which eventually started us working with business and industrial problems of leadership and morale. One might say that Dr. Will's efforts helped bring psychiatry into the medical mainstream in the same way that Dr. Karl's eloquent writing established psychiatry as a legitimate science in the public mind.

There were certain time periods when special areas of psychiatry were pursued. It seems that the concern of the 1920s was diagnosis, followed by an emphasis in the thirties and forties on treatment as new methods, especially psychoanalytic knowledge, became available. Then in the subsequent two decades, the fifties and the sixties, education was the major focus, with the beginning of the Menninger School of Psychiatry. As each preceding focus consolidated its initial growth, it became a platform on which the next phase was launched.

By a kind of logic that our past has already demonstrated, I think that the several decades ahead will see a dramatic growth of our work in application, a focus that in turn is based upon preceding developments in treatment and education. In this sense, our past is prologue, yet it is our future as well, for substantial growth in this rather undefined area of application depends upon the continuing growth and development of our clinical practice and our educational activities. Together they form a kind of three-legged stool laced together with the binding wire of research. It is through this kind of integration that our organization has been steadily growing.

Application is a term we hear more and more, and it should be explained.

I think our task is to expand our efforts to apply what we have learned about human behavior to other settings—to the educational processes of elementary and high schools, to business and industry, to the courts, to a variety of social systems that might find understanding of human behavior and motivation relevant to situations they confront. Pursuing such a course entails hard questions: How can this knowledge make a difference? How can we demonstrate that? Will more sophisticated ideas about people really help organizations and systems sustain the emotionally vulnerable and perhaps prevent them from becoming emotional casualties? Can we expect this kind of knowledge to help well people function even better?

It's a gigantic task, but its size is no reason to duck it. Moreover, I don't see us—whether we are psychiatrists or psychologists or social workers—undertaking such a task all alone. This work invites the contributions of many others in many other places and many other disciplines. The trick will be to develop a style of interdisciplinary work that taps the relevant parts of each area, and helps to introduce them into the structures of our social living in ways that benefit those who are part of them.

Psychiatry has to take a multidisciplinary approach to solving problems, but I don't believe this approach will reduce the importance of using individual treatment methods for patients whose problems require that kind of attention. Instead, I think this approach represents a valuable supplement to our individually oriented work: an understanding of what goes on between the patient and his environment may help us identify the problem more accurately and treat it even better. Witness the growing importance of family therapy as a way of approaching troubled people as a group, rather than singling out one person and treating him as "patient." There is a common tendency to see this issue in either/or terms—something that is not only unnecessary but, worse yet, obstructs the kind of integrated understanding of person/environment we should be seeking.

Another question asked is whether this broader approach will affect the basic philosophy of treating the individual. What is basic to us is not a certain style of treatment—i.e., one-to-one. That form has been around long enough to suggest that it represents a prime value. But it is what lies behind it that must be retained and coveted—an emphasis on the value of the individual, sick or well—an idea that he is important and worthy in his own right and not simply because of what he can do or achieve or produce.

Our cultural worship of the machine and the industrial genius which produced it has profoundly perverted this basic value, and has risked reducing us all to cogs in an industrial society that can replace us indiscriminately and without regard to any individualistic specialness that we may value in ourselves or others. The particular style of treatment— whether in groups, individually, as part of a family, with medications, or in any of a number of ways—is an expression of our commitment to a basic humanistic philosophy; it is this *substance* that is important, not the *form* of treatment.

This does not apply to psychoanalysis, traditionally a one-to-one treatment technique. Psychoanalysis is a method for the treatment of the *individual,* and isn't likely to be adapted to other forms. But even here, there is a tendency to confuse the method—the fifty-minute hour, the couch, the silent analyst—with the content, the theory, and the observations about behavior which this method has produced. It is this knowledge that can be generalized to other settings and other programs.

Some of the newer Gestalt approaches are being explored at the Foundation, as well as innovations such as guided imagery, biofeedback, and others. The image of our institution as some rockbound, doctrinaire expositor of the teachings of St. Freud to the exclusion of all else has never been true, and is even less so now. In fact, one of our exciting directions of inquiry is a systematic study of a variety of contemporary approaches to helping people—Rolfing, Gestalt, Primal Scream—and relating these methods and the theories that underlie them to our experience—learning strategies we can use as well as broadening our understanding of what helps make people better. Clearly, many things do. I think it is fair to note, however, that we haven't been so swept up with the preoccupation of the "new" as the only things worthwhile that we have turned our backs on forms of treatment that we have found successful and effective. There is a tendency in our field to grow disenchanted with a particular approach and cast it aside for something more novel and intriguing. The lack of solid data about improvement rates—for almost all forms of treatment—makes it hard to resist the blandishments of those who promote the novel and exciting, but it's even harder to demonstrate that these newer approaches are any better than the old. Nonetheless, we find this open, investigative stance a good way to extend our horizons and remain responsive to ideas which can add to what we are doing.

I have been asked, looking at society today, what I think is the major problem with which people are dealing. I ought to hesitate before the inviting pitfall of making such a sweeping generalization, but I can't resist. What has impressed me is the remarkable reluctance I note in so many people to deal openly and honestly with their feelings. Whether they offer explanations or rationalizations, whether they avoid or deny, whether they project onto some nearby victim, the problems seem similar. Feelings are perceived as frightening, as signs of weakness, as evidence of poor moral character. The effort to avoid one's feelings extracts a high toll. The distortions and maneuvers people go through to avoid feelings lead to all kinds of secondary consequences, many of them not even recognized by the victims.

I note, for example, the emotional poverty of the tough intellectual, the superficiality of the timid and intimidated, the paranoia of the fearful, the scapegoating of the anxious, and the loneliness of those so frightened of good, warm, close feelings of intimacy. Perhaps this is another price of our overly technological society; feelings are not a logical part of the system and there is nothing to do but avoid them— whatever the cost.

I suppose one consequence of refusing to be in touch with the emotional part of one's self is a tendency to dehumanize others as well as ourselves. At least one consequence of this alienation from the emotional self is the feeling so many people have that their lives mean little or nothing. Perhaps it is good that they have begun to worry about the emptiness of their world, full though it may be of material possessions. Having little touch with one's emotional self clearly makes it difficult to answer some questions I am occasionally asked: How does one decide what is really important? How does one set a goal that really makes sense? Without a better sense of one's self that comes from contact with one's feelings, these are hard—if not impossible—questions to answer.

Impossible as they may be, it seems that society is looking more and more to psychiatry to respond to these concerns. But I do not believe that psychiatry, as a discipline, should bear the primary burden of curing these social ills. I am aware that society expects a great deal of us— too much. In part it's our own fault. We too were carried away by the reformist enthusiasms of the mental health movement of the 1950s- 1960s and we oversold our product. At the same time I sense that many people have turned to psychiatry for what they might have sought, in an earlier time, from organized religion, or the church, or even the pastor. Paradoxically, it appears that people are turning back to their pastors now as pastors themselves have begun to acquire some needed psycho- logical sophistication. But it also suggests that psychiatry has insidiously moved into a role previously filled by the church.

I sense that this is partly an expression of a terrible state of perplexity and confusion that so many people are experiencing today. People are uncertain about just about everything: they are confused about handling their teen-agers; they are concerned about the proper roles of male and female; they worry about the stresses that produce ulcers or high blood pressure; and they question their own goals and direction. Of course our affluent society cannot only afford to ask such questions—less con- cerned than in years past about sheer survival—but it also can afford to recommend psychiatrists to help answer them.

We psychiatrists don't have all the answers. It seems to me the only way these problems can be solved is to develop the interdisciplinary approach I spoke of earlier to a higher level of effectiveness—embracing many social and scientific disciplines of knowledge. In fact, it seems that we are just beginning to realize that any attack on the major social ills we are experiencing will require vast organization of professional talent that will dwarf anything we've seen yet in the social science fields. I don't believe any discipline—including psychiatry—has a corner on knowledge these days. A perfection of the team approach and an enor- mous commitment of money and talent are called for.

As for psychiatry's role in this multidisciplinary approach, let's back up just a moment. I think "psychiatry's role" needs a bit more defining, lest it get lost in the morass of complexity of the problems I've alluded to. Psychiatrists must not lose track of the idea (nor should society let us) that it is our responsibility to treat the mentally ill—however de- fined. That's our first responsibility, and it can't be minimized, if for no other reason than the fact that society has given no one else that mandate. It is troubling to note that many of us have moved away from the direct treatment of the most seriously ill, and that our best efforts to develop more effective treatment strategies for these severely ill patients have not been outstandingly successful. This means that we have a long way to go to discharge this responsibility.

Many psychiatric hospitals are closing. In some states, the decision to close hospitals reflects a strategy for shifting the primary care of the mentally ill to the communities—and most communities are ill-prepared to handle the task. There is also a shift toward hospitalizing patients for shorter periods of time. Ideally this reflects better treatment programs, earlier hospitalization during acute stages, and more available treatment than was true in the past. Unfortunately, it also reflects a realization that third-party payments may be available for psychiatric hospital treatment only for short periods of treatment—30 to 60 days.

Of course this implies that long-term care will be available only to those with exceptional insurance policies or those able to pay the high cost entailed. It is profoundly troubling to see so little recognition that hospitals are necessary parts of the health system and that there must be long-term facilities if patients are to receive more than a new form of neglect that so blackened the escutcheon of psychiatry in an earlier time. We can hope that the process of social experimentation will demonstrate ways in which the advantages of community treatment programs can be combined with appropriate hospitalization, when necessary, in ways which can be afforded and paid for by the populace.

These issues seem terribly complicated, but there are a number of things the Foundation can do. First, we intend to explore ways of advancing our effectiveness with severely ill patients—whether through long-term treatment, judicious use of drugs, hospitalization, or a combination of these and other approaches.

Secondly, we must broaden our own community treatment programs —our aftercare programs are a beginning. I expect we will try such things as special programs for the especially vulnerable, the so-called high-risk patient: the illegitimately pregnant teen-ager, the first-time mother, the family with a mentally retarded child, the recently divorced mother with several young children. I expect we will develop a counseling service that will reach into the community.

I expect we will explore ways in which our clinical knowledge of children can help a variety of local child-centered programs, activities, and services—more than consulting relationships; perhaps new participatory programs with the schools, child-care centers, the pediatricians, and others. Further, I expect we will expand our efforts in certain specialized treatment programs—for alcoholics as we are now doing, acutely ill patients in our short-term unit, perhaps for drug addicts, or for seriously ill, long-term schizophrenic patients, and certainly in the fields of family and group therapy.

It is difficult to predict what other kinds of directions we are likely to see here at the Foundation in the fifty years ahead, but several trends are clear now, and will yield a number of program possibilities worth noting. Particularly challenging is the area of education. Under the rubric of a school of mental health sciences, we have begun to organize our thinking about a core-and-track system of professional education, which will bring all the mental health disciplines together for part of their training. But beyond this is the larger task of bringing social psychology, anthropology, even political science and economics into a relationship with the mental health sciences. This is a formidable task, but through programs of special study, an extensive visiting professor program, arrangements for special scholars from other disciplines, we hope to develop affiliations with universities and other centers with parallel interests. Out of this may come joint ventures, shared student-faculty exchanges, degree programs, and other means for expanding our opportunities for interdisciplinary collaboration.

From a slightly different approach, the Center for Applied Behavioral Sciences has been making progress in this effort to reach out to other areas for some time now. Our efforts to seek effective means of applying what we know to nonclinical areas has already led to the development of a very successful seminar program. Our experience with judges, executives, school teachers, educators, family physicians, city managers, and others has confirmed that this seminar experience is sufficiently basic to the nature of human psychology that it applies equally well to persons from widely varying occupations. The seminars seem to touch on issues which are significant to the lives of nearly everyone: issues such as personal value systems, self-perceptions, objectives and goals, and managing the normal swinging tides of feeling.

Our problem in this area now is one of marketing—how can we make this experience available to the great many individuals in positions of authority and responsibility for others? We're investigating the possibilities of modern audio-visual media combined with the small group experience, which may offer routes worth exploring.

Aside from the seminars, the future will confront us with opportunities we'll welcome. We'll be seeking better ways to manage community conflict; we'll be assisting groups with problems of leisure and retirement; we will offer programs that emphasize psychological growth, perhaps in the context of adult learning systems or grade and junior high schools.

There's an opportunistic slant to our position in this area of application—a position we can justify only as we evaluate the programs that these opportunities invite us to develop. The learning for us is surely as significant as it is for our client/consumers.

Research is a vital part of all these programs because throughout there is an emphasis on learning from what we do, although our future in research must be broader than that. An organization as knowledge-dependent as we, must have sophisticated methods for developing new knowledge. There is never sufficient understanding of psychological processes to permit us to say—as I have heard many who ought to know better suggest—that we already know it all, that we just aren't using this knowledge as well as we might. The latter part of that statement may be true enough, but the first part—never.

The most essential task facing the Foundation in the next fifty years will be finding better ways of helping people define themselves and manage their lives and worlds in more effective ways so that individuals may experience a greater sense of their own worth and significance. And I believe that's a task worthy of our efforts.

J. Cotter Hirschberg, M.D.

Dr. J. Cotter Hirschberg received his M.D. from the University of Chicago, and his residency training in adult and child psychiatry at the University of Colorado Medical School, Denver. Until 1952, Doctor Hirschberg was the Director of the Child Guidance and Mental Hygiene Clinic at the Medical School for the University of Colorado. He then went to Topeka as Director of the Menninger Foundation's Children's Division. In 1962, he graduated in adult and child analysis from the Topeka Institute for Psychoanalysis.

He is past president of the American Association of Psychiatric Services for Children, and has been Chairman of the Committee on Certification in Child Psychiatry of the American Board of Psychiatry and Neurology, and Chairman of the Board of Directors of the Topeka Public Library.

Today, Doctor Hirschberg is the William C. Menninger Distinguished Professor of Psychiatry at the Menninger Foundation, and is Dean of Faculty of the Menninger School of Psychiatry. He is presently on the staff of the Children's Division of the Foundation, and a training and supervising analyst in adult and child analysis at the Topeka Institute for Psychoanalysis.

Among the articles Doctor Hirschberg has published about child psychiatry are: "Children and Their Families: Function of the Community," a pamphlet published by the Hogg Foundation for Mental Health; "Termination of Residential Treatment of Children" and "The Role of Education in the Treatment of Emotionally Disturbed Children," chapters in *Residential Treatment of Emotionally Disturbed Children*; and with Jane Watson and Robert E. Switzer, the following "read-together" books for children and parents, *Look at Me Now!, My Friend the Babysitter, Sometimes I get Angry, Sometimes I'm Afraid, My Body—How It Works, My Friend the Dentist, My Friend the Doctor, Sometimes I'm Jealous.*

In this chapter, adapted from my conversation with him, Dr. Hirschberg discusses the Menninger Foundation's Children's Division and the types of patients seen there.

We work with children from all over the country, and from Canada and Mexico. One of the reasons we do not treat children from all over the world is that we insist on working with the families of the children. For the children who come into our hospital, we insist on regular—usually monthly—visits by the parents, and we maintain casework contact with the parents.

In our inpatient hospital program, the children are mostly from outside Topeka. We usually have four or five patients from Topeka and its environs, but of the total of about 65 to 68 patients who live in the hospital, their families reside in almost every state.

Most of the children who are here as inpatients come from the upper middle class or the upper classes. There are a few children in the hospital who are being partly supported by scholarship funds that have been given to the Foundation, and some of the children are supported by third-party payments, such as insurance. Hospital care is a tremendously expensive business.

We also have an outpatient department for children, and in our community clinics, children from lower socioeconomic backgrounds are treated. We have a community child mental health clinic in North Topeka and one in East Topeka; these accept payment according to the family's ability to pay.

I would say that approximately 70 percent of the children who are hospitalized here were referred to us by other physicians. These young people have had previous treatment in their own communities, and in various local child guidance centers. Approximately 15 percent come here on self-referral; their families have heard of us or know of other youngsters who have been helped here. Another 15 percent come here from a variety of other sources.

Now, in the community clinics, and in our sort of "drop-in" clinic for adolescents, as well as in our preschool therapeutic programs and our own outpatient department, the patients come from a far broader range of referrals. Many of these youngsters are referred by the schools. In our adolescent clinic, called the "Carriage House" (so named only because at one time the building was a carriage house), the teen-agers come in on their own—they more or less drop in; the word gets around that there's a place for them to go and talk out some problems. We don't carry on a formal therapy program there; we do work with groups and have a therapeutic activity program. In the other clinics, referrals come from welfare agencies, from churches, from the schools, and from other community agencies.

Most of the children who are inpatients are hospitalized here for the first time. They may have been in other outpatient treatment programs, but I estimate that less than 5 percent of our inpatients have ever been hospitalized before they came here.

Our inpatient children come from troubled families. This is not to suggest that there is a sort of history of emotional illness in the family; this is not necessarily true. It is very difficult sometimes to know whether or not the family is troubled because they have a troubled child —in other words, a child who is disturbed and will upset the family equilibrium—or whether troubles in the family played a part in causing the child's problems. Many of these young people would not be easy children to be with under the best of family situations. Most of the children who come here come from families who have had their own struggles and have problems. That is why we do not accept either children or adolescents unless we have a chance to work with the families. Families needing more help are referred to resources in their own communities.

In the main, by the time the family brings the child to us for hospital care, they are discouraged. They are wondering if the child can be helped. They have already tried a number of resources before deciding to bring the child here. Many of the families are very genuinely anxious about what it is going to mean to have the child in the hospital. Will he lose contact with them? Will he still love them? What have they done wrong? They are anxious and frightened, and struggling with their own feelings, and there is a sense of failure. We try to work with the parents, help them to understand and deal with those feelings, with their own guilt.

For the children, entering the hospital means facing many fears and anxieties, which are intensified by the fact that they do not come on their own initiative, but are brought by parents; they have been referred by physicians or schools. They are wondering what it will mean to be separated from their parents and from their friends. They generally have many doubts whether the hospital is going to be of any help.

Many of these young people come here angry. They don't feel they need to be in a hospital, and they see it as a deprivation, as an impingement upon their freedom. Many of them, without question, are confused. They do not know what is going to happen. They feel lost and have a low self-value; they're discouraged and depressed.

We will not take a child into the hospital, separating him from his family, unless we feel that it is a necessity. If we possibly can during our diagnostic process, we will refer a child and his family for treatment in their community, so that the child can stay with the family. It is of great value, if it's possible, for the child to be with the family and for the family and the child to work out their treatment process together.

Because our hospital patients are in a ratio of three males to one female, the pronoun "he" will be used throughout this interview, although we have inpatient units for girls from five through sixteen years of age.

So the decision to hospitalize a child, to take him out of the family for a while, is crucial, and we do it only when the degree of the child's problems requires it. Therefore, the children and adolescents in our hospital are disturbed enough that they haven't been able to sustain themselves, or their families were not able to sustain them within a normal community.

Sometimes, the child has caused such difficulties within the community that the public schools have said, "This child cannot be in school." And, of course, going to school is a major part of the growing-up process in this society.

Some of the children who have come to us have been involved with drugs, and they come here because they have not been able to successfully handle the problem, either through their families or through community resources. I am referring here, of course, to adolescents. In the past few years, though, we have had one or two children of junior high school age whose drug problems were serious enough to warrant hospitalization.

Children who are severely depressed and children who are suicidal can perhaps best be dealt with through hospitalization.

Most of the children here have been aggressive, angry, rebellious, defiant. They have what I would call acting-out problems. Perhaps one-quarter of the children are what I would call acting-out problems. Perhaps one-quarter of the children are what one might call "psychotic"— they have thought disorders, and perhaps they have been struggling with delusional thinking for a year or two before they were referred here.

We do not use the standard terms such as "schizophrenia," "psychosis," "depressive," in the sense that they are used to define an untreatable problem. We use new terms, descriptive terms, rather than "disease" terms. We do not feel that most problems are irreversible, and to many persons the label "schizophrenia" implies an irreversible disease. Another reason for our shying away from such terms is that we really believe that these are emotional illness-reactions, if you will, within the individual. The child's "illness" is his attempt to cope with internal stress or external family stress. So we do not see his problems as a clearly defined disease entity.

In determining a child's problems, then, we look at the set of interlocking systems in the child's life that has caused stress and to which he is reacting. We do not look for a "disease" that the child has. In other words, we try to find out how the child reacts within the family, how the family reacts together, and within the community.

On occasion, we have seen children who have not been helped here, and there are problems that we simply are not equipped to treat. For instance, we will not accept severely retarded children. This is not to say, of course, that such children cannot be helped elsewhere. In the area of retardation, for example, enormous strides have been made in the last ten years through the use of such therapies as behavior modification.

The average stay here runs about eighteen months to two years, although children are here for shorter or longer periods, too. During their stay, the children have quite a degree of freedom. About half the children are in individual rooms, and the other half are in double rooms; we do not have the dormitory-type of treatment program here, primarily because we designed the hospital to focus on individual treatment within a group program. All of the units but one are open; that is, they are not locked. One of the hospital units, which can house ten children, is locked. Their *rooms* aren't locked, and they have freedom of movement within the unit—but the unit itself is closed.

In the closed section, two of the rooms are double rooms, and the rest of them are single. A child in this closed unit still remains part of the total hospital program, and we are usually successful when we have those (more troubled) children in various programs in which the others participate. They do go off that unit to participate in activities, sports, various everyday things.

The treatment process itself does not isolate the child. We are constantly aware that one cannot treat a child without treating him within the context of his relationships with his peers, his family, and within the context of his school experience. The child is always a part of a larger complex—his school, family, friends—and to deal with him as if his problems are solely internal is to forget the larger social complex in which he interacts.

We are psychoanalytically oriented, both in our hospital and outpatient treatment programs. But few of the children are actually in analysis. I'd estimate that as many as 70 percent are in psychotherapy, another 20 percent are in family therapy, and perhaps 5 percent are in group psychotherapy. This would mean that about 5 percent are in analysis. We have some sixteen- through eighteen-year-olds who are in analysis. The couch allows for much freer introspection and a much greater degree of free association. This works well if the child does not have to have a great amount of contact with reality in the sense that he needs the reassurance of seeing his therapist in front of him.

Within the basic framework of our psychoanalytic, psychodynamic treatment program, we are eclectic enough so that we make use of different treatment approaches. For instance, when medication is indicated, we will use it; we make extensive use of educational and activity programs, and, as I've said, we have both individual and different group therapies. We do not, however, make use of behavior modification techniques. The children we treat respond to and need experiential, emotional, and intellectual insights into their dilemmas.

The entire hospital is actually the treatment program. We have a school program that is state accredited, and that goes from kindergarten through high school. A child can graduate from high school with us, or the credits are transferable with other schools in town. The usual procedure regarding school is that a child spends a period of time in our school, and then, before he or she is ready to leave the hospital, goes to the public schools here in Topeka.

We have a recreational activity department that offers all sorts of sports, competitive and noncompetitive. We also make use of all the local recreational facilities. What we try to do is to give the children a sense of being a part of the community; they use the YMCA, the local swimming pool, and they go to local churches and synagogues.

For those who have to be in the hospital—especially the children who have to be in the closed section—we have a gymnasium, craft classes and shops, an art department, a woodworking shop, and other facilities. These, of course, are open to all our patients, whether they can or cannot leave the grounds.

In other words, we have a full program, and we do not choose activities for a child only because they would be specifically therapeutic to a particular problem, but also because they provide a more complete life for the child.

The staff members who head these activities and work with the children in the activities have been especially trained by us or have been trained somewhere else to work with emotionally disturbed children.

The most helpful thing, I believe, in getting the child over his apprehension about being here is the availability of experience in normal groups—through the school and the various activities. That is why we make such an effort to make use of the community resources. We try to move our children back into normal groups of children as quickly as possible, even when they are still patients in the hospital, to help them become part of an everyday life again.

We also deal with this whole problem of what it means to have been in the hospital and what it will mean to go back into community groups during a child's therapy.

I've found that a child gains the most insight into his or her problems experientially—that is, having the experience of living with people and interacting with people who understand emotional illness. Reacting with people who give them different responses than they have been receiving gives them a chance to see themselves, not as someone whom they have made angry sees them, but as someone understanding sees them, someone who can say, "Do you know how I feel when you act this way?" or, "You know, I think you're angry with me now."

Insight does come from what I would call this corrective living experience. That's as important as the actual individual psychotherapy, analysis, group or family therapy, which works for intellectual and emotional insights into the children's problems. In whatever kind of actual psychotherapy the child participates, he proceeds at his own pace and is helped to think about the family and about growing-up experiences. At his own pace he becomes aware, within his relationship with the therapist, not only of what went wrong and how it went wrong, but of how to then use his experience with the therapist to discover patterns that made things not work. In other words, the therapist helps him understand his patterns of interacting with people by showing him how his experiences with a new person (the therapist) were similar to those with his family.

We also use therapeutic medications when they are necessary. My estimate would be that, sometime during their stay with us, about a quarter of the children will receive some kind of medication—sometimes a tranquilizer or an antidepressant. Sometimes, a child who comes here will be so severely upset and so confused that we really can't reach him and talk to him in individual psychotherapy without some sort of medication.

However, we have a ratio of about three staff people to each patient, so with that sort of staff availability we make use of people more than we do medication, you might say. Three-quarters of the children are never on any medication at all. In other words, we do not give medication because we don't have the time or the facilities to deal with patients; we give it only when it is truly necessary for the individual.

Any child who has been on medication is no longer taking it by the time he leaves us; we would not discharge a patient still on medication unless he was going to another hospital.

About 85 percent of the children who come into the hospital return to their homes and to their families. This is a very high figure, but it must be remembered that we are very selective about the children whom we take into the hospital; we always have a long waiting list. We don't take anyone into the hospital who doesn't first come here with his family for a diagnostic study. So our recovery statistics are far better than average because of the very careful selective process: we take children whom we believe we can help.

Some of the young adults who have been in a successful treatment process and go on to college from here—having completed the high school program with us—do not return to the home situation.

About 15 percent go on to other institutions, where the care can be of a longer range, less intensive, and therefore less expensive.

Of the 85 percent who have been discharged, roughly a quarter of them will continue psychotherapy of some sort in their own communities on an outpatient basis. The others who are discharged return to their families and their communities. Of this last group, about a third will seek further help as adults.

When a child is ready for release, he has experienced both inward and outward changes. While he is here, he has gone through a real period of growth, and the changes he makes are very apparent. The most important meaning of change to the child is that he is now able to resume the normal growth process. He has been helped through a very difficult period, and can now get back into normal activities and relationships.

The problems that brought him here have been sufficiently relieved so that instead of being blocked in his growth process, he can now make use of his peer groups and his own family and his own community outside the hospital. Inside the hospital, he was able to participate in activities and groups, which he hadn't been able to do before he got here. Yet, because the hospitalization did not isolate him from associations with other people, or his family, he is now able to continue the stream of growth on the outside.

If a child has a setback after he has been discharged, he most likely will be able to deal with it. Most children and adolescents make use of the gains they have made, so when they have trouble in the future, they don't have to regress as far back as they had been; they can use the treatment process to understand what is making them troubled again.

There is a small percentage of children who, when they have a relapse, will be just as ill as they had been the first time; if they return to us, we have to do the treatment process all over again, but make use of the insights and gains the child had previously achieved.

But, as I have said, in the majority of cases the children go on to lead normal, happy, productive lives. They continue school, go into useful careers, and lead healthy social lives.

We have an active research program going on that allows us to keep in touch with the children and families after they leave us. This follow-up study attempts to learn about the children one year, five years, ten years, and longer, after their discharge. Sometimes we see them and their families on a yearly basis.

In addition to the follow-up study, many of the children keep in touch with us on their own. We've had former child patients come by when they were married, for instance, to introduce us to their wives or husbands or to their own children.

Perhaps 10 percent have to be hospitalized again. Again, this may seem like an incredibly small percentage, but it does not include those patients who go elsewhere for further help; only the ones who return here. The stresses that happen to everyone—the everyday anxieties, difficulties with jobs and marriage, for example—can cause distress in a former patient, just as it would cause an illness in someone who had never been hospitalized.

A great amount of our treatment program involves working with the children and the families toward the task of leaving the hospital. That, after all, is our goal. Treatment termination, from our standpoint, is as much of the growth process as any other part—helping the child work through all the feelings of what it will be like to return home again. The entire process here relies heavily on experiences the child has. His working through his leaving the hospital can also be a health-producing experience, and an important part of his total treatment with us.

Stephen A. Appelbaum, Ph.D.

Dr. Stephen A. Appelbaum received his Ph.D. at Boston University, and teaches and practices psychoanalysis and psychotherapy at the Menninger Foundation. Author of more than fifty articles and one book on psychotherapy, psychoanalysis, and clinical psychology, Dr. Appelbaum is a Fellow in the Advanced Studies Program, Department of Education, at the Foundation.

Recently, Dr. Appelbaum has been researching the various "newer" therapies (See Part Six: *Some Newer Therapies*) to determine their potential for incorporation into the treatment programs at the Menninger Foundation. Here he discusses the new therapies and the scientific attitude in clinical work.

The Menninger Foundation could be called "traditional," in that developments through the years have been founded on a basically psychoanalytic point of view. It is traditional, also, in a scientific sense: whatever is done or changed is first subjected to systematic thought, and when possible to formal experimentation. As we have done through the years, we are approaching the challenges and opportunities offered by the new therapies and consciousness-raising procedures with an interested and, I hope, creatively skeptical point of view. Part of my work has been to familiarize myself with these new therapies, write about them, and report back to my colleagues about them. As we compare and contrast these new procedures and beliefs with our own, we often find the same things said in different languages. But sometimes we find differences in emphases and techniques which hold promise of being effective. By proceeding in this systematic way we hope to avoid faddism, the overenthusiastic and unsupported plunging into anything that holds promise. Such impulsive eruptions into action and fervently held beliefs are neither fair to patients nor, in the long run, fair to the ideas themselves. If one enters into activities without integrating them with other activities and other knowledge, and without providing some fundamental basis for confidence, at the first sign of their "not working" the activities are given up. Instead, they should be examined to see what went wrong, and what ideas and techniques can be saved.

Ours is also a strong commitment to diagnosis, on the grounds that individual differences among people are so pronounced that no therapeutic procedure is equally good with all patients. Rather, we try to understand each patient in as great detail as possible, and choose among the various interventions on the basis of that knowledge. I believe that diagnosis is the weakest link in the therapy delivery system. Adequate diagnosis, often including the intensive use of psychological testing, is one of the strong points of our work, and one not available in many places.

When one mentions diagnosis, many people immediately think of diagnostic categories, the nosological groupings such as have been codified in psychiatric texts and official manuals. These days many people complain that such pigeonholing merely results in pejorative-sounding labels being attached to patients. These people are, in my opinion, correctly arguing against the kind of diagnosis whose goal is only classification. The kind of diagnosis that we strive for at the Menninger Foundation begins with the diagnostic classification, and then goes on to describe in detail the person who falls within that large category.

Traditional nosological categorization is often a useful orienting device; if one's treatment decisions are as gross as the categories, then it is an appropriate and sufficient one. But the greater the number and range of interventions available, the more one needs to be subtle and precise in his diagnosis. One of the problems in research on psychotherapy has been its dealing with psychotherapy as if it were homogeneous, like aspirin—prescribed for just about anybody on the basis of symptoms. In fact, there are probably no two psychotherapies which are alike, just as there are no two people alike, no two patients alike, no two therapists alike, no two matches between therapists and petients alike. Thus, to ask in the abstract, which treatment is better is to turn one's attention away from the relevant questions, namely, which treatment is better administered by whom, under what conditions, and for what person? Each part of this expanded question requires a careful delineation.

Over a period of 15 years we did elaborate research in psychotherapy here, the Psychotherapy Research Project of the Menninger Foundation. In this project we examined patients before treatment, at the termination of treatment, and two years after that. Neither patients nor therapists knew that they were, in effect, subjects in a research study until the treatment was over, and so any influences such knowledge might have had were controlled. To some extent we also tried to control differences between therapists, for example using those with at least three years' experience, past their residencies. We assigned patients to various kinds of psychotherapy on the basis of an intensive diagnostic study. We even attended to the match between patient and therapist by judging whether the therapist's skill was the same with a particular patient subject as it was judged to be with his other patients.

One of our findings was that those patients who developed the greatest amount of insight did best of all the patients. Yet there was another group of patients who were judged to have developed little insight, to have accomplished little in the way of resolution of conflict, indeed not even to have been interested and adept in psychological phenomena, who nonetheless showed significant gains from their psychotherapy. This suggests that there are other factors in psychological treatments from which people can benefit besides the development of insight.

Overall, the study can be taken to support those who believe that the development of insight is the major factor in bringing about beneficial change, and it also can be taken to support those who say that an overabsorption with insight may result in lack of attention to, and exploitation of, other curative factors. The question of the place of insight in bringing about beneficial change is best dealt with by specifying how much and what kind of insight, developed in the context of what kind of relationship, between what kind of patient and what kind of therapist. This is the appropriate way to decide, in any particular instance, what kind of treatment a patient should have and what to attend to and emphasize in that treatment.

This, then, is the context in which our attempts to experiment with and evaluate the new therapies takes place. On the basis of this investigation I anticipate the following options: 1) That for some clinical problems we may practice one or another of the therapies more or less as it is practiced elsewhere; 2) that we may incorporate some of these procedures and thinking into our present range of interventions; 3) that we may continue largely as before, but with improvements through thinking through the issues raised by the new therapies, by taking seriously their criticisms and evaluating seriously their suggested alternatives.

Whatever the psychotherapeutic intervention, we have only begun to scratch the surface of the question of durability of change. Few practitioners have made adequate assessments of their patients at termination of treatment, to say nothing of assessing how life has gone for their patients years afterward. There is reason to believe that the time of termination is a poor time to evaluate the results of therapy. By definition it is a stressful time, and the opinions of both patient and therapist may be strongly influenced by their needs to view the treatment in particular ways. If the sole goal of the treatment was to overcome clear, delimited symptoms, that could at least be evaluated at termination. But the goal of many psychotherapies is to improve the pattern and quality of life. An assessment of that would require that the person have time to live that life and demonstrate what he has been able to make of it. In principle it would be best assessed at the end of the person's life. In the Psychotherapy Research Project of the Menninger Foundation at the follow-up point two years after treatment, we found that some people did better than was anticipated at the time of termination and some people did less well. But change of one kind or another was more the rule than the exception. These results suggest that adequate follow-up, probably a good many years after termination of psychotherapy, is necessary if we are adequately to learn about and judge many of the effects of psychotherapy and their durability.

I believe that the popularity of psychological treatment has exceeded its scientific status and its capacities for high quality training and practice. Such popularity deprives us of an incentive to evaluate carefully every aspect of practice and training. We need to provide ourselves with such an incentive, to be disciplined and evaluative, whether in formal research projects or in the individual practitioner's thoughtful assessment of his therapeutic experiences. In this way we can best take advantage of the yield from creative practitioners, giving each new school its due and each patient the best possible help.

CHAPTER *FIVE*

Treatment of a
Very Special Person: Ann
Hugo J. Zee, M.D.

The hospital experience of the young woman known as Ann, as told here by her doctor, Hugo J. Zee, of the C. F. Menninger Memorial Hospital, offers considerable insight into the humanizing effort in the hospital treatment of schizophrenics. Ann, who as a child appeared to be the model daughter—the "princess" of her parents—was actually a deeply troubled girl. It wasn't until she entered adolescence that her inner troubles became obvious in her behavior. Hospitalized by her r other at the Menninger Clinic, she received long-term treatment and eventually grew to lead a healthy, productive life.

The following account is abstracted with permission from Dr. Zee's article "Treatment of a Very Special Person," published in the Summer 1974 issue of *Menninger Perspective* (Volume 5, Number 2, pp. 4-11).

Although we hold no corner on the treatment of schizophrenia, the following account may serve as one approach in which a humanizing involvement is attempted, leading to a better "arrangement of affairs"—integration rather than exclusion of what was once considered alien.

The Patient

Unlike the majority of patients in our hospital who have already had a number of attempts at treatment, Ann came to us without a history of hospitalization. She had had three therapists prior to being referred here. The straw that broke the camel's back was that she had become a source of considerable public embarrassment to her only living parent, her mother, who had always placed a high value on what was proper and fashionable. In an unconscious effort to embarrass her mother, Ann would make indiscriminate, overt and coarse sexual gestures; she would mimic people in offensive ways, and use crude, vulgar, and loud language in public.

Apparently, these actions bothered her mother more than the fact that Ann often sat by herself, sometimes giggling, sometimes mumbling, often being unresponsive to her surroundings, obviously quite confused and indecisive. Indeed, it was her embarrassing and extremely offensive public behavior which caused her family to feel hospital referral was so urgent, although in private she had exhibited overt serious symptoms for three or four years prior to her referral. . . .

[Ann's] past history, especially her early life history, sounded like a fairy tale. It took years of painstaking effort to unravel what had been going on. Obviously, there was a need to hide a lot.

To hear her mother's version, Ann had been an adorable baby and although she (the mother) had some doubts at first about having the child, she repeatedly exclaimed that Ann was a delight and easier to rear than her other two children. Ann, so the story goes, was an active youngster, popular with the kids in the neighborhood, even a leader among them. She made good grades, showed an unusual sense of responsibility, and excelled in sports and other recreational activities. The mother added that she spent many hours with her and that there were many happy outings. In general, the description of Ann was that of a little princess. All this came to a sudden halt, so it seemed, once Ann became an adolescent and went to high school. . . .

Another story unfolded over the years as Ann was here in treatment. Indeed, although she was a planned baby, Ann's conception was more to appease her father who was gradually failing in his business and who needed an indication of his wife's continuing devotion. Although the mother hoped that after raising two children she could become involved in a career of her own, she made the sacrifice and became pregnant. She did in fact open a beauty parlor not long after Ann was born . . . a career that proved extremely successful. Meanwhile, Ann and her father became very close and spent much time with each other—especially when her father's business continued to decline while her mother's business continued to improve.

This reversal of roles in the family frequently has been noted in families of schizophrenic patients. In this case the mother increasingly assumed the role of the head of the family, while the father's role initially shifted toward assuming more motherly duties. . . .

Several years later, when Ann was still a child, her father died of a "heart attack" as the tale goes. Later we discovered he actually committed suicide. The full impact of this tragedy on Ann is still not known; the past history simply relates that there was no adverse reaction. By inference, however, we could assume that this had a profound effect on her. This was revealed in Ann's fear of developing personal attachments and her frequent feelings of responsibility for the deaths of people with whom she had only the remotest contact. The suicidal act put such a frightening sense of guilt on the family that the death could not be properly dealt with, leaving Ann alone with her grotesque childhood fantasies.

It took many painful sessions, sometimes over strong protests from her mother, but as the bits and pieces began to fit, a picture emerged of the worrisome, lonely, unhappy and overly compliant child Ann had been from early childhood. She had dropped hints indicating she thought her body was ugly, loathsome and evil; she didn't like to be touched, let alone cuddled, and she often suffered nightmares with recurrent themes of self-dissolution. Her mother's response to these troubled signs was to counter them desperately by organizing parties for Ann, providing her with fancy clothing, inviting friends over and even luring teachers into treating Ann in special ways.

. . . Rereading her chart, I was struck by what effort it had taken, especially on the part of the social worker, to keep Ann in treatment here. For a period of almost a year the social worker struggled with Ann's mother's reluctance to accept the treatment as a new way of dealing with Ann. She insisted her daughter was getting the wrong treatment, that we had read too much into things, that another doctor be assigned to the case, that different medication be tried. Several times she tried to dictate to us other forms of treatment she had heard about, or she would set deadlines by which time she said she would take her daughter out of treatment.

Eventually, these desperate attempts to deny what was gradually becoming obvious, to find blame rather than solutions, or to avoid feelings of overwhelming guilt within herself, gave way to acceptance; and with it came some change in Ann, as well. Such battles, of course, were not helped by the fact that often Ann didn't show much change. She sided with her mother in her denial; indeed, at times it seemed she was getting worse and feelings of despondency would settle on everyone involved.

No treatment of a schizophrenic patient is complete without family treatment as an integral part. The ties between the patient and the family are usually so loaded and so intense that unless we treat them with diligence, the treatment team doesn't have a chance to sufficiently loosen the patient from the family to engage him in treatment. . . .

But another reason the family needs to be closely involved in the treatment of the schizophrenic patient is that we can learn from them their specific ways of relating with the patient. This information is important because the treating staff often becomes involved in similar, if not identical, patterns. . . .

When I first saw Ann, what stood out most was the sharp contrast between her and her mother. While her mother made a striking, dynamic, engaging impression, Ann was dressed in dumpy dark clothes. She usually stood quietly by in a hunched-over, immobile posture, while her mother was obviously in charge of everything that went on. Ann was aloof, she answered questions in a detached, staccatolike manner, which made her sound like a robot. Occasionally, her severely drawn face would break into an inappropriate smile as she would make some vague sexual overture, which seemed aimed more to repel than to entice. In unguarded moments, she seemed to be mumbling to herself as though responding to hallucinations. When I took her for walks, she sometimes just wandered off as if she didn't notice me, although perhaps her intention was that I should go after her and catch her.

For quite some time there was little or no acknowledgment of me when I visited her in her room; she seemed more comfortable there than out in the hallway mixing with the other patients. Sometimes she complained that I controlled her body, that I made her do evil things. At one time she said it was her mind which caused some loud noise that was going on outside her room. Not only did she repeat, in an automatic way, some phrases I had used, but also her body posture would mimic some of my body movements. When she left her room, she moved slowly along the wall like a shadow, sometimes running into things as though she was not really aware where her body stopped and where the boundaries of the furniture began. . . .

The factors I have just described are all indications of Ann's extremely poor self-concept. One had the feeling that she sometimes didn't know where her body ended and mind began. . . . This sense of continuity existing between her body and the outside world is central to our theory of schizophrenia which stresses that *the* core problem with schizophrenic patients is a poorly established sense of self. . . .

Ann's poor self-concept was well demonstrated by her difficulty in recognizing or even acknowledging me. . . . I felt we had achieved some progress when she referred to me as "him." It was at about that point that I began to sit down beside her and tell her who I was, more emphatically and in concrete detail. For example, I would tell her that I was sitting beside her, I was sitting on a chair, she was sitting on the bed, that I was the tallest man on the Section with the shortest name. . . . I took her hand and let her touch my beard. Then I took her hand and let it stroke her own face, and commented on the differences between the two.

It took several days of these primitive ways of "getting acquainted" until she finally began to refer to me as Dr. Zee. . . .

Ann's wish for withdrawal to her private room seems to make sense if we realize how overwhelmed she felt by all the internal and external stimuli. By withdrawing, she was at least curbing some of these forces and by being able to control a much more simplified environment (i.e., the territory of her own room), she could begin to start putting some pieces together and at least have the gratification of some degree of mastery. . . . She could begin to put things in order at her own leisurely pace. Of course this meant tolerating a lot from her, a kind of meeting her at her own level—i.e., a messy room, a messy appearance. We gently coaxed her along to bring *some* order in her life, *not* (as her mother had done) *take over* her life. . . .

Another way of dealing with excessive sensitivity to stimulation was the use of major tranquilizers. These drugs do much to reduce the effects of excessive stimulation and arousal in such patients. For example, after Ann received the medication, she was able to move out of her room more spontaneously and more frequently. She seemed less afraid of people and she engaged in minimal conversation. She would accept help with minor chores such as fixing her hair or cleaning up her room, and she accepted being with others while eating her meals. . . .

Assigning Ann to someone who would spend a considerable amount of time with her (at first just to establish an acquaintance, but later to help her explore her inner life) was an extremely valuable, if not *essential,* learning experience from which Ann could correct some of her basic misconceptions about herself and others. I am talking, of course, of psychotherapy. Through the process of relearning how to relate more fruitfully to someone, especially in the sphere of intimacy which forms the substrata of our everyday living style, Ann eventually developed a greater trust in herself and in others. She was then able to become more successfully involved with the real world.

To assure that such a relationship encompasses the total self, a therapist must work in close coordination with the other treatment approaches; i.e., family, milieu and drug. . . .

Early in her psychotherapy Ann was mute with the therapist. However, with those least likely to be in contact with the therapist (like the night nursing shift) she confessed she heard voices telling her not to talk with him lest she be killed. To get some relief from this dilemma, she often experienced death wishes toward the therapist, fearing their fulfillment during his absences. . . .

Later, as Ann dared to be more open with her "secrets," she sometimes experienced extremely frightening episodes of retaliation from the "voices" for her disloyalty, or from the therapist for her death wishes toward him. During such times Ann's physical and psychological appearance was worse than ever—a discouraging sign unless one had a good overall understanding about what was going on.

Space doesn't allow a more complete summary of Ann's treatment. Suffice it to say that she excelled in English, a subject she pursued as she resumed her college studies after a number of years of hospitalization. Separating from the hospital proved to be very difficult, despite the fact that during the last years of her hospital treatment she established increasing contact with the community. On a lesser scale she saw leaving the hospital as a repetition of the separation from the family, so she experienced it as being "left on the North Pole at 3:00 in the morning." Reaching out to others still seemed a forbidding and frightening act. This separation phase was punctuated with suicidal preoccupations, some drug abuse, crises with those she was living with in town, running away from treatment back to the maternal fold and a destructive love affair. . . .

After an agonizing period of painful despair, Ann resumed treatment and increasingly was able to make more satisfying use of her talents. By now, some five years later, I have only sporadic contact with her, but she is well on her way in her career.

CHAPTER SIX

"I Have Everything to Live For"
Germaine Stuart

Germaine Stuart, an attractive, well-educated woman in her early forties, lives in New York with her teen-age daughter. She is presently
studying Yoga and Eastern philosophies and is active in various volunteer programs throughout the city.

In this chapter, Germaine tells of her hospitalizations in two private
facilities—Silver Hill, in Connecticut, and the New York University
Hospital's psychiatric unit—and her personal discovery and growth
since her hospitalizations.

Germaine Stuart

BB: Germaine, would you tell us a bit about your background?

GERMAINE: Well, I was born in New York City, but my family
moved to Washington, D.C., when I was very young, so I actually grew
up in D.C. My parents were upper middle-class people—materially, we
were pretty well off. I returned to New York when I got married—my
husband was a member of the foreign service. That was in 1955. We
lived abroad for about three years, then moved back to the city. In 1969
we were divorced. It was a pretty traumatic experience for me, emotionally.

BB: Do you have any children?

GERMAINE: I have a daughter who's thirteen now—a marvelous child. We have a great relationship. Open, honest. I think we talk about everything together.

BB: She lives with you?

GERMAINE: Yes, here in our co-op. I have a babysitter Maria— well, actually she is much more a member of the family than a baby-sitter—who used to stay with her when I was working. After school. And she was a great help when I was in the hospital. More than a great help—I wouldn't have been able to get through everything, I don't think, if it hadn't been for this woman.

BB: What brought you to seek professional help at the start?

GERMAINE: Well, I guess the divorce was the catalyst. As I said, it was emotionally traumatic. A messy affair. My husband had met a much younger woman through his work, and for almost two years, I knew he was having an affair with her. He'd had other affairs in the past, and I more or less tolerated his infidelities. But this was different. He wanted to marry her. For two years I fought it—which made it all the more difficult to accept, to deal with.

I couldn't accept that total rejection—especially because he wanted to marry someone else. And I focused all my anger and frustrations on her —"the other woman," "the home breaker." It was all her fault—that was how I was reacting. Well, we were divorced in 1969, and even then I couldn't accept it.

The culmination of this was in September of 1970. I was drinking heavily, going downhill rapidly. I was having severe depressions, as well as all the symptoms of alcoholism—blackouts, not remembering long periods of time. During this time, I was seeing a doctor, a psychiatrist, to whom my G.P. had referred me when I was trying to save the marriage. He was a marriage counselor—at least, that was how I originally started seeing him. My husband had gone to one session with him, then refused to go again, so I had been seeing him alone. After the divorce, I was still seeing him. Only then, it was no longer for marriage counseling, obviously.

BB: What was he treating you for—anything specific?

GERMAINE: For depressions. Since then, I've learned that I am a depressive and that it's probably a biochemical disturbance. At any rate, he was treating me with an arsenal of medication. I think that at one time, I had twenty-six prescriptions through him—Thorazine, Stelazine, things of that order. And I was drinking heavily then. He was aware of this, yet he never warned me not to drink while I was taking these medications.

About six months before my first hospitalization, I had asked this doctor to admit me to Silver Hill—a private psychiatric hospital in Connecticut, run by the Silver Hill Foundation. I'd heard of them, and knew they were good. I felt they could help me with my drinking problems, and with everything else. But he said that we'd be better able to work out the drinking outside a hospital.

BB: Was it this doctor, then, who finally admitted you?

GERMAINE: Not exactly. What happened was that I went to a doctor—a clinic—for stomach problems. A doctor there realized I had more than stomach trouble. He said I should go into a hospital. Well, the psychiatrist who had been treating me was out of town, so his associate admitted me to Silver Hill. The doctor from the clinic had said that I might have time to wait until my psychiatrist returned.

BB: You were treated for alcoholism at Silver Hill?

GERMAINE: No—for a nervous breakdown. You see, I wasn't sure that I was an alcoholic at that time. After all, my psychiatrist didn't seem to think so, and I trusted him. I *did* know I was depressed, and that my entire life was falling apart. I needed help.

BB: How long were you there?

GERMAINE: Three months. When I left, I felt on top of things; I felt marvelous. There's a psychiatric term for the sort of recovery I had then—it's called "flight into health." It's an enormous degree of recovery, not proportionate to the therapy or medication that one gets. I think that in my case, this "flight into health" had a lot to do with the happiness of my surroundings at Silver Hill, and with the fact that I had no worries about the home front. My daughter was being taken care of by Maria.

BB: Germaine, would you describe Silver Hill—the type of hospital it is?

GERMAINE: Well, it's a private hospital, in the country. I was very happy there. It's an open hospital, and I could have packed up and left any time I'd wanted to. Of course, they don't encourage that. As a matter of fact, they generally won't take someone unless they're going to stay a minimum of six weeks to two months. If a person needs only a few weeks' treatment, they refer them elsewhere. As it was explained to me, they found that when a patient leaves after a very short time, the chance of recidivism is quite high.

The grounds of Silver Hill are fabulous—it's like a luxurious country club. There's an Olympic-sized swimming pool, tennis courts, beautiful gardens. I saw a doctor three times a week. I didn't want to leave until I was ready. I thought that those three months were terribly beneficial.

BB: When you left Silver Hill, did you return home?

GERMAINE: Yes—but I also returned to drinking. I continued seeing my doctor from Silver Hill on an outpatient basis, and at one point, I told him, "This same old alcoholic pattern is returning." You see, when I'd been in the hospital, and when I'd started getting well, the doctors had been unable to pinpoint the alcohol problem. So, I returned to Silver Hill for a week to work out the drinking problem with my doctor there.

He gave me Antabuse—a drug that makes you violently ill if you take a drink—and suggested I go to Alcoholics Anonymous, which I did. I went to meetings for about a year, and at the time, especially because I had just faced the fact that I really was an alcoholic, it helped.

The problem had been that, even though I was seeing alcohol as a problem, I thought that it was related only to the emotional upheaval that my divorce had precipitated. It took me a while in AA to understand that what I was going through wasn't a one-shot thing—it had gone beyond drinking to deal with a specific problem. At one point, when I was in Paris to visit friends and not at all that unhappy at the time, I was consuming a bottle of wine a day in my hotel room. Just drinking for the sake of it—I had no pressures, no immediate unhappiness at the time. I just needed the drink.

At any rate, after about a year, I stopped going to AA. I think that the only thing about AA that bothered me—and still does—is the fundamentalist approach that some of the people there take: "Throw away all your pills, don't take medication." Well, these aren't doctors talking, and many people might be on medication for very good reason. I think that can be harmful. Besides, it had got to the point that I could handle it. I was taking my antabuse, which is an excellent backup in case the urge strikes. The drug stays effective up to five days after you've taken it, so you can't even decide to forgo a pill in a moment of weakness. You'd have to plan a binge—and that's not the way binges happen. I'd come to find that AA meetings, where everyone talks about drinking, were making me think about drinking more than I normally would. So I stopped going.

BB: And you don't drink at all anymore?

GERMAINE: No. Well, at first, when I was on the antabuse, I experimented a bit—I'm pretty inquisitive, and I suppose I just had to see for myself. I tried wine with dinner. I had a slight reaction and told my doctor about it. He increased the strength of my dosage. Some people need more than others, and after a few more "experiments," I learned that it wasn't something to play with.

BB: Are you taking any other medications now?

GERMAINE: My present psychiatrist has prescribed Elavil and Valium. The Elavil is an antidepressant, and like the Antabuse, I view it as a necessary medication—probably like a diabetic views his insulin. As long as you take it, the problem is under control. You know, I heard once that until insulin was discovered, diabetics were considered emotionally ill during an attack. But with insulin, they're normal. The same with depressives.

BB: I do agree with you there. There have been enormous strides made in the biochemical approach to emotional illness. How long have you been taking Elavil?

GERMAINE: This is fairly recent, and actually, the Elavil story is the story of my experience at New York University Hospital, and the things that led to it. You see, I'd been taking another antidepressant since the early 1960s when, about three months after my daughter was born, I went through a genuine postpartum depression. Then, I was given Tofranil, and had been taking it until about a year ago.

Well, last year, a number of things were happening to me—on the job (I was working for a foundation as the office manager and assistant to the president), and within my former husband's family. Let me explain: my ex-husband, who had married again and was living abroad, died. He'd been ill and in the hospital for several months before, so I knew he had been in serious condition. His parents had grown quite bitter toward me, and several incidents—little things that were petty but that all added up—had already happened with them. When it came time for the funeral, I received a note from them, asking me not to attend. I was hurt, but the funeral affair ended with me not going.

And then, I was having problems at work. Someone had been hired "over my head." She was supposed to have been a secretary to the president, but I soon discovered that she was hired more or less as an assistant to the president. I'd been asked to acquaint her with the office, and when I started introducing her as a secretary—which was what I'd been told she was hired as—she became upset and told me she'd been hired as the assistant to the president. Well, they "promoted me upstairs," as they say—gave me a new title—but my duties were diminished. The whole episode was upsetting. And in combination with everything else that was happening, I started spiraling into a depression.

BB: So it was outside pressures that precipitated your second breakdown?

GERMAINE: They contributed toward it. When I started feeling depressed about everything, I started self-medicating. I had all my prescriptions, including the Tofranil. Also, I wasn't seeing a psychiatrist in that period of time. But the Tofranil wasn't working. I was getting more and more depressed, and kept taking larger and larger doses.

Finally, I went to see a psychiatrist here in the city. He had been recommended by my doctor from Silver Hill. This doctor—whom I am still seeing now—was horrified at the strength of my dosage of Tofranil. He said I was suffering from a paradoxical effect: I was building up an immunity to the drug, and it was probably making me more depressed instead of helping to pull me out of the depression. He suggested hospitalization to overcome these effects.

I took a leave of absence from my work, and entered the hospital for three weeks.

BB: What was your stay at this hospital like?

GERMAINE: It was remarkably pleasant, and not at all disruptive to my life. That is, it caused much less of an upheaval than my stay in Silver Hill. In the first place, my daughter could come and see me regularly. This was reassuring to her, to see that Ten West—that's what the psychiatric ward at NYU Hospital is called—was a happy place and that no one there was terribly disturbed.

I should explain that at Silver Hill, during the initial treatment period of three weeks, you're not allowed visitors, and are allowed only to phone one person. So the first time, I hadn't seen my daughter right away—also, because it was out of the city, the distance created a problem. But at NYU, the mere closeness of the hospital made my daughter feel better.

The impressive thing about Ten West was the ambience of the place. I never felt as though I was in a hospital. We all wore civilian clothes; the staff is positively top-notch and I felt that they were terribly dedicated people. And the patients there were all incredibly tolerant of each other's moods. It was a sympathetic group of people—as a matter of fact, I made two very good friends there, and we still keep in touch. You know, it's very encouraging for the three of us to see each other now, to see that we're all well.

Ten West, you see, takes people for only short stays, and if a person is more seriously ill or needs a more structured environment, they won't go there.

BB: What sort of treatment did you have there?

GERMAINE: Well, I was there primarily to make the transition in my medication from Tofranil to Elavil. I was taking both—a combination of both—in order to make the transition. It's interesting that in Ten West, when the nurse gives you your medication, you have to take it in her presence so that no one ends up disposing of their pills in secret.

I also had my first experience with group therapy there. The staff would invite certain patients, who they felt would benefit, to participate in a group.

We went on outings, to museums and parks. Also Ten West has enough activities to keep a person busy all day long, but there are no demands.

BB: Did you see your own doctor while you were there?

GERMAINE: Yes, two or three times a week. And the rest of the time, I saw one of the hospital's resident doctors. You see, between your private doctor and the resident doctors, a treatment program is worked out for you on an individual basis. That was another thing that impressed me about Ten West—you see a doctor every day.

BB: Did you share a room with someone else?

GERMAINE: No—I had requested and got a private room. I felt that I needed it at the time, to work out my problems.

BB: What has your daughter's reaction to your hospitalizations been?

GERMAINE: Oh—this is very interesting. Actually, the word "interesting" is a bit cold in reference to this. When I spoke of my hospitalization at Silver Hill, I said that I'd had no worries on the home front. At the time, and from my point of view, this was true. But my daughter was going through something quite different than I'd thought she was. You see, Maria—the woman who has been with us for years—had told my daughter, Anne, about the fact that I was in a hospital. But as I've already explained, part of Silver Hill's initial treatment policy is that you can't have visitors during the first three-week period. So for three weeks, I didn't speak with my daughter; the only person I spoke with was Maria—about the logistics of the home, and so forth.

Well, Anne has very recently told me that during that first period of time, after I'd gone to Silver Hill, when she hadn't spoken with me, she thought I had died. She had convinced herself that Maria's story about my being in the hospital was a cover-up for my death. I was shocked when Anne told me about this. She hadn't let on about it one bit after she did come up to see me in the hospital. It wasn't until about six months ago, during one of our nighttime talks, that she brought it up.

At any rate, after three weeks, I was able to speak with her on the phone. Then, once she heard I was alive, she thought I'd been kidnapped —by the ubiquitous "they." And it wasn't until she came up to Silver Hill and saw the beautiful, peaceful surroundings that she realized I was all right. Once all her ideas had been calmed, she felt good about it.

But during my stay at NYU Hospital, Anne felt much better about things. I could go home on weekend passes to be with Anne, and we talked on the phone every day.

BB: Does your daughter understand about your illness—that you take medication for it?

GERMAINE: Yes. I've talked with her about all of this.

BB: Has anyone else in your family ever suffered from an emotional problem?

GERMAINE: My mother—she was also a depressive. But in those days, medications hadn't been developed to control the problem. She went on medication in her last years, but perhaps it was too late then. Also, she spent a short time in Silver Hill, and I think she was always apprehensive about returning there. She was old and lived alone, and had a real dread about being a burden on other people. But she always held together when I was in the hospital. When I would be getting better, she would break down. She died a few years ago. I'm only recently coming to accept her death.

BB: Germaine, since you left University Hospital, have you suffered from depressions?

GERMAINE: No. As a matter of fact, I feel better than I have during any time in my life. Of course, I'm taking the Elavil and I see my psychiatrist regularly. I think that one of the reasons I had a depression before I went into NYU Hospital was because I hadn't seen a psychiatrist for two years.

Now I see my doctor every two weeks, and I'm no longer in therapy for a specific problem. I'm in a more preventive type of psychotherapy —adjusting my behavior patterns, exploring myself. It's an upward thing, and the psychiatrist I'm seeing now is a doctor with whom I can work for the first time.

Then I also have the security of knowing there is a hospital like NYU in case anything does happen. Also, my relationship with Anne is extremely comforting. And aside from my ex-husband's parents, his relatives have been marvelous; they've sort of scooped us up and made us feel as though we are family members.

BB: Then you consider yourself cured?

GERMAINE: Well, I see my condition as a chronic thing, which needs continual treatment in the form of medication. My other problems—life problems, more or less—can be worked out between me and my doctor, and personally, I don't feel that I'll ever be hospitalized again. Had I had someone like this doctor in the first place, perhaps I'd never have gotten to the point of having to be hospitalized.

BB: So you would say that your life has changed significantly on a day-to-day level?

GERMAINE: Yes—especially the way I handle things now. If I get anxious now, I'll call my psychiatrist right away rather than wait for my appointment schedule. And I'm more aware of the signs of a coming depression. As an example, if I started taking afternoon naps, I'd call my doctor right away, because that is one of the classic signs of an oncoming depression.

I guess you would say my life has changed in other ways, too. I'm not working now—I've decided not to go back to work until my daughter is older. She enjoys doing things with me now; in a few years she may not —she'll be making her own life. I mean, I have the rest of my life to be a "career girl." Actually, I look upon my job ending as good fortune— the firm I was with was in financial trouble and laid off a number of its staff.

I should explain that when I was divorced, my ex-husband was very generous in his settlement, and I have no financial worries. I don't have to work, and in that way I am much more fortunate than most people.

BB: What sort of interests do you have now, Germaine?

GERMAINE: Well, I love the ballet—my daughter and I go often. And I'm involved in various volunteer work. That and travel, which I do quite a bit of. And skiing. I've also started playing tennis once a week with a foursome—that's great exercise. I feel much better when my body is in shape; I do setting-up exercises every morning.

I've also recently begun Yoga one morning a week with a group of friends. It was funny, I told my psychiatrist one day how good the Yoga exercises make me feel and started telling him that he should look into Yoga, that it would do a lot of his patients good; well, he pulled a pamphlet from his drawer and handed it to me. It was about Yoga, and he said he was going to suggest it to me. Yoga has opened a whole new dimension for me, and I intend to pursue it—to study the philosophy and beliefs behind it.

BB: Since your hospitalization, then, would you say that you've gained considerable insights into yourself and into what caused your problems before?

GERMAINE: Yes, definitely. As I've said, I see my basic condition as a biochemical problem and I have to have medication to control it.

But I've also learned a lot about my psychological problems in the past. When I was married, I was living vicariously through my husband. Even though you might say I participated—I was active as a diplomat's wife . . . the socializing, the hostessing and so forth. But I was totally dependent on him. I didn't possess an opinion of my own—they were *his* opinions.

Now I'm reaching the point of being an independent person, doing what I like. And I have to be careful not to become too dependent on my daughter, not to start building my life through her as I did through my husband. But I don't think it will be a problem, because I'm aware of it now. I enjoy living singly; I have no immediate intention of marrying again—perhaps when my daughter is older I'll start thinking about it, but for now, I enjoy my life without a man.

I've learned and accepted the fact that I can't do it alone—I need certain backstops: the medication, the psychotherapy, the security I have financially and in other ways on the home front. With my psychiatrist, I'm learning how to develop my own inner strength—my own personality, I suppose.

A while ago, I read the book about the "Type A" personality, and I've learned that that's a fair description of me—a compulsive perfectionist; I don't think you can change the Type A personality, but I think you can adjust to the circumstances of it; I'm trying to do that—adjust my personality to circumstances.

This has been a period of learning for me—of practicing the tools for adapting to situations. I remember that in the past I thought of suicide a lot; it was a seductive alternative during the times when I couldn't cope, but ultimately I realized that it would be terrible for my daughter. Now I don't think suicide would ever be a factor in the future . . . I have everything to live for.

Another significant change in my life has been with my weight. Before I'd entered Silver Hill, I was terribly overweight and that had done its share in contributing to my depressions; I lost weight there, but when I started working again in 1972, I started gaining again. Then, when I started seeing the psychiatrist I go to now, he sent me to a nutritionist to see if a nine-hundred-calorie-a-day diet would be safe for me. (It was.) I was on the diet while I was in NYU Hospital, so by the time I'd returned home, I already had a head start on the weight problem; I lost thirty-five pounds in six months, and today weight is no longer a problem.

BB: From the way you look today, I'm surprised that weight ever was a problem. But you seem to be handling everything marvelously.

GERMAINE: There is one thing I'd like to add that I think might be pointed out to other people—and that's about insurance. When I went into Silver Hill, my insurance policy would not cover any of the expenses; according to a clause in the policy, Silver Hill did not count as a hospital; a hospital, to them, was defined as an institution with an operating room. Well, Silver Hill, being a purely psychiatric hospital and not part of a general hospital, had no operating table, and I was faced with a fifteen-thousand-dollar bill to pay for myself. The hospital allowed me to pay it in installments, but I remember telling them jokingly that it would be cheaper for me to donate an operating room than to pay the bill.

People should check over their policies for those fine-print clauses. Today I can't buy major medical hospitalization insurance because of my history of two hospitalizations. Fortunately, I could pay for a hospitalization if I would ever need it again. But not everyone could.

BB: Well, thank you very much, Germaine. I'm sure that your entire experience will be encouraging to a lot of people.

PART TWO

Aftercare

It is becoming more and more obvious that aftercare—and I mean good aftercare—is absolutely essential for the person coming out of a hospital. It is a rare person, indeed, who can make the transition to the "outside" without any follow-up care.

The hospital treats a person in a crisis situation. But how can he or she be sure that a similar crisis doesn't recur? Where does one go to minimize the possibility of a relapse? If the circumstances of a person's life were trying before, they aren't going to have vanished while he was hospitalized. He must learn to cope and change things. And he needs a transition period to do that.

Aftercare is perhaps the touchiest subject in the area of mental health. It implies proprietary homes and poorly run halfway houses, transient hotels and neighborhood drug centers that become dealers' headquarters. But there are some good aftercare centers, run by concerned professionals, which should serve as a model for planned centers.

In this section two different types of exemplary aftercare centers for a person emerging from the hospital are explored. One focuses on psychotherapy, helping the person to gain insight into the specific problems that brought about his or her crisis situation; the other focuses on the entire realm of social and vocational rehabilitation. There are day care centers for recently emerging patients all over the country—the only thing we need is more of them.

CHAPTER SEVEN

The Karen Horney Clinic
Day Care Treatment Center
Louis Hott, M.D.

In 1955, three years after the death of Karen Horney, the clinic bearing her name and embodying her dream of providing free and low-cost out-patient care for all members of the community, opened its doors. In the 1930s and 1940s Horney distinguished herself as a pioneer in psycho-analysis in this country by challenging several Freudian concepts. The cultural, or social, conditions under which people live, she said, have a crucial impact on their emotional problems. She did not believe that a person's innermost self, his "real self," is the primitive, vile little "id" of Freud that had to be kept under control; the real self, she said, is a posi-tive thing, which must be allowed to grow. "I believe that man can change and go on changing as long as he lives," she wrote.[1]

Her optimistic, positive concepts of change and growth led to the development of a new school of psychoanalytic thought, and ultimately, to the founding of the Karen Horney Clinic under its first medical direc-tor, Dr. Paul Lussheimer. Today, the clinic is nationally recognized for its research into human behavior, its training of doctors, and its treat-ment and community programs.

Unlike many community clinics, its psychotherapy is almost complete-ly in the hands of psychoanalysts. Unlike many psychoanalytic clinics, its services reach people from every walk of life and with a broad range

1. See *Our Inner Conflicts*, by Karen Horney. New York: W. W. Norton (copyright, 1945).

of problems: the emotionally disturbed adult, adolescent, and child, the child with learning disabilities, the sexual deviant, the couple with marital problems, the retarded child and adult, the elderly isolate, the schizophrenic.

Part of its community program is the day care treatment center, which serves young adults who are emerging from a period of hospitalization. The five-day-a-week program is designed to strengthen the ex-patient's readjustment to community life through various therapies: individual and group psychoanalytically oriented therapy, occupational therapy, and milieu therapy (therapy aimed at helping the patient adjust to the practical aspects of his day-to-day life).

To be eligible for the day care treatment center, as well as for the other Horney Clinic programs, one must reside in the clinic's catchment area, which takes in the east side of New York City, from Third Street to Sixty-fourth Street. (All outpatient clinics in New York City are assigned geographical areas—"catchment areas"—by the city's mental health agencies.)

Dr. Louis Hott is the current medical director and chairman of the medical board of the clinic. He is also assistant clinical professor of psychiatry, New York University Schools of Medicine; assistant dean, member of the board of trustees, and faculty council, The American Institute for Psychoanalysis; and clinical psychiatrist, Bellevue Psychiatric and University Hospitals. In my interview with him, Dr. Hott offered several observations on his work with the day care treatment center, as well as his views on aftercare and follow-up treatment. In this adaptation of that conversation, Dr. Hott addresses himself exclusively to the aftercare program offered through the Horney Clinic.

Louis Hott, M.D.

For the patient emerging from a period of hospitalization, effective aftercare is essential if he is not to become part of the so-called "revolving-door syndrome." Studies have shown repeatedly that one of the primary causes of high readmission rates to psychiatric hospitals is the lack of follow-up and aftercare programs.

I think that effective aftercare should be based on three crucial considerations. One, that patients recently released from the hospital develop and maintain social contact with others; two, that patients in aftercare are given specific goals, even if they are limited at first; and, three, that the individual's own resources be tapped.

In our day care program, patients are with us five days during the daytime and return home at night; the cohesiveness with other people in the clinic can offset many problems at home and can overcome the social isolation of the emerging hospital patient. The idea is to keep the patients in a state of sociability, and to get them out of the environment that contributed to their illness.

Establishing goals for the patient maintains his desire to live constructively. Occupational and milieu therapy play large parts in this area; the patient's first goal can be something as simple as completing one task—making a pocketbook, perhaps. The important thing is that it's a start, a direction. Another goal follows, then another.

Tapping a person's talents often involves discovering what it was that he wanted to do, but for any number of reasons never did. In psychoanalysis I often ask patients, "When you were very young, what did you always think you'd want to be?" Everyone has some sort of talent, and an early career desire very often points to an ability in that area. Once a person's individual resources are uncovered, he or she can be directed toward tapping them, pursuing and developing those talents.

Through milieu therapy, group therapy, and individual psychoanalysis, we are able to guide patients in these three areas of psychiatric readjustment to community life. The clinic's maximum treatment period is five years, and if it is necessary in some cases, longer.

The approach to aftercare through the clinic is primarily psychoanalytically oriented. The changing clinical role of psychoanalysis makes this approach not only viable, but effective. However, when we speak of the changing role of psychoanalysis in the clinic, an important distinction must be made between psychoanalysis as a specific therapeutic method on the one hand, and psychoanalysis as a theory about human behavior on the other. When it is viewed as the latter, psychoanalysis becomes a means to influencing the community and to preventing mental illness or its recurrence.

The clinic is based in the constructive concepts of Karen Horney, and her theories about the effects of culture and society on an individual have been proven valid in our clinical experience.

Ours was one of the first community clinics to use psychoanalysis. We began with individual treatment, then enlarged our programs to include other modalities, including group therapy and the team approach. Psychiatric social worker, clinical psychologist, and psychoanalyst work together in the team approach, each contributing in the areas for which he is trained. The result of the team approach is a more complete picture of each patient from social-cultural, medical, and psychiatric points of view. The social worker is acquainted with a patient's family and cultural background, his schools, social agencies, and hospitals; the clinical psychologist may be asked to assess specific areas; and the psycho-analyst analyzes the patient, armed with this information.

The team approach enables us to screen patients for the aftercare program; we have psychiatric social workers and psychiatrists in the field who refer patients emerging from hospitalization to us.

The majority of the people who have been through our day care program recover and reenter the community; of the people who return at some point after their discharge, only a small percent have to be rehospitalized. Generally, with additional psychotherapy, the crisis that caused them to return here can be worked through. Remissions may occur. For a person with a fragile view of himself, anxieties and the pressures of day-to-day life can be a more frequent cause of panic than they are for a person who has never been hospitalized for psychiatric problems. But if there is a place for such a person to go, if he feels there is someone to turn to, he need not have to be rehospitalized.

For patients emerging from hospitalization to reach independence, it is important that they maintain a continuity with the outside; they must have the feeling that they are, indeed, on the outside, and that they can come to this clinic and present themselves as models of better and healthier people.

Perhaps the final most helpful aspect of psychiatric rehabilitation is the insight patients gain into the parts that they play in their own illnesses. We are always affected by society, but by guiding patients toward an understanding of their own potentialities, of the extent to which they can be constructive and positive, they can overcome the negative social effects through their own personal growth.

CHAPTER *EIGHT*

Fountain House
John Beard

Fountain House, the first psychiatric rehabilitation center of its kind in the country, was established in New York in 1948 as a voluntary, non-profit organization. Today it is located at 425 West Forty-seventh Street, two blocks from Times Square in New York City. Since its founding, Fountain House has grown from a small, social-recreational center to a prototype in aftercare facilities, with a network of comprehensive services available to ex-patients who are reestablishing their ties with the community.

But before there was Fountain House, there was WANA (initials for "We Are Not Alone"); and before there was WANA, there was an idea forming among patients and volunteer workers on the wards of Rockland State Hospital, New York. During the 1940s, a group of Rockland State patients got together with some of the hospital's volunteer workers, with the idea of helping patients obtain releases; once releases were obtained, the group would help each other to adjust back to community life. The idea became a reality with the help of Elizabeth K. Schermerhorn, a volunteer worker who was instrumental in bringing the patients together within the hospital and helping the group find meeting places in New York City after releases were obtained.

From 1945 to 1948, the WANA group grew; members met with increasing regularity and visited patients still in hospitals in the hope of hastening their releases; they helped each other find housing, jobs, financial assistance.

In 1948, again with the help of Mrs. Schermerhorn, as well as with the assistance of Mrs. Hetty H. Richard, a small brownstone on West Forty-seventh Street was purchased for the group as a regular meeting place. It was shortly after this that they became known as Fountain House—so named after the small fountain in the courtyard behind the building. That same year a Board of Directors was formed for the organization.

In the mid-1960s, the Fountain House organization built a six-story house across the street from the original brownstone. Every effort was made to preserve the noninstitutional, homelike quality of the brownstone. The succeeding six years saw the acquisition of five more brownstones and a country house. The country house can accommodate at least a dozen people, and gives members the chance to get out of the city, many for the first time in their lives. It also allows the staff a place to conduct small training groups and an opportunity to get to know members better by being with them for a few days or a week. In addition, Director John Beard has pointed out, this little 1780-vintage French Huguenot house, which is in Saugerties, New York, will be very useful for visitors who will be in training groups with the Fountain House staff.

Up to 2,000 people come to Fountain House each year. Anyone who has been in a public or a private hospital may become a member, as well as anyone who has suffered from mental illness in the past. Exceptions are made in the cases of diagnosed alcoholism, drug addiction, and criminal antisocial behavior. People can refer themselves for membership as long as they can provide a source from which their medical backgrounds may be obtained. Most Fountain House members come from state hospitals and from aftercare clinics operated by the New York State Department of Mental Hygiene.

One's membership in Fountain House can last indefinitely; however, if a person does not attend the program at least once for any three-month period, his membership is temporarily "canceled" in that his name is dropped from the active list of members. Whenever the individual resumes the Fountain House program, though, the membership is immediately reinstated and no application procedure is necessary. Nearly a thousand applications for membership are received annually; over 80 percent of the applicants have had diagnoses of schizophrenia; approximately 60 percent are men; nearly half the members fall in the age range of 25 to 40, with an overall age range of 16 to over 75. About half of the members are from Manhattan, and the others are from the other New York City boroughs.

The Fountain House staff numbers 65 today; 3 of the staff are part-time psychiatric consultants, available for emergencies and to consult with the other staff members on problems that may arise of a medical or clinical nature. The emphasis in Fountain House is on rehabilitation back into the community, more than on psychiatric care.

Fountain House has developed into a special kind of aftercare agency, a community-based rehabilitation facility. Its main thrust is toward establishing ex-patients' independence after release from hospitals through their prevocational day program, their transitional employment program, and their apartment program. It is a community of active, participating members, each member's contribution to the operation of the clubhouse based upon his or her interests and abilities.

John Beard is the Executive Director of Fountain House. Formerly with a county hospital outside Detroit, Michigan, he worked during the 1950s with a group similar to the original WANA, called The Detroit Friends Group. A psychiatric social worker, Mr. Beard came to Fountain House in 1955. From the time of his acceptance of the executive directorship until the present, the organization's rehabilitation program has evolved and the model that has developed led to the establishment of similar facilities in major cities throughout the United States.

In the following adaptation of my conversation with him, Mr. Beard discusses the Fountain House model in community-based rehabilitation, the evolution of the organization's programs, and the successfulness of those programs.

John Beard

Perhaps the most immediately apparent aspect of Fountain House's uniqueness is its history. The original objectives of Fountain House were conceived by patients in Rockland State Mental Hospital thirty years ago: to provide assistance to patients, which would enable them to leave the hospital and reenter the community; to come together as a group and alleviate the overpowering feelings of isolation, alienation, and loneliness which beset the recently released mental patient. After thirty years—years not without our own struggle and growth—those objectives remain. In the course of those years, WANA became Fountain House, and the ideals of the original patient-volunteer group have been molded into an active rehabilitation service that has become the model for other community-based aftercare facilities throughout the United States and in several other countries.

The design and scope of our programs has been determined by the original objectives of the organization's founders. In the past, and unfortunately in some instances today, the mental hospital environment was not neutral for the patient; it had an influence, a disabling influence in most cases that resulted in the patient's inability to function outside the hospital as an "average," responsible citizen. We feel that another kind of environment, different from the institutional milieu of the hospital, can have the opposite effect for the released patient. We believe in the importance of people to a person, and Fountain House tries to provide an environment in which the importance of people can be reestablished for ex-patients, especially those who have had negative experiences in their relationships. We try to serve as a bridge for a released patient, helping him to establish the human independence he may have lost during the hospital experience.

Fountain House is more interested in how a member *can* behave than how he does behave at the time he joins. So we have expectations of our members which, in a sense, are similar to the aspirations a family holds for its members. When a member is in a setting where others have aspirations for him, he will be encouraged to meet his potential; and the members who perform well at Fountain House, within such a setting, gain a concept of their future through relationships with other people.

Both staff and members often refer to Fountain House as a family, and in many respects we are. But for a family to be a family, it must be able to meet a wide range of its members' needs. The variety of services offered through Fountain House can be found through separate agencies: housing, prevocational activities, transitional employment, social-recreational activities. But when a member receives these services through Fountain House, he is not getting them in a fragmented way; each area is organically part of the whole, meeting one or more of the range of a member's needs in a unified way similar to the unified way in which a family meets its members' different needs. In the family, you know how a child is doing in school or at work, how he is doing socially; you know how he is physically, and you know where he lives. To best meet our objectives, the family model in this sense serves better than a focus on only one aspect of rehabilitation.

But what about a member's own family? Does Fountain House alienate members from their families? Although members' families do not participate in the agency's programs, they are welcome to visit, and Fountain House staff are available to talk with parents. However, we think that the best way for a member to restore his relationship with his parents is for that member to become strong himself; and the best way for a patient to strengthen himself is *not* to sit at home with his life going nowhere and with nowhere to go. Very often, members have poor relationships with their families, and the home setting is not beneficial. We have seen that most parents feel positive about the fact that their child (most often an adult himself) has a place to go.

Eighty-five percent of our members are single and have never been married; of the remaining 15 percent, most are divorced or separated. Some of our members are mothers whose children were taken into custody by the state at the time of their hospitalizations. A mother has to get back on her own two feet before the state is going to give her custody of her child again. But if she comes out of the hospital to go home and take care of the family, chances are almost nil that she will get any supportive, rehabilitative feedback; she will be confined to the home by her mother/wife role and very likely will not get her life together again.

The Fountain House experience, then, far from alienating the family, is able to help members to restore their relationships with their families.

Fountain House services are geared to help formerly hospitalized psychiatric patients deal with several specific community adjustment problems.

The apartment program, begun in 1957, grew out of the urgent need by many members for adequate housing. A number of people were coming to Fountain House during the day and returning to the hospital at night because they had no home. There were members who were living in lonely, shabby rooms, paying exorbitant rents; others were living with their families in adequate housing, but their poor family relationships were resulting in their inability to adjust to community life.

Most former mental patients are unable to sign a lease for a variety of reasons: they are unemployed, they have none of the required references, they have no experience, and thereby no self-confidence at finding an apartment. The problem was becoming acute; it was impairing some members' ability to adjust to life outside the hospital. So the apartment program was born. Former patients could not secure leases, but Fountain House Foundation could.

We rent apartments in the name of Fountain House and sublease them to members. Today we hold leases on over forty apartments in New York City boroughs, each with a living room, bedroom, kitchen, and bath. Most of the apartments are shared by two members and they share the actual rent of the apartment. However, if only one member lives in an apartment, he pays only half; we think that it is more realistic for us to assume the cost. Vacancies are rare, and it takes very little time for an apartment to be filled.

With help from the community, Fountain House furnishes the apartments with essentials. If a member wants a telephone, he pays for it himself. We don't provide television, radios, or stereos; we aren't running a hotel service, but are giving people a start.

The primary aim of the apartment program is to provide decent housing at a reasonable cost. As one of the Fountain House services, it is related to the entire rehabilitative environment of the agency. Small groups of apartment residents meet each week with staff members, often in each other's apartments, to discuss problems that may have arisen: housekeeping difficulties, problems between roommates, and so forth. Each apartment is set up to take an overnight guest; in this way patients not yet discharged from the hospital can visit Fountain House overnight and become better introduced to the total environment.

Today, the need for housing programs such as ours is more urgent than ever as public hospitals begin discharging increasing numbers of patients. Fountain House can reach out and contact many of these people (but many more community-based centers must be initiated). Our rehabilitation services are not limited to the structure of Fountain House. Both staff and members maintain contact with dropouts, for example, and with members who have been rehospitalized. The members play a highly consequential role in our reaching-out efforts through visits to dropouts' homes, through hospital visits, and through hosting visiting patients in their apartments.

Members' involvement in delivering services is one reflection of the principles by which Fountain House operates. It is reflected again in our *prevocational day program*. We believe that each member, no matter how socially or psychiatrically disabled he is now, has a contribution to make to the operation of Fountain House. I am not talking about make-work; I am talking about tasks that are valuable and whose value is appreciated both by staff and other members.

With a physical facility the size of ours, many day-to-day tasks must be performed: housekeeping, cleaning, and cooking, for example. Both staff and members contribute to the maintenance of the houses. We do not employ outside help to clean—members and staff share the responsibility for this. Clerical work is done by members and staff; a daily newspaper, a monthly magazine, and numerous reports have to be prepared; food must be purchased, meals must be prepared and served; the Fountain House thrift shop has to be run, and merchandise for the shop picked up, sorted, priced, and sold. These and a variety of other activities are well suited for the vocational rehabilitation of severely disabled members, and they could not be completed without the assistance of the day-program members.

Of vital importance in the prevocational program is the way in which the participants' views of their disability change as they perform these jobs; members begin to realize their own potentials, their own abilities. The recognition paid them by staff and other members for their work contributes to this shift in self-concept.

Day-program members are given the opportunity to choose the kind of work that interests them and that has the degree of responsibility they can handle. Because they are members of a club, however, the work that they contribute is done so voluntarily, and it is apparent that members themselves do not view these job contributions as structured rehabilitation, but as their individual parts in a family effort in which both they and the staff participate side by side.

The purpose of the prevocational day program is to provide the more psychiatrically disabled members with opportunities to develop work potential, and to reverse the process of institutionalization that they had undergone in the hospital.

With the success of the day program, staff members began asking why, if members could work responsibly and effectively at Fountain House, couldn't they do the same in industry and commerce? Certainly there were numerous relatively simple jobs to be had in businesses, and many of them seemed suitable for a *transitional employment program*.

We had seen success with a similar idea in a Michigan mental hospital where I had worked as a social worker on the back wards; the part-time jobs we had secured for patients were not only performed well, but the work experience also had a positive rehabilitative effect upon the patients. So the Fountain House transitional employment program was initiated. Our first placement was a messenger's job with our printer, and the program has grown to include some 200 members whose combined annual income in 1974 was approximately $400,000.

The idea behind transitional employment is to create an approach for members to regular employment; the program eliminates the obstacles to securing a job. Interviews for employment are among the greatest obstacles to a recently released mental patient. The ability to pass a job interview does not necessarily reflect the ability to do the job—the two are not equivalent. Another obstacle is the patient's negative attitude toward going out on his own and looking for a job. This, too, is eliminated with the transitional employment program. Members are hired for jobs here at Fountain House, they are assisted in filling out application forms, and they do not have to have job references.

We had very little difficulty finding and securing job placements with industry and commerce, and our arrangements with businesses are simple. Once a position is secured (usually through staff enquiries), a staff member performs the job for the first few days. Most of the placements are entry-level, so staff members have little difficulty performing the work. When the staff member gets a thorough understanding of the job requirements, as well as an experience of the atmosphere of the work situation, the member assumes the job. The position will remain filled by that member for an average of five months, at which time he will either go on to another placement or, if he is ready, take a full-time job of his own. The staff member who initiated the placement follows through in the continuing management of that placement, seeing that it is rotated and filled by a series of members whom he trains for the job.

Members participating in the program help motivate other members to avail themselves of transitional employment by serving as examples, and through group discussions and presentations.

Some members are ready for independent employment after their first placement; others have to have two or three placements first; still others fail on their placements and return to Fountain House. But a member's failure does not result in rejection and isolation; we accept failure as an educational experience in rehabilitation, knowing that the member has tried and that an unsuccessful trial does not always reflect his disability. We do not view vocational disability as a psychiatric condition, because it is often a consequence of external factors whose alteration or elimination can result in the member's ability to perform well.

Although staff and participating members encourage other members to become involved in the transitional employment program, there is not an oppressive pressure on people to go to work. But Fountain House, as an environment that is reflective of the community, has a value system, and one of the important values is to provide the opportunities for people who want to get back to work; thus, we emphasize work opportunities. However, we are not rigid, and would not exclude people from membership who prefer to participate only in our social-recreational program.

The *social and recreational program* for some members is an introduction to Fountain House, the first program with which they become involved; participation in the social program often leads to participation in the day programs. Members also in the day programs, those who are independently employed and no longer day-program members, and members who do not participate in the more intensive rehabilitation programs are among the two to three hundred people who come to the clubhouse for the evening and weekend activities.

Members gather in the clubhouse living room to chat with one another or simply to relax alone. We have a library and a music room, a television room and a game room, which are all busy; the snack bar, where a cup of coffee can still be had for five cents, is popular as well. More structured activities are also available for members with special interests; with the help of volunteers specializing in an area, members participate in a poetry group, a photography group (we have a fully equipped darkroom), cooking classes, drama, a sewing class, a choral group, and a creative writing class. The clubhouse classroom, where a current events course is held, is generally busy. Musical programs, from folk music to classical, are another attraction.

Saturday nights usually see a dance at the clubhouse with live music provided, sometimes by the Fountain House dance combo or by a volunteer community group. In the spring and fall members in the drama group present their plays, and during the holidays the clubhouse is open for holiday activities and dinners. We have regularly scheduled films and talks on arts and crafts. Fountain House also provides for its members free tickets to many of the cultural events in New York City.

The evening and weekend program, though not viewed as a rehabilitation program that can significantly alter the vocational adjustment of severely disabled members, enables the former patient to overcome his feelings of isolation and alienation from others. In this way it is important to the whole of Fountain House services.

Evenings at the clubhouse are also used for group meetings and discussions to cover areas of members' experiences in other programs. One evening a week, the members of the transitional employment program have dinner together and in small groups exchange information and insights about their work experiences. People who are about to make the transition from our program to independent employment will also make use of the evening clubhouse program to meet and discuss this new step in their lives.

The Fountain House staff has work schedules that include the evening social program; this is essential in order for the staff to have contact with members who participate solely in the social program and with members who are making the adjustment back to the community and are thereby no longer in the daytime programs. It is also essential because the Fountain House staff does not maintain a "we/they" relationship with the Fountain House members. There is no departmentalization; the roles of the staff do not necessarily reflect their training. We have professionals among the staff such as social workers, psychologists, rehabilitation and vocational counselors, as well as people with liberal arts backgrounds and no specific training in the area of psychiatric rehabilitation; we also have staff members with no college education.

In each of the seven units which comprise Fountain House, a group of staff is responsible for a group of members; each unit is like a family, and staff in each unit is responsible for transitional employment and apartment programs, and in part for its own prevocational programs.

In the same way that we want former patients to feel like people and not mental patients, we want staff to feel like people and not social workers. Members and staff must relate on a person-to-person basis in a noninstitutional setting, because that is what Fountain House is about. Social workers at Fountain House do not conduct regularly scheduled "interviews" with members; the work is carried on as a natural part of the functioning of the organization. Formalizing the relationships can lead to a "we/they" split and erode the bridge of trust and unity that is felt by members and staff alike. In every area of Fountain House activity we try to minimize the gap between staff and members by establishing real relationships and thereby develop a real sense of caring. I think that there is a significant difference between this approach and the more institutional approach of disabling people by infantilizing them.

The results of a nine-year follow-up research project, published by Fountain House in 1974, detail the extent to which Fountain House has met its objective of reducing the number of released psychiatric patients who return to the hospital. As opposed to a 74 percent rehospitalization rate for patients who did *not* undergo rehabilitation, only 37 percent of those former patients who did experience full rehabilitative services returned to the hospital; in other words, the rehospitalization rate was halved. In the case of rehospitalization, there is a difference, too, between the amounts of time each group spends in hospital: 4.1 years for the patient who has not experienced rehabilitation services, as opposed to 2.1 years for patients who have. Again, exposure to rehabilitation almost halves the length of rehospitalization.

The success of Fountain House has resulted in several factors: the cooperation of businesses in placing former patients in industry and commerce; the staff's extraordinary energy and dedication; a substantial income from both government and private sources; and the establishment of other agencies similar to ours, such as the Rose Garden in Rockford, Illinois, Horizon House in Philadelphia, and Threshold House in Chicago. The Fountain House model has also been explored and developed in Australia, Pakistan, and Poland.

CHAPTER NINE

"There Must Be Something Good Out There"
Peter Nelson

There were no circuses, no Little League games, no summer camps in Peter Nelson's childhood; there were only the walls of Rockland State and Pilgrim State Hospitals. Although he was never diagnosed as emotionally ill, Peter was hospitalized at the age of seven, and finally released when he was nineteen.

Now in his early twenties, he is a special member of Fountain House, and plans to attend New York University to take a degree in social work.

Peter Nelson

B.B.: Would you tell us a bit about your family, Peter?
PETER: We lived in Harlem. There were three of us in the family. My father divorced my mother.
B.B.: You lived with your mother?
PETER: Yes, I lived with my mother, my brother, and sister.
B.B.: What kind of family life did you have?
PETER: It wasn't so good. We were a poor, black family and my father left my mother. When I got older I tried to realize just what was going on in the past . . . and I mainly got the feeling of being very poor. We were in one bedroom, all together. I slept with my brother.

B.B.: But were your relations good among yourselves?

PETER: No, not very good. My mother: I never called her Mom or anything. I always called her by her name. I don't know how that came about, but it just came about.

B.B.: Were you the oldest of the children?

PETER: Yes, I was. I was a year older than my brother. My sister was two or three months old when my father left home. She was born in about '55 or so.

B.B.: She's much younger than you and your brother?

PETER: Yes, she is.

B.B.: When did your father leave the nest?

PETER: I don't actually know the date, but it was when I was about seven or eight years old.

B.B.: Did he drink?

PETER: Oh, I'm sure he did. He often offered us some of whatever he was drinking.

B.B.: Did he hold a job?

PETER: Well, when I was on my way to the hospital, I saw him working. He was working as a furniture mover, moving furniture. So I guess he was holding a job.

B.B.: Did your mother work?

PETER: Well, I noticed that my mother wore a white uniform and white stockings and shoes, so I guess she worked as a nurse or a helper.

B.B.: Would you say there was a background of mental illness in your family?

PETER: I don't know. From what I hear, my mother had to put my brother in the hospital when she came in to see me one time, but that's the only indication of anything. But if it was like my hospitalization—I never got treatment when I was in the hospital.

B.B.: What led to you going to the hospital?

PETER: Well, I guess it was on my mother's part. She was afraid. I was staying out at night when I was eight, didn't get back home until the morning. Then she'd give me a beating, and I'd do it again. I wouldn't go to school. She'd give me a beating. This happened pretty constantly all along, so she was bothered that I wouldn't listen to her.

B.B.: Were you committed?

PETER: Well, yeah, by her. I had been out all night, pretty much as usual, and finally she put me in the hospital.

B.B.: Had you stayed overnight with friends?

PETER: It wasn't exactly what you would call "staying overnight with friends." We had what might be called a little game. There were eight of us and we just sort of took subway train rides like the kids do today. You see little kids on the trains, just riding around. We used to do that, and if a store was open, like Macy's, we'd go there, and we did little things, bad little things sometimes, but we stayed out mostly all night.

B.B.: What hospital did she commit you to?

PETER: Well, she put me in Bellevue Hospital, and I stayed there for a couple of months. After that they let me go. I went back home and I did more or less the same things over again. And then she said, well, why should she take me back? I said, "Well, then I'm not coming back here anymore." And I didn't take any feeling about it when she said it, of course; I have no feelings about that. And so I went to—they transferred me to Rockland State Hospital.

B.B.: How long were you there?

PETER: I was there nine years. It was about '57 I went there.

B.B.: So when you came out you were about sixteen?

PETER: Well, when I finally came out I was nineteen. I went to Pilgrim from there. They had transferred me again, and I was there for two years.

B.B.: How would you describe those two hospitals? Where did you get the better treatment, do you think?

PETER: Where did I get the better treatment? Well, like I said, there was no treatment needed for me. What I had been put in for was juvenile delinquency, really. When I went there, they didn't give me any medication. Of course you got your regular polio shots, and all those sorts of shots.

I thought they were giving me treatment, but after I got older, I realized they weren't. I didn't get any sort of pills or anything except when I got into fights. If I was fighting and acting up, they would give me medication—drugging me up to keep me down. That's the only medication I ever got from the hospital.

B.B.: For what reason did they release you?

PETER: Well, I had been there so many years, and finally as a young man—I'm sure the doctor read my records and, you know, saw there was nothing really wrong with me. This is something that's always been on my mind. You know, I was afraid to ask to go home, or anything like that, because where would I go? My mother only came up to see me, when I was in Rockland, about five times.

And the only reason she came was because the doctor wrote her a letter, or called her to get up there, to come see me. She (the doctor) was a very nice young lady, and she liked me. She was worried about me, so she called my mother, because she noticed that I had no visitors from my family. And when my mother did come up, I was glad to see her. Because I did miss home life. I cried a little bit.

I try to think about it now. What kind of young man would I be if I hadn't spent almost twelve years in hospitals, even though they were custodial? I'd have spent those years on the street, probably.

B.B.: Your hospitalization, then, was custodial. It was just keeping somebody who wasn't sick?

PETER: That's right, and the kids who went home came back so many times. I saw this—I said, "Well, I hope when I get out that I don't come back, because there must be something good out there."

B.B.: I gather you were in a locked situation.

PETER: I was in a locked situation for a year or so; then they let me down in the open wards, where you got your parole cards, and you did special things for attendants and so on.

B.B.: But were the staff and attendants nice? Did they treat you well?

PETER: If you were nice to them, they were nice to you. But if you weren't, they got on your back once in a while and they did things that they weren't supposed to do.

One time an attendant hit me; I just said to myself, "This can't be done. I'm going to do something about it." So I took off. We were coming out of the lunchroom, and were going on the outside to get back to our building (we ate in another building), and so I decided what to do when this attendant put his hands on me. I jumped over the fence, and, if I remember correctly, there was a main office there, where the big chiefs were. Yes, I remember, because when I got my parole card I always went up there, and I carried the building reports up to the administration office. And so I said I would go up there, 'cause I knew where the office was.

You know, I went up there and told one of the doctors what happened. He drove me back down and kind of just dropped me in my supervisor's hands and said, "Take care of this problem." At that time, there wasn't anything done, of course, but when I went back to the ward the attendant got me put on buffer again: you know, working on the floor with big buffers. They were made from an iron pipe and a big block, with pieces of blanket wrapped around. . . . The buffers were to shine the floor. You had machines, and then you had the other buffers for people to pull by hand. They were big heavy blocks.

B.B.: The attendant had something against you?

PETER: Yeah, he had something against me. He sure did.

B.B.: And getting put on the buffers was dirty work.

PETER: Dirty work.

B.B.: Well, how did you feel when you finally were released?

PETER: I was scared. I was scared when I first wanted to tell them I wanted to leave. Suppose they said no, you know? But then I said, "Well, I should run away before I ask them, because this way they can't say no to me or hurt my feelings." Then I said, "Well, I can't do that 'cause then I really would be scared if I went out by myself."

So, instead, I thought they might give me some sort of help, and I figured I'd ask them.

When I finally saw the doctor, I said, "You know, after being in for all these years, I would like to get out."

He said, "Why would you want to get out?"

I said, "Well, I've been in here long enough. There's no life in the hospital for me. I want to go out and make my own life now."

And he said, "Would you go back to your family?"

I said, "Well, not exactly. I'm sure they can't be found at the moment." The staff had tried to contact them, but there was no luck on it. They had moved.

B.B.: What was most helpful in overcoming your fears about getting out?

PETER: Well, when I got out I was with somebody who was going out the same time as me, and we got on a bus with a group of other patients who were leaving or going to another hospital. We went to the Welfare office—and it was a good feeling when I got off that bus.

And now, I was worrying about where I was going to sleep for that day. You had to go to Welfare; you waited there for several hours until your name was called, and they finally call your name, and you get this piece of paper, and you're told to go to this address. They also gave me a check; it was a piece of paper to me, with a couple of numbers on it. I didn't know what it was, so I just took it to the clerk at the hotel.

B.B.: They gave you a place to sleep?

PETER: Yeah, they gave me a place to sleep, a hotel around Forty-seventh Street. I got a dingy room . . . I just stayed there. Well, I had to have something to eat, so I stayed there for a good couple of hours, and then I went out, when it was nice and late and dark. There was a store open next to the hotel and I just went in there.

And when I wanted to go out and see what was going on around me, I just went out and took a walk. Of course, I got lost; then I found my way—somebody directed me back.

B.B.: Did you seek a doctor?

PETER: Well, when you get out of the hospital, they assign you to a clinic, so I went to a clinic, and began to go once a week; it's called the

Lower Manhattan Aftercare. I was seen by a doctor and a social worker for about two and a half months. At the time, they didn't really do very much for me, in terms of finding a job or helping me find some sort of club to go to.

B.B.: Would you say that you were lonely at the time?

PETER: Yes, I was—I was very lonely. When I was going to the clinic, I found my own job. I worked in a one-man owned factory, making buttons and buckles, on Twenty-eighth Street. Things were going well while I worked there, and I continued at the clinic. I reported to my social worker about how I was doing on the job.

B.B.: Were they helpful specifically?

PETER: They gave me hints, about not being late, getting out of bed in the morning; not much else. They did suggest Fountain House, however, in terms of socializing with people. I worked for about three and a half months at the factory, and then things weren't going very well. My back hurt, and it was boring, too. At first, I didn't want to go to Fountain House, because I wanted to stay away from mentally ill people. I didn't see myself quite as I saw other ex-patients. Then I decided to go, when they suggested it again, to try it out. Fountain House did help, in terms of work.

B.B.: What was the Fountain House experience like?

PETER: I met a social worker, first, and saw some friends I'd known in the hospital, and that gave me support—I wasn't scared then, and I filled out the application for Fountain House work.

I was assigned to the warehouse unit, where you put tickets on clothes donated for the Fountain House Thrift Shop, by Alexander's and other stores. The social worker prodded me to get in on time, though I wasn't paid.

From there, we had a twelve o'clock lunch, which cost thirty cents. I was crazy about that. I met other members. I talked to them about what Fountain House was doing for them, and I decided to stick right with it.

It took about four and a half months before I went on my first job placement—at Chock Full o' Nuts. I stayed there for about a year and a half. Then a check came in the mail from Fountain House, which surprised me; it turned out that they wanted me to work on Sundays and train members who were going to work for Chock Full o' Nuts. I was pleased; no one had told me. Probably the Fountain House worker in charge of Chock Full o' Nuts was responsible. Usually they do talk to a member first.

Then I went to Sears Roebuck in New Jersey, as a porter and a mental health worker. I was to run this Fountain House placement. I stayed there for about six months and then went to Alexander's on Fifty-ninth Street, as a stock man and still as a mental health worker—training Fountain House members who came down to work at Alexander's.

I was approached by our program director to see if I'd like to join the staff at Fountain House, full time. At first, I decided not to do this; it was too much responsibility—it meant being in charge of people's lives. And I wanted to get on with my education. I was going to a business school, studying typing and accounting. I had been to a school in Rockland; it was not very satisfactory, but I had the rudiments of an education. Anyway, I told Esther, program director, that I wasn't sure about being a full-time worker for Fountain House yet, and she said I could reconsider later.

I continued with the job, and worked sometimes seven days a week, at the Fountain House Snack Bar—which I ran every Sunday for a stipend —as well as the job.

After a couple of months, Esther asked me again. I took a week and a day to decide I would like to try it. I saw the director, Mr. Beard, and I was assigned to the dining room unit, on the staff, on February 21, 1971. I was also helping place members on jobs. This went on for about two years.

Then I was transferred to the Snack Bar, with three other staff members, as the assistant to the unit leader. Here members are trained for work at Chock Full 'o Nuts.

Now another staff member and I are running the Sears placement group from Fountain House. I've been running a group apartment program out in Queens with fourteen members. I lived there for a time.

Then I asked to move to the new Fountain House halfway house, a new project where patients come directly from the hospital, on Forty-seventh Street, as a staff member. This is in the process of being set up; at the moment only staff live there.

B.B.: What are your plans for the future?

PETER: I am now going to NYU and getting my high school diploma. I'll enroll in college and take courses in psychology there, and continue to work as a social worker.

B.B.: That's great, Peter. Are you doing all right in your studies? When do you think you'll get your diploma?

PETER: My marks are good, and I think I'll graduate this year.

B.B.: What was most helpful, overall, in your reaching this point?

PETER: Well, nothing bothers me now. I have the patients to work with, the members, to help from returning to a hospital. What helped most? Realizing that if I was kind to someone else, they'd be kind to me.

PART THREE

Individual Psychotherapies

TRADITIONALLY, psychotherapy has been practiced on a one-to-one basis. The psychotherapist and the patient meet in private over a period of time and work on the patient's problems. How the psychotherapist interprets his patients' problems and how he goes about treating them, as well as the type of education and training the psychotherapist has received, define what sort of therapy he practices.

One of the most intimate relationships in our society is the one that develops between the psychotherapist and the client; so choosing an individual therapist according to your specific needs is of prime importance.

Of course, every psychotherapist is different from every other. But basically, individual psychotherapy breaks into two broad branches: the psychoanalytically oriented (or medical-model) approach, and the behavior-oriented approach. In practice, a psychotherapist will rarely fall at one pole or another, but will make his point of departure from some point along a continuum between the two.

Psychoanalytically oriented therapy is based of course in psychoanalysis, which takes a long-term approach to a person's problems. Pure psychoanalysis can take several years. As the term implies, one's psyche —self—is analyzed. The patient ("analysand") is guided back over his personal history, back through childhood, with the purpose of discovering the roots of his problems. Once such "insight" is gained, it is reasoned, the patient will understand the problems he suffers today and can change. Based originally on the work of Sigmund Freud, psychoanalysis has undergone many changes.[1]

In psychoanalysis you are treated by a medical doctor with specialized training in psychiatry and psychoanalysis. Part of his training requires that he go through psychoanalysis himself. A purely psychoanalytic therapist is nondirective, that is, he or she does not advise, but guides you toward understanding yourself through understanding your past.

Behavior therapy is generally a shorter-term process. The therapist is very direct, because he is dealing with *symptoms,* or the obvious, visible parts of his patient's problems. Very strictly speaking, a behavior therapist will "cure" someone of biting his nails without going into *why* he bites his nails. To practice behavior therapy, the therapist does not have to have a medical degree; he can be a psychologist, that is, he has a Ph.D. in psychology (in some states, an M.A.). Of course, psychiatrists who have medical degrees may also practice behavior therapy.

Behaviorism is based on theories that were developed in laboratory experiments, conducted in the early stages of behaviorism on animals. The father of behavior therapy in this country is Joseph Wolpe, of Temple University, Philadelphia. The discipline became more sophisticated and refined with clinical studies of patients and the work of such behaviorists as Victor Meyer, who found he could treat patients who suffered phobias with behavior therapy without dealing in the causes of their fears, and C. R. Hull, who wrote a classic book on the subject (*Principles of Behavior*, 1943). Behavior therapy caught on in this country during World War Two.

A psychiatrist can prescribe medication, which a psychologist is unable to do. The clinical psychologist is more limited in the type of therapy he can practice in that he cannot conduct psychoanalysis.

Today, most psychotherapists take what is called an eclectic approach to psychotherapy. Armed with the knowledge of several different types of psychotherapies, which lie between the poles of pure psychoanalysis and pure behaviorism, the psychotherapist often selects an approach to fit an individual person's needs.

1. One of the seemingly more superficial changes is the shift from "the couch" to "the chair." Freud asked his patients to lie on a couch, facing away from him, and this became a recognized feature in treatment. But Freud had never intended "the couch" to be a feature, apparently. Frederick Perls relates that Freud simply didn't like to be looked at—hence he put patients on a couch and sat behind them!﹐ An important anecdote to remember when you're getting to know your own psychotherapist.—BB

Many people, when they emerge from a period of hospitalization, will seek some sort of follow-up care with an individual psychotherapist; the kind of therapist a person sees, of course, is dependent upon his problems, the degree to which he feels he has been helped—or hindered—by hospitalization, and—most important—the trust he has for a therapist.

CHAPTER TEN

Psychoanalysis
John Schimel, M.D.

Dr. John L. Schimel, a psychiatrist in private practice in New York City, is an outstanding psychoanalyst who treats people who have been hospitalized, as well as people who have never been in a hospital.

In addition to his own practice, Dr. Schimel is the Associate Director of the William Alanson White Institute of Psychiatry, Psychoanalysis and Psychology in New York City; an Associate Clinical Professor of Psychiatry at the New York University Medical Center; and Adjunct Clinical Professor of Psychiatry at the Albert Einstein School of Medicine.

He received his medical training at the Georgetown University School of Medicine and served his psychiatric residency at the Bellevue Psychiatric Hospital and in the U.S. Army during World War II. He did his psychoanalytic training at the White Psychoanalytic Institute.

Dr. Schimel has published four books on adolescence: *The Parents' Handbook on Adolescence* (World); *How to be an Adolescent and Survive; Your Future as a Husband;* and *Your Future as a Wife* (the latter three with Richard Rosen Press). He has also had over a hundred articles published in professional journals such as *The American Journal of Psychiatry, Contemporary Psychoanalysis, The Journal of the American Academy of Psychoanalysis,* and in such popular magazines as *Redbook, Family Circle,* and *Pageant.*

This chapter is based on my conversation with him, discussing such points as who enters psychoanalysis today and why; families' and society's attitudes toward mental illness; Dr. Schimel's views on hospitalization and the present mental hospital situation; and his approach to psychoanalysis.

John L. Schimel, M.D.

Most of my patients are from the metropolitan New York area, and most are from the middle class. I treat various groups—doctors, artists, students; many are professionals. As a matter of fact, for some time about half of my patients have been physicians or members of physicians' families. I also see a number of businessmen, and this is at least in part due to my downtown New York location; they're working in the neighborhood or nearby and my office is accessible.

I once published a list of reasons why patients choose me—"rational" reasons for choosing a particular psychoanalyst. It included such things as: "You were the closest doctor to the Queens Midtown Tunnel"; "Your waiting room was so small I was sure your fees would be moderate"; "I had decided to see a gentile analyst" (I'm not); and so on.

The point is that people choose an analyst for a variety of reasons, and sometimes the reason seems quite unrelated to the person's problem. Yet I've never seen anyone who came for treatment who did not, in fact, need it. When we get into the real reasons a person seeks treatment, the answers aren't nearly as simple as my list of "rational" reasons for choosing an analyst.

The shorthand way to answer why an individual seeks psychoanalysis is to say that patients come out of desperation, and that it's usually as a last resort. They've tried everything else and nothing has helped: counseling, talking to friends and family, or some other sort of treatment. Many come at a physician's advice; nearly all the people who enter treatment with me already have been put on some sort of tranquilizer by their physicians.

However, most patients are forced—and this is on a philosophical level—to see a psychiatrist because of social pressures. It can be a husband or wife threatening divorce unless the other goes into treatment; it can be a law firm telling an associate that he will be passed over for partnership unless he gets help.

I don't mean to say that nobody chooses it; it *is* a choice, even if it's a last resort choice. People used to come into psychoanalysis more voluntarily, it seemed, because at one time getting psychoanalyzed was very fashionable among certain groups. But even these were people who needed help.

My patients are primarily neurotics. I occasionally see a patient suffering from a severe depression. Over the years I have treated quite a range of patients, including schizophrenics. Patients are usually seen by other professionals before they are referred to any analyst, so that I tend to see certain kinds of patients. This can be thought of as a screening process.

My referring sources tend to screen for economic reasons, too. If someone is poor, he may not be referred to me because I am in private practice. But he may be referred to one of the clinics with which I am associated—the New York University-Bellevue Hospital clinics, the Albert Einstein complex, or the White Institute (I teach and supervise younger professionals in all three places).

Occasionally, I see a patient who requires hospitalization, often a young man in his teens. In such cases I may refer the patient to the High Point Hospital in Port Chester, New York; the Hillside Hospital in Glen Oaks, New York; the Austen Riggs Center in Stockbridge, Massachusetts; Chestnut Lodge, Rockville, Maryland; or the Sheppard-Pratt Hospital, Lawson, Maryland. These and other hospitals are excellent, and over the years I have come to learn the particular strengths of each. But at the point where I hospitalize, treatment by me has ended with that patient and is taken over by the staff of the hospital.

Sometimes I, in turn, get referrals from the hospitals to which I refer patients; and sometimes patients will return to me after hospitalization; but more often an ex-patient will receive aftercare through the hospital system. A young boy, for instance, whom I may hospitalize at Hillside, will be treated there for six months to a year, and then move to a Hillside Hospital Halfway House. The ex-patient's reentry into the community is handled in stages and supervised by the hospital's social worker. Very often the therapist who treats the patient in the hospital will continue to see him after hospitalization.

In order not to be misleading, I should add that the number of patients whom I have hospitalized, and who have come to me after hospitalization, is small, so I cannot generalize about the average problems of hospitalized patients; I can only speak from my own experience.

Now, as to my own patients and the types of problems I have dealt with, I am better able to draw some sort of generalizations. First, it may be important to understand that psychoanalysis today differs from that of the "old days." Eearlier, in classical psychoanalysis, there was an injunction against making any important decisions or life changes during the period of treatment. Today, however, many do not believe in that; all kinds of changes necessarily take place during therapy, particularly with younger patients.

Very often people in psychoanalysis change their careers or begin to work for the first time. In the case of youngsters in their late teens, I encourage them to take a more active part in life, to go out, establish themselves as people less dependent upon parents and family. On the other hand, I occasionally see an adolescent who has become socially paralyzed and who does not even attend school, and for whom home has become a sort of private sanitarium. In such an instance, the course of treatment is often designed to help him back into the mainstream of life, back into the community, to school or a career. In the course of such changes, he will quite naturally move the center of his life out of the home.

One trend I have seen changing among patients in psychoanalysis over the years has to do with divorce. During many years of practice, almost no divorces occurred among my patients; but today that has changed. A change that takes place in the patient during therapy may lead to the end of a marriage. Sometimes the change takes the patient into another marriage, and sometimes into a needed resting period.

The attitudes of the families of patients coming into therapy vary greatly. For instance, about a year ago a man in a serious depression came to see me; he couldn't work, he hadn't been out socially in a good many years, and his home life had gone completely to pot. Now he's back at work; he goes out again; and he's cheerful some of the time. He's still a depressive type of person, but now he is able to carry on a normal sort of life. In this instance, the wife and his entire family were quite grateful.

Of course, there are other attitudes. When I am treating one party in a marriage, all kinds of reactions and attitudes may be displayed by the other. Husbands or wives may be terribly apprehensive because they have heard that many people get divorced after they have gone into analysis.

And there's another type of reaction that a marriage partner may have when his or her mate goes into analysis: something that they feel belongs to them—that is, the confidences of the partner—is now being given to someone else. A triangle develops. In some of those instances the spouse, whether it's husband or wife, will try to undermine the treatment. A husband, or sometimes a parent, may react by refusing to pay the bill. That hasn't happened lately, but it can happen.

You can see that the attitudes of families vary greatly. I have been treating an adolescent girl who is an actor-writer. She has taken enough pills at times to almost kill herself; her family would love to have much more contact with me—and I do talk to them. There is no one else they can turn to except me. I'm sure that sometimes they'd like to kill the daughter and get rid of me, too (they have said it to me), but they're stuck with both of us. They resent the fact that I'm the only one who can reach her.

And of course, there's always guilt. Families often feel that they have caused the problem, or have, at least, contributed to it. Along with the guilt—on that same level of reaction—there still exists the social stigma of being treated for an emotional problem. That is changing, of course, but the social embarrassment is still there. We all saw what happened to the vice-presidential choice on the Democratic ticket in 1972 when it was discovered that he'd had shock treatment; Mr. Nixon thereupon became busy denying he'd ever seen a psychiatrist, and President Ford was checked out closely to be sure he'd never had psychiatric treatment before he was selected as vice-president—he was asked if he'd ever even had any contact with a psychiatrist. So the business of social stigma is not a dead issue.

These matters are further complicated by the existence of automated records kept on Welfare clients, Medicaid and Medicare patients, and others. The result is a pooling of information, which creates the possibility of a leakage of confidential information. Insurance companies now demand a patient's diagnosis as well as other information; if you give out that information, even with the patient's approval, it goes into a computer somewhere, and who knows what happens to such information or what it may eventually be used for.

Getting back to practice and the patients I see: most of my patients receive long-term treatment, that is, two years and up. I do not see patients every day, but two or three times a week, occasionally four times a week at the beginning. With adolescents and young people, I start with twice a week, and that seems to work as well as the three-times-a-week schedule I tend to maintain with older people. Each arrangement is worked out on an individual basis.

The insights that come during analysis, the time it takes, and the process different patients undergo to reach them vary greatly. Briefly, the whole idea of insight has to do with two areas: one area of insight concerns the patient learning better about who he is and how he perceives the world and how he misperceives it; the second area has to do with the patient understanding more about the behavior and significance of other people in his life. As either one or both of these areas begins to become clear to the patient, he generally begins to function better, as well as to become more hopeful about his own life.

So, if a man comes in and says that he is terribly depressed and that he can't understand it—he can't work, even though his boss seems to be sympathetic and patient with him, and his wife and children appear to love him—well, he hasn't a clear and insightful perspective of himself and certain areas of his life. To him it seems that everything is all right; it's just that he's depressed. Well, I then have to elicit more information about the family situation; and as more and more information comes out, we may learn that he is actually involved in a malevolent relationship with a significant person in his life. He may begin to see that he is actually involved in a difficult relationship with his seemingly loving wife (or, a wife in analysis may see this about her husband); he may discover, for instance, that she repeatedly disparages him. This may be hard to see at first, but realizing what is actually going on in his life is the kind of thing that helps the person emerge from the prison of his mind: to know what hit him and where he hurts. It is important to point out that the end of the road is more often a compassionate understanding through divorce.

The termination *process* in psychoanalysis starts long before the actual termination. During the preparation for termination I tell a patient that I would like to see him in three months—call me in October, for instance, to review what's been happening. That might result in one visit, or a series of visits. Or, the patient may never call at all. I always leave a standing invitation, that the door is always open, and that if anything comes up, to please get in touch with me. No matter how busy my schedule, I can always make room for former patients—and I always do.

When treatment is being terminated the patient usually has a mixture of feelings, chiefly apprehension on the one hand and pride on the other. Generally, the person goes on to lead a much better life than before treatment. I have had some successes in treating people who had been quite severely disturbed. Some severely disturbed people may, however, have problems that I can only envision being treated in a hospital situation.

Now, concerning the hospitalization, there are a number of problems inherent to that whole process. If I see a patient who seems to require hospitalization, I must be extremely careful in making that disposition. The manner in which the beginning of treatment is handled is terribly important. When hospitalization is indicated, it is best that it be accomplished quickly. I'm reluctant to hospitalize and, in my practice, I rarely find occasion to do it. It is usually the outcome of a calculated risk. There are consequences to hospitalizing someone; his identity as a helpless member of society is being established right then and there, and that may have an enormous effect on the patient's future. Hospitalization confirms for the patient the idea that he is out of control. As a communication from a professional it can have a determining effect on the future of the patient. So, in deciding whether or not to hospitalize a patient, I am making a crucial choice. If a patient is truly suicidal, for instance, he should be in a hospital for his own protection. That is the other side of the risk—should I fail to hospitalize a real suicidal or homicidal patient.

I have mentioned a number of excellent hospitals. People with money can go to such hospitals if they are informed of such resources. But there are divisions along socio-economic lines. There are many who have to go to state hospitals. When I served in the admitting office at Bellevue Hospital and at St. Elizabeth's Hospital, the people I saw were poor. But I do think that the state hospitals have done a lot for a lot of patients—not necessarily in terms of organized programs, but sometimes custodial care can help interrupt mental illness. Sometimes, just getting away and into a hospital environment helps some. I used to see repeaters at Bellevue Hospital and often I would hear: "I can't stand it on the outside anymore."

There is much discussion about a locked versus not-locked situation. Addressing that point, I'd say that the question is not necessarily one of good versus bad. In the first place, almost all hospitals contain locked wards, at least in the sense that the admissions ward is generally a locked or closed ward, even in the best places. After an initial period the improving patient is given increased privileges. If the patient is a suicide risk, it is perhaps best that he is in a locked ward, at least for the admittance period. I think that it's the overall care sequence that is what counts, more than whether a hospital is locked or not.

Now, there are so-called day hospitals, where a patient can spend his daytime hours in the hospital attending group therapies, going to classes, and doing occupational therapy, and can then go home and spend the night with his family. There are also night hospitals in which the patient may work outside during the day and receive group therapy and other help in the evenings. Sometimes the same facility is used for both. These and other innovations have been going on during the past ten to fifteen years.

Most hospitals rely heavily on drug therapy, particularly for schizophrenic and depressive patients. I believe that drugs are often essential in the hospital treatment of an illness. The problem often comes with the release from the hospital: a patient may stop taking his prescription and end up in the hospital again. There are aftercare clinics with programs for patients discharged from state hospitals in nearly every state. But they're not always convenient or accessible to the patient. Some ex-patients come in for only one prescription and never appear again. There may be no follow-up with the patient. And the situation isn't as simple as the fact that the patient merely isn't taking the drugs that have been prescribed. Often there is no one to see to it that a patient continues the medication. We do not know what kind of people take the prescribed drugs and what kind of people stop. In fact, we don't even know if the total situation is really better with the use of drugs, or not.

Patients go into a hospital, receive medication, seem to get better, and are diagnosed as better, then are released. The result is a revolving door situation. Once outside, a patient may get worse again because he stops taking his medication. He may get worse for other reasons, too, of course—such as losing the protection that the hospital affords. At any rate, he is often readmitted. In many hospitals, the total resident population is much smaller than it was forty or even ten years ago—but the readmissions rates have risen tremendously.

We just do not know the consequences of sending people back into the community who are not well enough, and often this is because they *seem* better, as I said, due to medication, which may stop when they're released.

Many people who are being released today are destined to return in a few months. What has been attempted in California, and is being done in New York, is, I think utterly scandalous: the state hospitals are being emptied, and here in New York you see many people raving in the streets. So we have shifted the burden from the state hospitals, where people live in a more or less protected environment, to Welfare, with which many of these people cannot connect; in effect, we have gone to the Middle Ages, with a vast floating population of mentally ill people who cannot take care of themselves and with nobody to take care of them.

But despite the problems in the field today, I do think that psychiatry is helping more than it once did. For one thing, there is a freer interchange of ideas among the different schools of therapeutic thought; we aren't nearly as isolated as we once were. Some of the advances made in behavioral therapy are good and have interesting applications. I'd have to reserve judgment on some of the newer ideas in therapy, however.

I am a psychoanalyst, and as such belong to the American Psychiatric Association and to the William Alanson White Psychoanalytic Society. I am also a member of the American Academy of Psychoanalysis, which includes psychoanalysts from the newer, so-called neo-Freudian schools. We exchange information and ideas, and this is done more freely than had been the case in the past.

One of the popular assumptions is that psychoanalysts do not get into the public system of mental health care because the money isn't as good as in private hospitals and in practice. This is a false picture. About half of the heads of departments of psychiatry in medical schools, for instance, are held by psychoanalysts. There are a great many psychoanalysts in public programs. At the Bronx State Hospital, for example, many of the leading psychiatrists are trained psychoanalysts. The director, Hugh Butts, is a trained psychoanalyst. And Leon Salzman, also an important psychoanalyst, is the hospital's deputy director. A number of Bronx State Hospital's progressive programs were initiated by the former director, Israel Zwerling, also an analyst. Places like Bellevue Hospital are sprinkled with psychoanalysts. One William Alanson White Psychoanalytic graduate is the director of one of the largest community psychiatric programs in the country, the Philadelphia Child Guidance Clinic.

Psychoanalysis is not limited to the wealthy. It has evolved and is a more dynamic treatment than it was in its earlier classic forms. Psychoanalysis is a total treatment—viewing the person as a whole, and guiding him to a happier, more productive life.

CHAPTER ELEVEN

Eclectic Therapies
Herbert Walker, M.D.

Dr. Herbert Walker practices what has come to be known as eclectic psychotherapy. Dr. Walker employs an effective blend of behavior therapy, hypnosis, directive psychotherapy, and psychotherapeutic drugs.

Dr. Walker, Associate Clinical Professor of Psychiatry at the New York University School of Medicine, received his training in psychiatry at the U.S. Naval Hospital, Bethesda, Maryland, and was a Resident and Chief Resident Psychiatrist at New York University Medical Center and Bellevue Hospital. In addition to his private practice in New York City, he is an assistant attending neuro-psychiatrist at Bellevue Hospital and attending psychiatrist at the Manhattan Veterans Administration Hospital. He is a diplomate of the American Board, Psychiatry and Neurology. Dr. Walker has published articles on his eclectic approach to psychotherapy in the *Journal of the American Medical Association* and the *Journal of Behavior Therapy and Experimental Psychiatry.*

Adapted from my interview with Dr. Walker, this chapter discusses his approach to psychotherapy and his personal views of his profession.

Herbert Walker, M.D.

Today, more and more psychiatrists are using an eclectic, or pragmatic, approach to treating patients. The term "eclectic" therapy implies exactly what it would seem: a treatment method that draws from all the theories known in psychiatry to this time, and confronts a specific problem with a therapy that is fitting. Eclectic therapists are armed with the knowledge of Freudian psychoanalysis, and use it as a basis for diagnosing a patient's problems, but not necessarily as a treatment method.

In my own practice, I use behavior therapy (behavior modification), some drug treatment when it is indicated, ego-supportive—or directive —psychotherapy, and hypnosis. I will address myself to each of these kinds of treatments as I use them in my practice, and as they are employed generally by eclectic psychiatrists.

Behavior therapy is essentially a therapy that is symptom-oriented. That is, it deals with the symptoms themselves and not with the person as a whole; the objective of such treatment is to alleviate a type of behavior that is harmful, inappropriate, or otherwise disturbing to a person. This involves a very direct therapy, with the patient taking a "student" role, and the therapist, a "teacher" role.

The basis of behavior modification is that most of the ways we react to any given thing—an object or a set of circumstances—is learned. If a person's way of reacting toward something is harmful, or causes the person difficulty in his life, then that behavior can be changed via relearning a new response. The person himself will not change, but his inappropriate or harmful behavior will. In other words, we examine the way a person responds to something (the stimulus) and call that response a learned piece of behavior. Using techniques developed in experimental learning and behavior psychology, we teach the patient to overcome that inappropriate mode of reacting.

In teaching a person to overcome a maladaptive response, of course, we teach him how to change the way he reacts to something. If a person is always extremely anxious on an airplane, for instance, I would first have to study that anxiety response. So I would set up a situation in my office that is very similar to the atmosphere—the milieu—of a plane. (This can also be done with imagination.) I can then observe what sets off his anxiety, and from that insight, can outline a program to help the person learn new and adaptive responses, which will eliminate the anxiety by replacing it.

Behavior therapists study the patient's symptoms very carefully, outline an almost recipe-type of treatment program with the patient, then execute the program. I almost always teach a person relaxation exercises and give a patient material to read that relates to his or her problem. I encourage the person to experience those things that frighten him (or produce maladaptive behavior)—first *in vitro* (in my office), and then, gradually, in his own life *(in vivo)*. *How* the symptom developed is not the matter at hand in the treatment program—only the elimination of the symptom via relearning a new response to a given set of anxiety-producing circumstances.

It is a fairly well-known fact that behavior modification consists at least in part of approval and disapproval. The patient is rewarded in some way that fits his case for appropriate (adaptive) responses to the symptom-producing stimulus, and is in some way punished for maladaptive responses, usually by approval or disapproval of the therapist or a peer. Some therapists use aversive techniques. For instance, the patient may, through systematic desensitization or inhibition, be taught to overcome a phobia or fear; he is encouraged to experience the phobia and to carry out the phobic behavior—the way he reacts to this fear. Gradually, using approval-disapproval and teaching the patient relaxation exercises, he learns to get over the anxiety, to react differently. I encourage my patients to do in the office things that frighten them, or to fantasize the situations that frighten them; in a relaxed, protected environment the relearning is then eased, and confronting the problem is easier.

Behavior therapy is very effective in the treatment of psychosomatic types of problems, phobias, and sexual problems such as impotency. (The success of Masters and Johnson, certainly, is attributable to behavior modification.) I have found in my practice that behavior therapy, as an adjunct to the other types of therapy I describe, is effective in treating depression if the therapist is very, very active, and if the depression is focused around some type of obsession, as is so often the case.

In treating depression along behavior-modification lines, the therapist has to forcefully discourage the patient from thinking about or talking about the things that are depressive to the person. Of course, as I have said, this is effective when the patient is in the midst of a depressing obsession. With this sort of thought-stopping treatment, a therapist might apply a very mild shock to the patient's skin in order to help the person stop a rumination or obsession about something that is futile or upsetting.

Another facet of behavior therapy is called assertive training, and I believe that it is particularly helpful for people outside the hospital; it provides them with techniques, teaches them devices, to become more appropriately assertive over their thoughts and therefore over their lives. It teaches people *appropriate assertiveness*; in other words, how and when to be assertive, when it is appropriate to be assertive, and when it is inappropriate. Frequently, depressed patients are inappropriately non-assertive.

As I have implied earlier, behavior therapy derives from experimental psychology—most people who practice behavior therapy exclusively are psychologists, as a matter of fact, and not psychiatrists. People generally will associate behavior psychology with Ivan Pavlov and B. F. Skinner—both well-known for their experiments with animals and modifying animal behavior and reactions. Of course, we have never made the direct jump from the animal laboratory to the human situation. Behavior theorists such as Joseph Wolpe of Temple University, Philadelphia, (who is the father of behavior therapy in this country) have shown how behavior therapy can work for people. I have had the privilege of a sabbatical with Dr. Wolpe.

My own philosophy is that behavior therapy should only be used as an adjunct to psychotherapy—directive or ego-supportive psychotherapy. Behavior modification is good as an immediate, alleviatory therapy, but the patient who is deeply troubled must learn to deal with the problem, as well as altering the effects of the problem.

I also use *hypnosis* in my practice, and like behavior therapy, it is limited in the extent to which a patient may be helped by it. Hypnosis seems to produce an alpha wave rhythm, which is similar to the alpha rhythm one gets in transcendental meditation or from certain other Yoga exercises. It is effective in a relatively small percent of the general population; only about 20 percent of the population are able to be hypnotized into a deep trance.

Hypnotherapy has a very checkered past since its beginnings in eighteenth-century France by Anton Mesmer; it wasn't until 1946 that hypnotherapy was recognized by the American Medical Association as an accepted form of medical practice.

I feel that hypnotherapy can be most effective in helping patients overcome a habit such as smoking, for relaxation and changing attitudes and motivations. A paper, published by Dr. Herbert Speigel and his associates, reports a 20 percent success rate after one session of hypnosis with smokers, and I find this extraordinarily encouraging. But again, even hypnosis as a "cure" for symptoms should be used only as an adjunct to other types of psychotherapy. It seems as though the ultimate success of habit-breaking through hypnosis is contingent upon the patient's ability to pursue the therapy with self-hypnosis exercises.

The hypnotist must be cautious, because his suggestions—the post-hypnotic suggestions used to remove a habit or a maladaptive symptom—may be harmful to the patient. It may result in what we call "symptom substitution"—that is, the replacing of one maladaptive response with another—unless the patient is instructed in an adaptive (healthy) type of reaction to use in place of the maladaptive symptom. I have reported such a case in the medical literature.

The type of therapy that I think is most helpful in keeping patients out of hospitals is *directive psychotherapy*. Patients out of hospitals who have had long-term psychological problems are generally extremely fearful—fearful of themselves and therefore fearful of their judgments. One of the major shortcomings of American psychiatry has been an apparent inability of therapists to direct the patient—to help patients make decisions as, for example, an internist would. An internist will say to a person who has had a myocardial infarction [heart attack], "You may not walk up stairs." Yet a psychiatrist is often hesitant to suggest to a patient that he may or may not do something—act in a way that has always resulted in emotional troubles.

This hesitancy to be directive in psychiatry is the consequence, I think, of neo-Freudian thinking; intervention is considered theoretically incorrect. In my own practice, eclectic in style, I use insights a la Freud to help the patient understand his or her behavior, but as a psychiatrist, I deal with the patient in a very directive manner.

A very important point should be made here: in guiding the patient, especially in helping the patient understand his or her behavior, the psychiatrist must not be judging *mental* behavior; the therapist must always remember that behavior is individualistic. Each person behaves differently from every other person; and every type of behavior—even behavior that does the individual no good—is simply *different* from others. There is no such thing as *right* behavior and *wrong* behavior. (I am not referring to criminal behavior.) This is a bit different from the view taken by my Freudian colleagues; my point of departure is more existential, taking into account the here and now rather than the how and why of a person and his psychological problems. I think it is very important—important to the extent of being the goal of therapy—to help the patient get over a psychological problem as rapidly as possible. When the immediate, visible, pain-causing effects of, say, a depression are overcome, then we can get down to dealing with the behaviors that set up the depression so as to prevent a recurrence.

I see many patients who are in depressions, and I have found that prescribing a rather vigorous physical exercise program for a depressive person is a great therapeutic boost. I think that exercise is the *sine qua non* for a person to have a healthy mind—the healthy mind-healthy body equation is one in which I believe firmly. Dieting, nutrition, and very careful attention to one's physical health will provide a basis that will make the active and more direct psychotherapy more effective and lasting.

I help my patients by encouraging them or discouraging them just as I did when I was a general medical practitioner in Maryland. I would tell a patient, "Look, you take your pencillin for five days and stay in bed." In my approach to psychotherapy, I am that directive; I encourage a patient to indulge in a certain kind of behavior if that behavior is going to help him or her.

I prescribe medications as part of my practice, but I keep in mind that patients may become dependent upon medications, and that some people cannot take certain drugs. What is one person's cure may easily be another person's poison. So it is extremely important for a psychiatrist to remember the *individual* in every phase of treatment—and the medication phase is no different.

It is becoming more and more apparent to the psychiatric community that at least schizophrenia—and even some severe depressive behavior—has a biochemical basis. Freud himself pointed out that one day analysis would be anachronistic. Even behavior therapy will be insufficient in treating certain psychological maladies—and this will become increasingly obvious as the psychiatric profession discovers the biochemical, or organic, basis for psychiatric problems. My own feeling on the subject is that schizophrenics are suffering from a biochemical imbalance, and that correcting this through medications, as well as understanding and environmental manipulation, is of the utmost importance.

At the present time, though, all psychological disturbances do not seem to have an organic basis—and even in the case of schizophrenia, an illness for which the greatest evidence has been presented in argument *for* a biochemical cause, medicine has yet to concede a hundred percent to medical therapy. Therefore, the wisest approach at this time would seem to be a pragmatic approach: to study the patient's peculiar set of problems. This is my approach. After learning what the individual patient suffers from—what sort of reactions trouble him—I help the person alter his behavior so that he doesn't get ill, doesn't get depressed again, doesn't get into an obsessional type of neurosis again, and doesn't return to the hospital.

It should be part of the psychiatrist's role to help the patient stay out of the hospital, just as it is part of the internist's role to keep his patient out of the general hospital. Being hospitalized is an extremely shattering experience, often less therapeutic than helpful; it disrupts not only a person's day-to-day life, but his feelings of validity as a functioning human being as well. It is telling someone, "Look, you can't make it on your own—we have to lock you up to save you from yourself." The person may become, or at least feel like, a victim, and sometimes he may actually be a victim. The case of electroshock is too often a case of the patient receiving unnecessary treatment, and philosophically this makes the patient a victim, indeed. I do feel that in some cases ECT is necessary, but only rarely. The recurrence rate for electroshock patients is quite high, so if shock treatment is, as some claim, beneficial, why isn't the effect lasting? Why do ECT patients exhibit a high rate of rehospitalization? I encourage patients not to have electroshock treatment, except in extreme cases. Usually, through a combination of antidepressant drugs and directive modes of psychotherapy, I am able to avoid recommending ECT for even seriously depressed patients.

In my quite active New York practice, as well as in the past as coordinator of the residency programs at Bellevue and NYU Hospitals, I have seen few cases where ECT was actually indicated—that is, where another approach would not have been equally, or more, effective.

The primary concern of the psychiatrist, after all, is to aid the patient toward feeling better—and the results should be to the patient's long-term benefit. The patient is an equal human being; any treatment must be human if it's to be effective at all.

CHAPTER TWELVE

Child Psychiatry
Milton Senn, M.D.

Milton Senn, Sterling Professor Emeritus of Pediatrics and Psychiatry at Yale University, is one of America's pioneers in child psychiatry. As early as the 1930s Dr. Senn began building the bridge that would unite the practices of pediatrics and psychiatry. He has been in private practice, and today he is retired.

Dr. Senn received his medical degree from the University of Wisconsin, obtained specialized training in pediatrics at Washington University, St. Louis, Missouri, and proceeded to Cornell and the New York Hospital Medical Center to teach pediatrics. Later he worked with patients in the New York Hospital-Westchester Division, White Plains, New York; although his patients at that time were primarily adults, his interest in child psychiatry led him to further his training at the Philadelphia Child Guidance Clinic. He then returned to the New York Hospital-Cornell Medical Center as a professor of psychiatry and pediatrics. In 1948 Dr. Senn became the Director of the Yale University Child Study Center and Sterling Professor of Pediatrics and Psychiatry.

At Yale, Milton Senn emphasized the importance for pediatricians to incorporate psychology in their practice—to understand children and to see them as normal human beings involved in the complexities of growth. The marriage of child development and pediatrics continued to be Dr. Senn's goal, both in theory and in his own practice, for over a quarter of a century.

In my conversation with him, I asked Dr. Senn about his experiences as a child psychiatrist, the types of patients he treated, his treatment approach, and his opinions about current and past methods in child psychiatry, as well as the general recovery rate for children in psychotherapy.

Milton Senn, M.D.

When I became interested in child psychiatry in the 1930s, my goal was not to have a career as a psychiatrist, but rather to return to pediatrics with a better understanding of children's development. Curiously enough, in those days little was being done in the field of child psychiatry. Most psychiatrists seemed to have very little awareness of children, even psychologically. They primarily dealt with adults, and the clinical studies that were made during that era were usually retrospective psychological studies on adults, such as the case histories presented in the field of psychoanalysis.

At that time, the traditional therapy practiced in the child guidance clinics entailed working with parents and children in a team approach. This was in no way the group or family psychiatry, which is practiced today; at the Philadelphia Child Guidance Clinic, where I received my training, our teams consisted of a psychiatrist, a social worker, a psychologist, and very often a pediatrician. As a rule, the psychiatrist dealt with the child, and the social worker with the parents. The philosophy of working with children was primarily based on the thinking of the well-known American psychiatrist Adolf Meyer, at John Hopkins, often called the Father of American Psychiatry. He emphasized the role of the milieu of the child as a force in his life, and the need for changing it in circumstances where the child was in trouble, as in removing a child from his home and placing him in an institution or changing his school. This frequently entailed working with the family through the courts.

Yet, even in the mid-thirties, we were no longer satisifed with simply dealing with the milieu at the Philadelphia Clinic. Along with others, I felt that one had to know more about the inner feelings of the child, about interpersonal relationships—and that took me into psychoanalytic training.

At Yale I emphasized the importance of understanding children as normal human beings in a very dynamic process of growth. I tried to stress the role of the pediatrician or general practitioner in a child's development. These are the doctors whom a child is most likely to see when sick, and it is important that they understand the relationship of specific problems to development, and of their roles in enhancing the development of each individual.

I felt that the role of the pediatrician was one of prevention, dealing with families where there were impending difficulties, and working with the parents even more than working with the children who were disturbed, either neurotic or psychotic.

Many children's problems that were being treated by psychiatrists were not those of psychosis. In pediatric practice one doesn't see young children in states of manic excitement or severe chronic depressions. Of course, one sees depressive moodiness even in younger children, and both older children and adolescents occasionally may show signs of acute depressions, which are troublesome. Most children who are in psychotherapy are children who are suffering from crises, reactions to very specific circumstances in their lives. You might call them "neurotic" reactions, involving anxiety and other feelings. An example is the so-called "reactive depression," where the symptoms are primarily despair and despondency. At times children act out against society in anger, in acts of violence or delinquency.

Such children, whom psychiatrists see a lot of these days, have outbursts of uncontrolled feelings. We term this acting-out *impulsive-control disorders*. These children and adolescents sooner or later get into trouble with the law. That brings them into the courts and possibly into child guidance clinics, particularly the former if they are from the lower economic classes.

If they are upper-middle class or upper class and act out with this sort of anger, they tend not to get into the courts as much, but into the hands of private psychiatrists, where the problem is dealt with in a different way.

In New Haven, where I practiced, the children I saw came from primarily white middle class families, but increasingly from lower economic classes, especially from black and Puerto Rican families.

As a rule, there was no history of mental illness in the children's families, but the behavior problems were emotional responses to stress and strain within the family; for example, a death of a parent. In such a circumstance a child may react with either physical illness (or the symptoms of a physical illness), depression, truancy from school, or something else. How that child's reaction to the specific situation is handled may further decide whether or not more serious behavior problems follow. A child in a reactive state may do extreme things that get him involved with the law; he may join others who are also reacting with various types of acting-out aggression, such as vandalism. Community resentment against such group behavior is strong, but the solution of this social problem varies with social class.

If the groups of children or adolescents who get into trouble with the law are middle class people, people with some money, the law often steps in and says that the child and his parents *must* have psychiatric treatment.

In contrast, the poorer family, the family without money, who cannot buy psychiatric help, doesn't get it. Sometimes lower class children may be sent to a child guidance clinic that is attached to a family or juvenile court. But more likely, the child of poorer parents (and his parents) will be judged as delinquent, scolded, and punished in some way—as if punishment is going to help the child and his parents to "reform."

Such difference in the way that society looks at the problem is widespread. If you have money, a child's problem is psychiatric; if you are poor, it's called a crime and treated punitively rather than psychiatrically and supportively.

The psycho-pathology that affects a child often stems from anxiety in the parents, sometimes related to their depressions or psychoses; out of the parents' problems come problems in the child as a reaction to the parents' pathology. There may be an identification with one parent, wherein the child assumes the parent's symptoms. A child may identify with her mother's anxiety by withdrawing, not wanting to go to school. Or a child may identify with his father by having anger outbursts if he sees his father behaving that way.

Of course, what happens to individual families is related to what is happening in our society in general; psycho-pathology in families and individuals is closely intermixed with social pathology. For example, people of the middle classes move around a lot more than they used to. I recently interviewed a young woman whose parents had moved seventeen times in fifteen years. She is now twenty-three years old and she's quite troubled emotionally. She feels that she has no home base, no stability. The reasons for moving were all connected to her father's employment, and businessmen's moves of this sort are quite common today.

Also, the excessive competitiveness of our culture could be called a cause of social pathology, and of some children getting sick. There is pressure on everybody, the need not only to compete, but to beat. It's similar to the expectations of the national economic growth; it has to be up-up-up. And a person's performance has to be up-up-up from the time he or she is born. If it isn't, the person is deemed a failure by our social standards. You can't be on a plateau; you can't reach a point and say, "Gee, I'm glad just to be here." You're pressured to go higher. And I call this kind of competitiveness syndrome "social pathology." It is this kind of social pathology that has an effect upon children.

The competitiveness of our society demands constant change—upward. But children need continuity. They don't need constant uprooting; they don't need undue pressure to compete. Particularly in the early years, children want a chance to be related to by other people in a very personal way. They don't want relationships from an array of adults, and they don't want a frequent change of people, but they do want continuing nurturance from one person. And it's difficult to provide that these days. The family is breaking apart more often, and there is the growing problem of disunity that faces children today.

There is a great difference between the way an adult will come to a psychiatrist and the way a child will. An adult seeks help more or less directly, although sometimes, of course, other adults step in and guide or force him toward help. With children, it's altogether different. A child or adolescent *rarely* presents himself for psychiatric treatment. There is usually someone else who is concerned about the child. Often, a parent comes with a complaint about the child's anxiety or depressed mood or temper outbursts or drug use. Or perhaps the child is doing unusually poorly in school. The school behavior of a child is very often the precipitating factor that will lead a parent to seek professional help for a child. The teacher or principal of the school may recommend psychiatric help, calling in the parents and telling them, "Look, either you get help for this child or we kick him out of school."

The precipitating factor may be the parent's inability to cope with their child. They cannot deal with his "bad habits," or his moods, for example; or the child's behavior among his peers may cause their parents to complain to the family, and they can't contend with such criticism. Often, it is the parents who are primarily the "trouble," certainly the troubled. They go to a child psychiatrist seeking help for their child, but it is also help for themselves they more or less unwittingly seek. And so you have two or three patients, really. The child may basically have the same symptoms as the parent(s) or he may not. But the crux of the issue is that the parents are involved, usually in the formation of the child's difficulties, and are always reacting with their own anxieties to the child's difficulties.

This was already recognized in the 1930s; hence, the team approach where, as I said earlier, a group of professionals worked with different members of a single family. Child psychiatry took a turn away from the group approach for a time, with the emphasis on the one-to-one, more psychoanalytically oriented therapy; and the parents often were left out. Today, therapists recognize that parents are so involved in either the cause of the child's problem or in its effects on others, that they must be involved in its resolution.

Now we deal with both parents and child, and often with the troubled child's siblings. This means that entire families are seen in therapy, and not always just one family alone. Very often, a session will include a large group, comprised of several families where the children have been the reason for seeking help.

About drugs. In the actual therapeutic treatment of children, I prefer less drastic measures than drugs. Today, however, medicines are being used increasingly in child psychiatry. They are used by psychiatrists primarily for what are termed "acting-out children," children who, when they are in school, are so restless that they disrupt the group; they do not learn and they prevent others from learning. If they are on tranquilizing drugs, their behavior can be controlled; they are no longer disruptive, since they are no longer driven by this inner drive to move about.

Sometimes these children are labeled "minimal brain-damaged children." In America this diagnosis is quite frequent; it is a puzzling condition, because there is little or no actual *evidence,* by physical standards, of brain damage. Yet, these children behave as though the brain were damaged. The label includes "minimal" because of the "soft"—less serious—diagnostic signs.

That type of child, in the hands of some psychiatrists, is treated with drugs—usually amphetamines, which reduces the hyperactivity. This is seemingly a paradox, since amphetamines ("speed") tend to "excite" adults. But in children, they act more as tranquilizers, at least as far as overt behavior is concerned. They help the child to focus his attention, to concentrate.

Many people are concerned about the use of drugs with children. In my practice, I shied away from drugs as much as possible, although some highly ethical, highly repsected child psychiatrists are proponents of drug therapy.

My own approach is more direct. I believe that most children should be treated on an interpersonal basis by persons skilled in psychotherapy. This is to say that children should be dealt with on a relationship basis, the job of the psychiatrist being to help a child rearrange his or her life and to help reshape the circumstances of that life. To change schools, for example, as well as to get at the root of the poor learner's inability to learn; or to help the parents learn to cope with their child's behavior.

I am more concerned with prevention—attacking the potential causes of a child's problem before the problem results in trouble. We realized long ago in medicine that you don't wait for a child to get sick with diphtheria and then treat the disease with an antitoxin. Medicine developed methods of preventing diseases; with that successful model of prevention, psychiatrists have sought means of preventing psychological problems by intervening in some way.

But that is difficult. How does one intervene in a family where problems seem inevitable? Perhaps no intervention is desired, as when the parents and others involved with the child may have no insight into the problems. But even if you have a child's and the parents' willingness, how can one institute appropriate measures of intervention? Frequently, both parents and child resent what intervention implies. Even when a parent or a teacher is the prime mover in seeking help for a child, resentments can arise. Both teacher and parent may feel that they have failed; they consider intervention a poor reflection on them and their competence. Parents feel that the psychiatrist is "showing them up," and as a consequence, often do not like what he suggests as preventative steps in dealing with their child's difficulties.

When one has a crisis situation, though, wherein the family and child are upset to an extent that shatters—or threatens to shatter—their lives, it is no longer a matter of prevention. Now one must act, intervene; as when we have to remove the child from the home or hospitalize him. (Of the children I have treated, a relatively small percent—less than 10 percent—required hospitalization.)

Wherever possible, we try to return children and youths to their families after hospitalization, because we think that a family is the appropriate place for a child. Even though the family may have provided a poor life for the child, the child removed from the family will continue to try to return to it. Children will seek out their families.

We see this sort of thing happen even in the case of separated parents; the child builds up a fantasy about the absent parent and tends to glorify him. The child wants to seek him out, to be with the parent. What children in this situation are actually doing is seeking reassurance about the closeness of the ties between the parents and themselves. Where there had been no such good relationship, and hence the search is unrealistic, we discourage it. Children, like adults, try to forget the unpleasant and painful aspects of family life and glorify and fantasize it in ways that are not going to help them deal realistically with their familial problems. Where the family is the root of the child's troubles, and he has been helped psychiatrically to cope, the rational step is to allow him or her to deal with the real situation, and not to avoid it.

In children the degree of therapeutic reserve—the lasting effects of therapy—is very high. There is a fantastic drive in young people to recover, to learn, to cope, just to be better off. This is not to suggest that there is no danger of relapse. But parents, teachers, and doctors (not only psychiatrists) can do a lot by understanding children—how they feel, what their special problems are—and by being supportive psychologically in times of crisis.

People are becoming much more tolerant of emotionally troubled persons; and I am seeing a far greater understanding among parents of children with emotional problems. There is still a stigma attached to hospitalization for an emotional illness, but it is slowly and noticeably diminishing over the years. Even among the medical profession there is a greater tolerance for the mentally sick. It's curious that medicine hasn't always been tolerant of people who are emotionally ill—even doctors, too frequently, still *blame* a patient for his or her mental upsets.

The entire field of child psychiatry is changing with the times—we are viewing children and children's problems within the context of society, and treating them accordingly. Much more must be done in this field. All of us need to learn more about children and their development, and of the influences of society on individuals and on families.

Only then, and with the recognition of what is normal and what is harmful and a willingness to change that which does us ill as a society, will progress continue.

CHAPTER THIRTEEN

"The Total View"
Larry Farmer

Larry Farmer is the pseuodnym for a professor at a major metropolitan New York university. Since he left college, he has been in therapy with numerous psychologists and psychiatrists, treated primarily for depressions.

Today in his forties, and with the help of a psychiatrist he feels is right for him, Larry has learned to overcome the problems that led him to therapy years ago. For those who have traveled through the maze of psychotherapies as Larry has, his story will surely strike some familiar chords.

Larry Farmer

B.B.: Larry, you have seen several psychotherapists over the years. What originally led you to seek out professional help?

LARRY: Well, for a number of years I'd had a feeling that there were some very major and unresolved problems that I would have to deal with sooner or later. These vague feelings became more identifiable, came to a culmination during a period at college, when I simply wasn't doing any work at all. I was just sleeping all the time and lying around, getting more and more depressed. I felt that things were getting rather drastic, so I had to do something, so I found a psychiatrist.

B.B.: Was he helpful?

LARRY: Moderately, as far as I could see then. He was rather a classic, unimaginative doctor. At the time I had no basis for judgment, and I had that sort of casual attitude, where you accept the usual psychiatric jargon and the psychiatrically oriented outlook of parents who were quite literate people. We had a number of psychiatrists in our family. But he seemed all right, and I did get through school. It wasn't until several years after I stopped seeing him that I realized he hadn't been all that helpful.

B.B.: Were you hospitalized?

LARRY: No, I wasn't.

B.B.: When did you decide to go back into psychotherapy with another doctor?

LARRY: After I left college, I moved to New York and started working. I saw another doctor here briefly, then I stopped for a period. I moved around a bit, working in various other places, went to a number of other psychiatrists for short periods, and then finally saw the doctor that I'm seeing at this moment.

B.B.: Were your parents supportive about your psychotherapy?

LARRY: They were pretty decent about it. My father is a chemist and took a very sane and balanced view of things. My mother's primary concern was financial. She was worried about how much it would cost. But, as I say, they were enlightened and sensible about it. They did not get alarmed and they didn't pry too much. Of course, I hadn't lived with them since I'd begun college, and I think they saw me as more of an adult working out my own problems.

B.B.: Was anyone doctor more helpful than the others?

LARRY: The one I see at the moment. This is after I've seen a number of doctors. I really don't believe that just any doctor can help any person. The doctor I see now has done more good than the others put together. It was partly because of my shopping around that I can realize this.

B.B.: You said before that when you were in college you would lie around, feel depressed? Do you still get depressed?

LARRY: Yes, but not to the extent that I used to, by a long shot. There was a period when I was very, very depressed and made a couple of suicide attempts.

I don't get anywhere near that any longer. Every few months I feel sort of down about something, but it's not depression in the sense that it once was. It was really totally debilitating or totally alarming or just frightening. I mean, now it's upsetting and by definition, depressing, but it doesn't last very long, only a day or so.

B.B.: Were you ever at a point where you couldn't function?

LARRY: I would think so, yes. I mean, during the worst period, which was a couple of years after I moved to New York, there was a period when I literally couldn't do anything; I was in a terrible state. I couldn't cross the street; I would like stand there for the light to change, from red to green or whatever, so I wouldn't have to make the decision whether I was going to cross the street. That sort of thing. It had got to a point where I simply couldn't trust any judgments of my own; I was in a total, total state of chaos.

One reason that I so appreciate the particular doctor who I'm going to at the moment, is that she simply cut through all that stuff, and, well, in a relatively short time, got rid of the ghost of my past, totally debilitating treatment. As I say, it was a combination of my own problems, but I think they were augmented by the nature of certain kinds of therapy that didn't help me.

B.B.: Do you feel you have come out of this with more insight into yourself?

LARRY: Oh, yes. I think I'm a naturally insightful person and rather introspective in any case. I think that there have been, occasionally, rather startling insights that I have gotten, and I think that simply through some process, the dynamics of which I don't totally understand, there were certain things that simply changed in and of themselves as they've been discussed in therapeutic situations or simply as time has passed.

One of the problems is that it can be overdone a bit—you know, the self-speculation.

I see my doctor now once a week; I find that very helpful. When I was seeing other doctors, I saw them as often as four times a week. I don't feel that that, which was encouraged by them, was ideal, although at the time I felt in no position to pass any judgment. But I do think that that situation meant that every single thing I did was sort of put on ice until I got into the doctor's office and discussed it. I've come to feel for myself that this once-a-week thing is more useful, because there are six days when I have to do things on my own.

B.B.: Has your current therapy produced a change in your lifestyle?

LARRY: "Lifestyle" tends to mean how you decorate your apartment. I have a job, and I'm relatively happy. I'm doing what I want to do in terms of my free time. In those ways, yes, it's produced changes.

B.B.: Yet you will still have at least short-lived, minor depressions. Can you think of anything that triggers one of those depressions today?

LARRY: Time going by when I'm not doing what I want to. The awareness of the difficulty of certain things that I am trying to do in terms of career. I don't mean teaching; I also have aspirations in art. The problems involved in that. My lack of recognition, and that can be very depressing. But other than that, I can't think of any specific things.

B.B.: So you really cope quite well with life from day to day?

LARRY: I think relatively so. I'm markedly optimistic about things and I think that I deal with them much better than I used to. I know, for instance, that if I get depressed, it is nothing like it once was; therefore, it just doesn't seem to be something to get that excited about.

B.B.: When you were in New York and upset, and seeing the doctors who were not as helpful as your current one, did your problems ever interfere with your work?

LARRY: At one point, yes. This was during the period that was so difficult. I remember very clearly, that I was sort of vaguely looking for jobs, but, at the same time, getting panicky every time I got near one. I'd give myself these crazy speeches as I approached the place where a job existed, and I'd end up either not going in for the interview or deliberately muffing it so that I simply couldn't be hired.

I was never fired as a result of my condition. I was just voluntarily unhired.

B.B.: Would you say your social life has improved with your general improvement?

LARRY: I suppose so, yes. Well, the reason I say I suppose so is that in some ways I think I have less social life, than, I'd say, ten years ago and that's okay with me. So it hasn't improved in the sense that I go out more or see more people, but I guess that I do what I feel like doing, which is the important thing.

B.B.: Have you always had good close friends?

LARRY: Right. That was never a problem. I mean, I've always had a number of friends—close friends and good friends. I get along quite well with people.

B.B.: Were your friends helpful to you when you were down?

LARRY: Yes, they were . . . sometimes it was surprising who was particularly so. I mean, either people who you really didn't think really had much feeling for you, or, quite frankly, you had much feeling for, came through in surprisingly articulate and sensitive ways. Most people I knew were quite nice to me.

B.B.: And some of them are still close friends?

LARRY: Yes. Right.

B.B.: Do you feel they understood your problem at all?

LARRY: Well, in a way that one can understand someone else having problems. I don't think you can fully understand what another person is going through.

I've had people talk to me about certain kinds of terrors that are very exotic and unlike anything that I've ever experienced, but I do believe them and can sympathize with the fact that they might have felt them, even though, you know, I'm so far away from them.

B.B.: Larry, what would you say are the basic differences between the doctors you saw who were not helpful and the doctor who is?

LARRY: Okay. I would say that the essential difference is between a kind of doctrinaire approach, as opposed to a more personal one geared to one's own needs. In other words, the doctors who I felt were not particularly helpful or, in one case, actually harmful, were people who, it seemed to me, were after psychiatric insights that would fit some theory. There seemed to be a kind of doctrine that they clung to, needed, and explained everything in terms of, and hid behind in a way.

My present doctor seems to me someone who deals with the person, each person, in a very individual way, without using some classic explanation that presumably satisfies everyone. That's one difference.

The second seems to me a certain amount of balance and humor on the part of the doctor. Granted, at certain moments when you're feeling very vulnerable, you're probably not wise to hide behind a chuckle. But the total absence of any balance in perspective, at least when a doctor is talking to a patient, makes things that aren't all that serious seem tremendously serious. My present doctor is a well-read, intelligent, and enormously humorous person, for whom humor is a balancing and sensible thing—and that to me is a relieving situation in the therapy.

I guess another thing has to do with worldliness. A number of the doctors I had before, it seemed to me, weren't very worldly or sophisticated outside their profession. You know, they seemed to have once been hard-working, earnest, dreary students who went to medical school and became doctors, so their experience of the world is confined probably to the people they see in their office and their wives' friends.

My present doctor is a more sophisticated and worldly person, and I find that relaxing and helpful. It is nice to have someone who's read someone good besides Thomas Mann, the only respectable author most psychiatrists seem to have read, and who can take seriously, you know, allusions to things that are important to me. Literature is important to me. That's a very trivial-sounding comment, but it isn't really trivial, because, again, for some of these other doctors, I think it was threatening to them, I really do. I don't think that's arrogant, but I do think a few of them minded that I had read more than they had.

I guess, finally, the thing that is extremely important would be that I really like this person as a person. Some of my past doctors claim that that isn't all that important. I think it's very important. My doctor today is a woman I respect as a person, as much as I know her. She's a woman I have a really warm feeling about—and that feeling carries me through very difficult periods, when I don't agree with her, for example, or when I feel that I'm being criticized, or when things in therapy are unpleasant or difficult.

In the earlier cases, where I was dealing with certain enigmatic figures who deliberately refused to reveal anything about themselves, it meant that I had to go on faith, and I'm not a great one for faith. I don't find it a very compelling emotion.

B.B.: You want someone you can empathize with.

LARRY: Right, and whom I feel I have a very personal response to, and who has a personal response to me. As I say, I have evidences of genuine concern, genuine generosity, thoughtfulness, and human treatment, which in this kind of situation seems to me to count much more than all the expertise in the world.

I've seen doctors who are world-famous men—one man especially had an enormously high reputation. And the session with him was about as devastating as any single experience I've ever had in my life. I think the man was a savage. I really do believe that a psychiatrist's reputation in his field has nothing to do with whether he's a good practitioner or not. I think therapy is more an art than a science, and that's what you have to look for; someone who's feeling the vibrations.

B.B.: In very general terms, what did this "savage" doctor manage to do?

LARRY: Well, he so discouraged me about myself. He saw me at a time when I was enormously vulnerable, and anything I thought I was thinking was questioned, defined as a means of hiding something that I didn't want to say. I was being told that the reverse of what I was thinking was probably true, so I was ready to believe anything that anyone said about me. You know, if someone said, "You're a murderer," I would have said, "Yes, you're right," because somewhere in my mind it probably was true.

This person's attitude was essentially: I might as well give up, as there was nothing either worth dealing with or worth trying to save in me, and, as far as my life was concerned, I probably should get some sort of menial job and just survive. He was really quite horrible. Really horrible.

Let me just add one other thing to an earlier question that you asked. I think one thing that's very useful is for the doctor to point out, not continually, but often enough, the parts of you that are working well. I know the purpose of seeing a psychiatrist is to deal with problems—but if the emphasis is exclusively on the things that aren't functioning too well, or the problems, you begin to feel that that's the whole story. That is all you are. A product of these things that aren't working up to snuff. One thing that my present doctor does do, which I find helpful, is to point out things that are going well, and things that I have done well. To have the total view. So that you do not begin to think that you are nothing but a malfunctioning creature. My current doctor does not have the kind of ego needs that some of these other analysts had, which were devastating. With someone like the one I'm going to now, you can begin to see yourself in a more real way, and you can even start to like what you see.

CHAPTER FOURTEEN

"To Live from Day to Day"
Elaine Farland

Elaine Farland's children were teenagers when she was hospitalized the first time for a severe depression. She was rehospitalized many more times. Fortunately, she could afford excellent care although there were times when the care was far from excellent. In fact, it was exceedingly bad, money or no money.

It wasn't without long searching that Elaine found a psychotherapist whom she could trust, and whose work with her has made psychiatric hospitals a thing of the past in her life. Presently in treatment with a psychotherapist who practices both behavior therapy and directive therapy, she has been able to return to her career as a writer.

Elaine Farland

B.B.: Elaine, would you tell us a bit about yourself, your background?

ELAINE: Well, I'm fifty-six. I was born in New York City. My family was well-off. I was brought up a great deal by nurses and governesses. I wasn't very intimate or close to my parents, because their life was very active and social. I had a brother and sister whom I was very close to, but we had different nurses and governesses who never got on. Intimacy was difficult, so I grew up to be quite a lonely child. My father and mother had an unhappy marriage; they were divorced when I was about ten. We certainly did not lack for material things. I think the lack was for intimacy, coziness, and constant love from the same people.

I grew up with the knowledge that my grandfather had committed suicide. I knew this upset my father. Then, when I was older, my brother became mentally ill.

B.B.: But what brought you to seek professional help?

ELAINE: I had a complete—well, laymen would call it a "nervous breakdown." My doctors called it a psychotic depression with delusions and hallucinations. It was obvious that I needed help: I was suicidal; I was completely nonfunctioning; I was terrified to go out; I was terrified to be closed in. I was suffering acutely all kinds of painful feelings of inadequacy. I thought I was crazy, and all in all I had really folded into a person who had to be locked up for my own safety . . . not "locked up," but protected, let's say.

B.B.: You were hospitalized then. How many years ago was that?

ELAINE: That was about ten years ago. I was hospitalized several times for different lengths of time. The first time was for four months, and the final time was over a year. Other times it was for two or three months. My treatment varied—anything from shock treatment to drugs to psychotherapy or all of them put together.

B.B.: What sort of hospitals were you in?

ELAINE: Two places I was in upset me very much, because I was locked in. I already had violent claustrophobia, and on top of that I felt stripped of my dignity. I felt more like a prisoner than a patient. I have much to say on the subject of incarceration being punitive, and unnecessarily so. You haven't done anything wrong, after all. You are sick and looking for help. Although I had to be protected, I don't think I had to be locked in my room, which was the situation in these places.

B.B.: What kind of treatment did you get in the final hospital?

ELAINE: My doctor tried many drugs. It wasn't until later that he gave me shock treatment, when the drugs seemed to fail. I suppose that eventually you could say the shock treatment enabled me to leave the hospital. I don't think that I was cured by it, because I had to go back to a hospital on other occasions.

B.B.: Do you remember how you felt when you left the hospital on these occasions?

ELAINE: Yes, I was very scared. I was afraid to go home to my children, for fear that they would think I was "crazy," which I think they partly did, because I don't think the situation was well handled at home. I went home to an unhappy marriage, and all in all I was terrified to face the world and what "they" would say and what "they" would think. You get used to the hospital, it seems safe after a while—if it is a good one. You get a case of "hospitalitis," which is really not healthy. You don't want to come out and face the problems of the world again—they are frightening.

B.B.: What was your family's attitude toward your illness, Elaine?

ELAINE: I think they had trouble understanding it. My friends, too. Unless you have had someone very, very close to you who has suffered through a mental illness or unless you have gone through it yourself, I think that it is extremely difficult to understand.

B.B.: Did your doctor explain your illness to your family?

ELAINE: He tried. My brother understood, because he had been sick himself. I don't think the rest of my family really grasped it. They tried. They tried to be kind, but it was really more than they could understand. There is so much feeling and anguish in mental illness that unless you have suffered it yourself, it is extremely difficult to articulate it to somebody else.

B.B.: What was most helpful to you in overcoming the fears you had when you left the hospital?

ELAINE: Well, before I was fully released for the last time, I made repeated short visits home which, at first, were most discouraging. But my doctor stood behind me so that I could overcome the sense of hopelessness or defeat. He told me I was really better and that he thought I could cope with living outside the hospital. I had a very helpful, a very kind, and a very excellent doctor. I was extremely fortunate, after having had some very bad ones, that I *finally* found an excellent one.

B.B.: Do you suffer upsets now?

ELAINE: Yes, and it's on a cyclical basis. I'd say it seems to come three or four times a year, about the same time of year. I don't really know the reason *why*.

B.B.: What are your symptoms during one of these upsets?

ELAINE: I get panicked, extremely afraid of situations and people, and I withdraw into myself (which is the worst thing you can do). Sometimes I get suicidal, which is frightening in itself—and then I have to go to the hospital for protection.

B.B.: Do you think that there is anything special that triggers these upsets?

ELAINE: Not to my knowledge. They are totally unrelated to what is going on in my life at the time. I've come to know that they are partly chemical, partly hereditary and that is why drugs help, and partly past environmental. That is why psychotherapy helps.

B.B.: Are you seeing a psychotherapist regularly now?

ELAINE: Yes, I do, on an outpatient basis. I have great confidence in him.

B.B.: What is his approach?

ELAINE: His approach has been excellent for me. He is a psychiatrist who specializes in behavioral and directive therapy and hypnosis. Now we have been over and over the past together, the tragedies and all the other things that hurt. We've discussed these, he understands them, but he dwells on the present and he says not to anticipate the future unless you can anticipate it with some degree of pleasure. He is trying to teach me to live from day to day. He emphasizes positive thoughts, rather than negative ones.

We discuss current problems, fears, and how to handle them. Sometimes I act out a situation that is fearful to me, in his office, in what I feel is a protected, safe environment. After a while, I begin to see how groundless some of the fears are. He tries to change my attitude toward situations, if I can't change the situation. With very painful episodes, he uses mild hypnosis, and has taught me how to make use of it when I am not with him—a form of self-hypnosis. He has taken me almost totally off drugs, and I've been better than I have been in a long time. I have not been hospitalized for over two years. He has helped me through some bad times.

He has taught me how to stop hyperventilating. Hyperventilating is a vicious cycle; you become panicky for no reason you can find. You breathe too fast and too much, and this makes you more panicky—or if you hyperventilate you start to panic. I don't know which comes first, the chicken or the egg.

Hyperventilation has many side symptoms. You think that you are suffering from air hunger, that you can't breathe, and you get more and more scared, your limbs feel numb and you have chest pains. All in all, you think that you really are going to die, but if you can learn to stop it, you can stop the panic. My psychiatrist has taught me breathing and relaxation exercises, so that I have overcome this problem.

B.B.: How else has your psychotherapist helped you?

ELAINE: He has taught me that I have certain rights: I have never asserted myself really. I don't mean in an aggressive way at all; I mean that I never spoke up for myself, but now I know how to do it politely but firmly, without getting angry. Anger is futile, really, although at times everyone should be entitled to blow his top.

He introduced me to Recovery, an organization of ex-mental patients who believe in self-help. Recovery teaches you that situations may be distressing, but they are not dangerous; that you should try to substitute objective and positive thoughts for subjective and negative thoughts. It is not always easy to do, and in fact I am often unable to do it. It teaches you that there are many others like you, and that a sense of humor is a pretty good thing to have about yourself.

My doctor has also helped me understand the difference between real fear and what he calls "free floating fears," which are almost impossible for me to explain. I mean, I'm afraid of being stung by a bee; that is real fear, because it can kill me and I carry a bee kit. That is a realistic fear. But I had many fears and I didn't know where they came from. They were not valid, they were not appropriate in what is a happy life. Most of them we have been able to pin down. We are trying to talk myself and my way out of these fears. If they get too uncontrollable, then I take drugs for a while. I think that I have improved a lot, because, as I said, I seldom take drugs now, and these "free floating fears" are much less frequent.

B.B.: How do you cope with life from day to day? Especially when you're depressed.

ELAINE: Well, I'm not depressed right now. When I am, I don't cope very well, I'm apt to withdraw, I get quite frightened, in fact I get panicky that this will be a "bad one" again. Recently, through my doctor's help, I have come to realize that it doesn't have to get all that bad if I get immediate and proper help. But still and all, these panics do stop you from functioning well as a human being. I have learned how to get out of them, usually without help.

B.B.: You mentioned the Recovery meetings. Have they been a great help? Do you still go regularly to them?

ELAINE: No, I don't. I read the book, and I try to practice what they taught me. I think I learned a lot from them. And if I want to, or need to, I will go back. Right now, my doctor is the greatest help.

B.B.: When were you last hospitalized?

ELAINE: Well, I was hospitalized two summers ago. I was heavily drugged, too heavily drugged, I think. I have a very low drug tolerance, and am extremely sensitive to them. Since I was taken out of the hospital, and have had this present psychiatrist, who took me off drugs gradually, I feel that I am much better. I think I was in a chemical bind from all those drugs—I didn't have a chance to see if I was going to get well or not get well on my own. After all, my chemistry might have changed over a period of years, and I think it has. Without drugs, I can feel my gut feelings, which were numbed by drugs, and I can see myself as I really am, and where I want to go.

B.B.: What are your interests now?

ELAINE: My interests are pretty much what they have always been; my husband, my children, and my home. I read, I write; I've had a few books published. I love the land, and to grow things. And I am deeply involved in helping mentally ill people.

B.B.: Has your present doctor helped you to gain insights into yourself?

ELAINE: Oh, yes. I understand myself better than I did. It doesn't always help to know, to have gained these insights because in spite of the knowledge and the insights, you can get a depression; but it does help a great deal in many ways to cope with situations. You learn to avoid them if it doesn't hurt anybody else, or if you have to face them, you learn to face them—hopefully with an improved attitude.

B.B.: You mentioned that at one point you were overdrugged. Could you explain that?

ELAINE: I went to a neurologist who said that I was losing my coordination. I was having double vision. I couldn't even sign my name; my handwriting had gone completely to pieces. I couldn't drive. My speech was slurred. I couldn't walk straight. I couldn't hit a tennis ball. People who didn't know me would have thought I was drunk—stoned. This was a consequence of all the drugs.

B.B.: How many drugs were you taking?

ELAINE: I couldn't list them, there were so many. Too many. The neurologist didn't *promise* that my coordination would come back. But it has. I can drive again. My handwriting is legible again. And I can see properly and I can walk straight. I can hit a tennis ball and my speech is unimpaired. People who know me know I don't drink, and I guess they thought that I was overdrugged. It was tough to get off all those drugs. The neurologist said he bet I couldn't do it without going to a hospital, but I did it *without* going to a hospital. The withdrawal symptoms were rough. But now, with my psychiatrist's help, and only very occasional drugs, I am incredibly better. Don't get me wrong—I am not denigrating drugs. I have needed them badly. But I think that giving me the right drugs, and the right amount at the right times, required exceptional knowledge and perception. I have worked through some pretty bad depressions, with no thought of ever going back to a hospital. I feel pretty stable, and the hopelessness I used to live with—that all my life there would be repeated hospitalizations—has left me completely. That is the greatest victory of all. I am very optimistic these days, and grateful for the skilled help and care I have received.

PART FOUR

The Group Experience

MENTION THE TERM "group therapy" to half a dozen people and you will probably get as many different responses. Perhaps the most revolutionary development of lasting effect in psychiatry has been the shift to group psychotherapy. And like all such revolutions, once the first step is taken, the movement gains a momentum of its own; new and increasingly bolder concepts are tried; ideological schisms occur; offshoots of offshoots appear, until the term "group therapy" by itself can literally mean hundreds of different things.

Originally, the concept of psychotherapy within a group developed in answer to needs of emotionally troubled people who live in our "other-directed" society. In his book *The Lonely Crowd*[1] David Riesman explains in detail the idea of the other-directed person. In our society, where mass media communication and our daily personal and impersonal contact with other people are a condition of our lives, other people are the central force and problem; people are more aware of each other and of their own ability—or lack of it—to communicate with others and to understand what is expected of them from "the others." A minimum of success at being an "other-directed person" is required of us all if we are to be emotionally healthy.

1. See *The Lonely Crowd*, by David Riesman. New York: Doubleday & Co., Anchor ed. (1953).

135

For the emotionally troubled person, dealing well with other people is one of the biggest difficulties to overcome. The solution to this problem in psychiatry is to put patients in a group situation where, under the guidance of a psychotherapist, group members talk about their problems —especially their problems in dealing with other people—with each other. The group serves as a controlled mirror of the society in which you live, so communication and participation are its key elements.

This is the more conventional group; it is not by any means the "encounter" group or the "weekend marathon" group. These developments in group therapy came about in the late 1950s and new approaches along these lines are still coming onto the scene. The newer approaches more or less take the idea of the "other-directed" person for granted and go on from there to deal with developing "human potential," as well as dealing with the emotional problems of people. (Some of these newer approaches are examined in Part VI.)

This section looks at two groups based on the conventional approach —meeting the needs of emotionally troubled people in modern society by helping them understand their problems with other people. In a good group, with the help and support of the group therapist and members, you learn to develop new ways of relating to others and of coping with your problems that involve others. For many, the solution to adjusting to our world has been found in a conventional therapy group.

CHAPTER FIFTEEN

The Institute for Self-Awareness
Father James Lloyd

Father James Lloyd is a Catholic priest who received his Ph.D. in psychology from New York University. He was trained in psychology by several New York psychiatrists and psychologists and has interned at Seton Psychiatric, New Rochelle Guidance Center, and the Institute of Physical Medicine and Rehabilitation.

Father Lloyd is associated with the Church of St. Paul the Apostle, New York City, and the Communications Office of the Archdiocese of New York. He is Director of the Graduate Division of Pastoral Counseling at Iona College, New Rochelle, New York. A member of both the American Psychological Association (Division of Psychotherapy) and the American Association of Marriage and Family Counseling, he is presently an associate professor of psychology at Iona College.

He has also taught courses in psychology at the New York Institute of Technology, where he was an adjunct professor.

In addition to his individual and group practice, Father Lloyd moderates the radio program, "Religion and Psychology," which is broadcast on WABC-FM, locally in New York City.

In this chapter, adapted from my interview, Father Lloyd tells about the people who enter his groups, his approach to group therapy, and his views on religion and psychotherapy.

Father James Lloyd

It would be difficult to pinpoint specific reasons why people choose to enter therapy groups; for every person there is a different reason, a different problem. Broadly speaking, the people who come to see me do so because they hurt—not for physical reasons, of course, but because they are in some sort of personal pain and want relief from it.

People seek me out in particular for a variety of somewhat more definite reasons: a person may have been referred by a former client, for example; this happens often—I find that many of my clients have heard about my groups through word of mouth. Then, because I am a Catholic priest as well as a psychologist, certain people choose me because of the seeming "protection" such a choice would give them from the social taint of needing psychotherapy. To some people, the idea of going to a psychotherapist implies something horrible or cynical, at least unconsciously; seeking psychological help is a sort of taboo. They might think: "I should be able to handle this myself; it's sacrilegious to have to go to therapy. But this guy's a priest, and after all, I've been brought up to go to the priest with my problems . . ."

I don't want to imply by that observation that all my clients are, or must be, Catholic; I see people of all faiths and people who have no religious beliefs or affiliations.

My groups are comprised of both whites and blacks from every socioeconomic strata. I do not charge a fee, and that is certainly not a minor reason for my large practice. I ask that people contribute five dollars a month if they can, to help pay for the rent of the room we use in the rectory; as long as I get enough to pay the rent, I don't ask for more.

My smallest group has seven people, and the largest, nine. In groups larger than that, a group member is more able to "cop out," as it were —to melt into a corner and reap no benefit from the group experience. Each week I see thirty people, primarily in groups, although I also practice individual psychotherapy.

My clients' age range runs from the mid-teens to about sixty, with the mean age at about thirty.

Most of my clients don't really know much about themselves; some are seriously upset, and some are simply confused. A lot of the confusion is the "who-am-I" sort of thing; people want to find out something about themselves and what they want to do with their lives.

My thrust in the group experience is aimed at two things: one, for the person to know who he or she is; and two, for that person to discover what other people think of him. Self-knowledge and feedback are the primary goals of each group.

To put it another way, I would say that there are certain types of *cells* that contribute to a person's psychological makeup. *Cell A* (called Joharcis Window) contains what you know about yourself that other people also know about you. In therapy, the goal is to enlarge upon this area.

Cell B contains what you don't know about yourself, but what others do know. This is your blind area, and through group feedback, *Cell B* will be decreased.

Cell C is what I call the Secret Cell. This is the area in which you know something about yourself that you have kept sufficiently hidden from others. Through self-disclosure this cell will decrease in the group process. You will tell things about yourself that others didn't know; so as *Cell C* decreases, *Cell A* expands. That is what I aim for.

The group experience here is not psychoanalytic; psychoanalysis deals with what I would call *Cell D*—that which is unknown to both the individual and others. We don't touch on that area in our group. Our process is more interactional, a developmental process based on the model of Abraham Maslow's self-actualization theory. The emphasis here is not on pathology; we do not talk so much about what is wrong with a person as we do about what positive aspects of the person should be expanded.

Our model, then, is actualization rather than the older type of model, which was a medical-psychological one that assumed something was wrong with the person—that there was a disease to be treated.

In my group work, the theory is that if we concentrate on the positive side and help people to be the best that they can, the negative side will be annihilated almost automatically. If we were to focus on what is wrong with a person, saying, "You're wrong, you're doing terrible things," their feelings of self-rejection would be intensified. And that is precisely what we don't want; we want self-acceptance through positive self-knowledge.

Because I was trained as a Freudian, I probably use something of a Freudian model for my interior diagnosis of clients—at least for the purposes of clarification and to establish some sort of working base. But from there on, when I think in terms of what is going on *now* with a person, I become more eclectic in my approach.

I have drawn from the ideas of Carl Rogers, who developed the system called client-centered therapy; the process is focused on the patient and it hooks into the Maslow theory quite well in this sense: Rogers holds that the person should get the feeling of acceptance from the psychotherapist. It should be a nonjudgmental acceptance, an unconditional personal regard. No matter what the patient says, the therapist accepts him or her without condemnation. This, again, involves the development of a warm, trusting climate. Rogers' theory is that if you have that kind of atmosphere, there is an inherent thrust toward emotional health in the client. With the proper kind of climate, a person will be able to hear what he is saying and without judgment from the therapist he will be able to reflect upon it. The therapist, in Rogers' model, asks clarifying questions but does not judge nor say, "Now, this is what you should do."

Some therapists work the opposite from this; they set up the goals along their own set of criteria.

However, I do find that I am often trying to move people in a certain way. Even though I am trying to be objective, I sometimes find myself feeling that I know what is best for a client. As a matter of fact, I've done a little bit of research on this, on my radio show with psychologists; I've asked the same question of people every week, and the general feeling from the responses is that it's impossible for the psychologist to be objective. It is impossible not to transfer your own values onto the patient at least in some way—your own values manage to get through.

Contrasting my work again with psychoanalysis, I am more interested in what is happening to people at the moment. If we go back to the past —which we could easily do—the process becomes much slower. I think it's much more efficient to ask, "What are you feeling right now? I would be interested." Interest, anger, joy—whatever it might be—I think that this is important in terms of self-awareness.

I know that many people are not in touch with what they're feeling. It would be comparatively easy to go back to something that happened when a person was five years old, to try to discover why that person is out of touch. But that might be intellectualizing—and that is the exact opposite of what we aim for in our groups; and, of course, we must remember that we interpret our past in terms of what and how we are feeling today.

The group therapy I represent should not be confused with encounter groups; ours is a slow process, an ongoing process that does not end after one weekend. Each group meets once a week for an hour and a half. I believe that the slow process has a much more lasting effect than the weekend marathon encounter groups have. I am not trying to find an aspirin for my clients; I'm looking for people to change their lifestyle, if they must, in order to say, "Look, I'm enjoying myself." I'm looking for lasting, permanent changes.

We urge people to express what they're feeling, so the feeling level is very important in my therapeutic model; we stress identification and verbalization of emotions.

People who come into the groups may have a lot of fantasies at first about what's going to happen to them emotionally if they say a certain thing. They're afraid to express anything, so one of the first things to be done is to get at that initial feeling—fear. The group helps the new client identify the fear of saying anything; once he identifies it, it can be expressed, felt, understood.

Expression of fear is extremely important, because if it is not got out it can turn inward and become intrapunitive. And when nonverbalized fear becomes intrapunitive, it often takes the form of setting oneself up for negatives, living with defeatism: "I'll beat hell out of myself one way or another as a lifestyle," and at the same time wondering, "Why do things always go so poorly for me? I don't know why I'm living this way." So there is no understanding and no self-awareness as a result of allowing fear to go unidentified and unexpressed.

It goes without saying that one must feel at ease in a situation before he or she is going to allow much to be exposed about his or her feelings. One of the most necessary—and in our groups, successful—aspects of a group experience is the climate of safety a person feels; people feel safe here to say whatever they want to. Overcoming a group fear is a difficult thing to achieve. But it is essential in order to have a cohesive feeling among group members. If we don't have that, then we're playing games, and the difficulties that can arise from game-playing can be insurmountable.

One of the interesting things about these groups is that it isn't I who offers the insights. It is the group members. In fact, they are really the therapists. I facilitate; I'm almost, if you will, a guardian, to make sure that nobody gets hurt. I intervene at certain strategic points—but the group members are the ones who get and relay the insights. Sometimes they're cerebral, which is often unfortunate because the experience is often intellectualized. But if an insight comes at a gut level, if it's personal, there is no question that the clients expand themselves. They receive a wider range of options: "I don't have to act this way—there are other ways of acting, and it's my choice."

This is one of the things we emphasize here. You don't have to do things a certain way; you don't have to feel compelled in one way, in a determined way. If you *want* to act in a certain way, then that is an avenue we can explore.

People undergoing the group process here will be constantly reminded of the good that comes from applying their insights outside the group. A part of our theory is that any sort of group is a social microcosm—a reflection of society as a whole—and that what goes on here might easily be applied outside. Once a person has worked out a problem within this social lab and is able to enlist that new way of acting without the group, he finds that it becomes a part of his life—and life itself becomes more enjoyable for that person.

The process involves a lot of interaction, which gets intense at times. Members confront each other: "Why are you saying that? What does such-and-such way of dealing with this situation get you?" But people open up to one another. Many are opening up to others for the first time in their lives.

Our clients range from people in search of richer lives to people who have been severely upset. Generally, I don't work in group with a person who is in the midst of an emotional crisis. If a person has been hospitalized for a severe upset, and if he has become stable—has been helped by hospitalization—he now needs expansion. In that case, he is ready for a group, because the problem is no longer medical—that is, it's no longer to be treated on a medical model; but it is developmental. And development, expansion, are what the group process is all about.

Of thirty clients, I believe five or six have been hospitalized at some point in the past. The process of developing self-awareness within a group assumes a certain amount of anxiety tolerance. There are the initial fears of opening up to the group, as I discussed earlier, and the emotional interaction of the group; people who do not have a tolerance for this would find the experience of a group very trying, would drop out, and wouldn't benefit. So we are talking about people who are fairly healthy but confused.

An important part of my group work is to aim for the proper composition of each group. I have to be a bit selective in putting people into groups, and this is both for the individual and group welfare. Some people simply won't fit into any group therapy process; certain people are blockers—they become too anxious to function effectively. Others are monopolists or withdrawers in a group situation. Some people can be quite manipulative in a group and can continue using therapy—individual or group—as a lifestyle. They may not want to get better, but they've made therapy and their problems—the continuance of them—a way of life. I cannot work with this kind of person. We're talking about *moving* here—not running in place.

When a person comes to me, I may not necessarily suggest a group. If a person is frightened or extremely shy, I feel that his difficulty in opening up can be sufficiently basic for putting him into individual therapy. I don't want the group experience to be traumatizing—the group is so open and direct: "You so-and-so, why don't you say anything?" To an extremely sensitive and closed person, this is a judgment.

Some people have problems that they are reluctant to discuss in a group at first. For instance, if I have a patient who is homosexual and is hesitant to discuss his sexuality at this point, I will see him individually. If, through individual therapy, he can discuss it with me, the feeling of safety begins to develop. He'll soon get to the point of feeling easier about discussing his sexuality with other homosexuals in one of the groups. At that time he'll be ready to share. I can prepare him for the group sharing, and then, within the group he'll be able to deal with his pain and hopefully reach a sustaining change in the way he deals with himself and others.

If someone comes to me whom I do not feel will be helped by my sort of therapy, I will refer him to another psychotherapist. If someone (a new client or a former client) who is in the midst of a crisis approaches me for therapy, I will refer him to a psychiatrist. I do not refer people to hospitals, nor do I prescribe drugs, because I am not a medical doctor.

The length of time a person remains in a group is highly individual. It depends upon how long it takes any person to reach a certain level of comfortable and enjoyable living without the assistance of therapy. Most of my group members remain for about a year; some leave after three months; others, after two years.

The changes that people make as a result of group therapy are variable and are subjective matters. We usually do intragroup evaluations of each other. Generally, there are positive changes, but sometimes not. If not, we want to know why, and we work on the problem.

We've been doing a very interesting piece of research, trying to see the relationship between successful psychotherapy and improvement in one's financial status. It's remarkable that people will be able to ask for salary raises or take risks doing new things if they've been successful in therapy. One of the indices we have for success is the degree to which a person is able to take more risks, to be bolder about his or her station.

This is not to say that I believe group members should go out into the world and make outstanding professional achievements. I am interested in people enjoying their lives more, instead of finding life threatening, dull, uninteresting. I'm interested in the self, in the person owning his own self, rather than in what I might call the American heresy of productivity. I think it's neither healthy nor personally helpful to be driven by the idea that we've been taught to embrace as a value system—that you're good *only* if you produce, get results, set a sturdy track record of achievements. Rather than placing joy in achieving, one should place it in owning one's self.

The main thing is to learn that by taking risks and making changes in your lifestyle, the roof does not fall in—on the contrary, living becomes more worthwhile, truly exciting.

If a former group member has a temporary emotional setback, or if a critical situation develops in his life, he may return to the group. But that situation usually entails a crisis kind of counseling—one to three sessions of talking through the problem. Generally, a person who returns to the group because of a setback, snaps back very quickly. In the groups, we talk about the criteria for psychological health. When someone is feeling, say, a regression, he or she is usually able to tell the group, "I know that I'm going to be better in a reasonably short period of time. Right now it's very painful, but this is not a permanent situation." And that person gets immediate feedback from the group.

But if the person feels—and acts—as if there is no future, as though everything is bleak, that's a referral situation.

I do not have the finances or the facilities to conduct thorough follow-up care or studies. There are people who, when they leave the group, might ring me up a year or so later with something to discuss. This sort of check-in happens, but not on an organized basis. The doors are always open for people who desire to keep in touch or who may need some follow-up short-term counseling.

People have asked me about the effects that psychotherapy—both receiving and giving—has had on my religious convictions. Like many of my Catholic colleagues, I believe that going into therapy has enhanced, rather than detracted from, my faith. And I think that this holds true for most people of religious conviction. Practicing therapy has put me and many of my colleagues into a much more authentic relationship with God and has made us better priests, better people.

The idea some Catholics have that therapy will somehow impair their faith concerns me. Therapy puts faith on a more real level; it helps a person get rid of religious superstitions, distortions, "magic," inauthenticities, which are many times at the seat of a person's problems, and which many people *mistake* for religion. Freud, for instance, saw people with the religious distortions, which were actually classic obsessive-compulsive neuroses—he rarely saw authentic religion! So I believe that if one is religious—whether Catholic, Protestant, Jewish, Moslem, Hindu, whatever—and experiences psychotherapy, his faith can only be improved.

CHAPTER *SIXTEEN*

Recovery, Inc.

The phrase "The Four Steps of the Example" has a vaguely Eastern ring to it, almost as though it were a translation from the Hindi. Actually, it describes part of a twentieth century, purely Western method in the self-help group process known as Recovery.

Two features of Recovery set it off from any other form of group: it is entirely operated, supported, and controlled by lay people, all of whom are patients or ex-patients of mental hospitals or outpatient psychotherapy; and it adheres strictly to one method aimed at helping people to maintain their emotional health.

To understand the Recovery method, we have to understand a bit about its origin and evolution. The organization was founded in 1937 by Dr. Abraham Low, then Associate Director of the Psychiatric Institute of the University of Illinois Medical School in Chicago. His purpose in forming the group was to guide formerly hospitalized patients toward self-leadership and thereby prevent relapses; but as his research and study with the first groups expanded, he found that his particular group approach also benefited people who suffered from chronic nervous symptoms.

Originally, meetings were held in the Psychiatric Institute and conducted by Dr. Low; in 1941 Recovery left the Institute and incorporated as an independent "association of nervous and former mental patients," with Dr. Low as the medical director.

From 1941 to 1952, Dr. Low continued to supervise meetings, but he and the members were evolving a systematic method that would eventually lead to a completely self-help group. Self-help ideas would spring up among members, be tried out, and be incorporated or discarded. Then, in 1952, the groups—or panels as they are often called—began operating without professional supervision, led entirely by patients or former patients trained in the self-help approach that is unique to Recovery.

Today, Recovery, Inc., is nationally recognized by the psychiatric profession and has chapters from coast to coast in the United States and Canada.

The result of these years of development is a method that has helped thousands of people maintain a perspective on their lives through practicing (in Recovery language) self-leadership. Three fundamentals are essential to the Recovery approach: members study the lectures and literature of the late Dr. Low, including his book, *Mental Health Through Will Training*; members attend meetings regularly; and they practice the Recovery principles in their daily lives.

A typical Recovery meeting opens with a reading from Dr. Low's book or a recording of one of his lectures. Next, members relate experiences in their daily lives when they applied Recovery principles. Each experience is told according to a format developed during the organization's formative years. This is "The Four Steps of the Example":

I. PARAGRAPH 1, beginning with "Several weeks ago . . ." describes the *event*, which is to be reported as panel example. It mentions various things which were said and done, the persons involved, the time of day when the event took place, the place, and the temperamental reaction of the patient ("I began to work myself up").

II. PARAGRAPH 2, beginning with "Before long . . ." describes the *symptoms and discomfort* they produced.

III. PARAGRAPH 3, beginning with "Suddenly it came to me . . ." describes the *spotting* of temper, of the working-up process, and of the absurdity of the philosophy of right and wrong, further the emphasis on the Recovery concept of *averageness* ("These things will happen in married life").

IV. PARAGRAPH 4, beginning with "Before I had my Recovery

training . . ." describes the temperamental reaction and symptoms which the patient would have experienced in former days.[1]

The Four Steps are adhered to strictly, and panel leaders are present to assure that examples do not wander from this outline. Each example takes about five minutes and is followed by a ten-minute group discussion.

After the structured panel discussions, more informal and spontaneous discussions begin as the panel breaks up into smaller groups. During this "mutual-aid" period, members bring to each other a more personal experiential understanding of Recovery self-help. Psychiatric advice does not enter in, neither during the formal panel discussion nor during the "mutual-aid" period; members deal only with the areas of experience where they practice self-leadership: challenges at their jobs or in their educational pursuits and within their families.

Recovery has its own terminology, which helps members define and use the self-help techniques. As one member relates:

"When I would wake up in the wee hours of the morning with fearful feelings, racing thoughts, and panicky ideas that I would again become mentally ill and have to be taken back to the hospital, I would practice *spotting*. This means recognizing that these are only nervous symptoms, distressing but not dangerous, as I had been told by my psychiatrist. They did not indicate the return of mental illness. I practiced the Recovery self-help technique of commanding my muscles to lie quietly on the bed, and the principle of bearing the discomfort of the tenseness until the nervous symptoms gradually diminished.

"After leaving the house . . . I might meet a friend or acquaintance on the street and immediately I would feel very self-conscious about having been hospitalized three times for mental illness. But I started practicing two principles that were firmly established by Dr. Low as he developed the Recovery method: (1) No one shall be held responsible for the ailment he suffers; and (2) there is no hopeless case among nervous and former mental patients, regardless of the duration of the condition.

"I practiced *averageness* with my friends and acquaintances by commanding my muscles to make me walk up to them, shake hands, smile a little, and chat for a while. In this way I demon-

---

1. Excerpted from the pamphlet, "Recovery, Inc.—What It Is and How It Developed." (Recovery, Inc.) Chicago, 1973. P. 28. Reprinted here by permission.

strated to myself that I could choose to look at my past mental illness in the same way I would look at pneumonia or any other physical illness.

"I also practiced *endorsing myself*; that is, giving myself credit and self-approval for my efforts to overcome my shame and self-condemnation for having been a mental patient. . . ."[2]

Recovery does not replace a member's psychiatrist; meetings serve to complement a person's psychotherapy. Group leaders are trained in the Recovery method and are themselves former patients and lay people. As the organization stresses, they do not diagnose or treat emotional problems. Psychiatrists may refer patients to Recovery, but the organization expects members to follow the authority of their doctors.

Professionals in the field of psychiatry, as well as nonmembers, are encouraged to attend Recovery meetings and observe the group process; but professionals cannot become group leaders.

Adult men and women from every social and economic strata are members: people recently released from mental institutions; people who have visited or are visiting a psychiatrist but have never been hospitalized; people who have been diagnosed by their physicians as having nervous, rather than physical, disorders; people who constantly suffer from tenseness or self-consciousness and feelings of inadequacy; people who have problems dealing with their tempers.

Recovery, Inc.'s national headquarters are in Chicago, and its Board of Directors are all former patients, lay people who work as unpaid volunteers. It is a charitable organization supported financially by contributions and the income from the sales of Dr. Abraham Low's literature and recorded talks. There is no compulsory fee for members.

2. Ibid., pp. 11-12.

CHAPTER SEVENTEEN

"One Step at a Time"
Carl Schmidt

When Carl Schmidt read Shakespeare, the line, "All the world's a stage. . ." must have leapt out at him. He emigrated from Germany with his family to London, where he studied acting during World War II, and then moved to the United States in the early 1950s. His debut in New York wasn't on the stage, however—it was as a night clerk in a hotel. Professional and personal struggles eventually led him to Recovery, and he has been a member for over ten years.

Carl tells here about his struggles with emotional problems as a young man, about his gradual and painful recovery, and the professional advances he has made since his participation in Recovery. He lives in Manhattan today and is a group leader in the self-help organization.

Carl Schmidt

B.B.: How old are you, Carl?
CARL: Forty-eight.
B.B.: Are you married?
CARL: Single. I've never been married.
B.B.: Tell me a bit about your family.
CARL: Well, I was born in Germany. My father was Jewish, and we had to leave Germany in the thirties; we moved to London, where I grew

up. My father died in England, and my mother returned to Germany and remarried. My sister remained in London, and is married also. I came to New York in 1952.

B.B.: And what kind of family life did you have? Was it a happy one?

CARL: No, I don't think so.

B.B.: What were your relationships with your parents?

CARL: My mother was a very erratic person, and my father was rather withdrawn. My mother more or less managed the home, and my father devoted most of his time to his business. I wasn't very close to him.

I would say that my mother was quite emotionally unstable. Her mother was very affected when all this Nazi thing came about. If I remember correctly, she was committed and she took her life in a mental institution.

B.B.: What brought you to seeking professional help, Carl?

CARL: Well, I had studied to be an actor in England. I never really pursued my career in England, you know, because when my father died my mother had returned to Germany, and I felt rather isolated. My father's family had all left England, and I had some cousins who had gone to New York. One of them was an actress, and I had corresponded with her. I felt I was not getting anywhere in London. I felt, I guess, lonely. Also I'd always been curious about coming to this country, so I migrated. That was in 1952.

In New York, I began working with an off-Broadway children's theater and that led to a tour with the children's theater. I toured around the country for close to a year, and during that time started to feel depressed. I'd never really admitted to myself that I was suffering from depressions—I always figured everybody had depressions. It never occurred to me that this was something unusual. But I'd always had a little difficulty communicating with people.

After the tour I worked in a job in summer stock for a while. I was out in Princeton with the theater when I guess the depressions really got worse, and I just withdrew. I felt things were closing in on me, and I walked out in the middle of the season and I went back to New York.

I got a night job in a hotel, and I found I had difficulty sleeping; I was feeling very depressed, still, but I liked life so much that I felt, well, the only thing to do was seek professional help. It had never occurred to me before.

I had heard about an outpatient clinic, but that there was a waiting list of a year. I felt kind of desperate, you know, so I went over there and filled out a form. They said, "Well, what brought you here?"

I don't know whether it was spontaneous or not, but I said, "I'm feeling very suicidal and I've got to see someone immediately."

They gave me a very good psychologist. He saw me first at the clinic. I guess I saw him there for nine months before he left the clinic and said that he was setting up an office of his own. Of course, I would have to pay. At that time I was not holding down a very satisfactory job. I was mostly in hotel jobs, so he recommended that I come to his group, which was cheaper. That's how I joined his group.

B.B.: Did you find the group helpful?

CARL: Yes, but I always had difficulty, I always felt very much like I was an outsider. I got some help from it, but I think I was pretty sick.

Now, while I was in the group therapy, I heard from my mother. I hadn't seen my family for several years. I had come to realize that my mother had been a rather damaging influence on my life, although I had always been fond of her. She had started writing these letters about how unhappy she was. She had remarried when I was in California with the tour, and she wrote that she wanted me to come over to visit. I said, at first, I was not able to leave my job, and that I was in therapy. Well, she said that she was going to send me the money to come over, which was very unusual for her because she very rarely helped me in any way. I mean, when we left Germany in the thirties, I was thirteen, and she immediately put me to work. I had to leave school and go to work. I'm only going back to that to point out that she never really did anything for me, so the gesture of her suddenly sending me the money to come to Europe . . . I should have known there was some catch behind it.

Well, it seemed that her marriage was a little bit on the rocks and she was using me to hold it together. She wanted to show me off as the good son—her husband's children, apparently, had rebelled against her, had left, you know, removed themselves from the situation and gone off and married. I was to be the example of the perfect son, but, of course, I wasn't.

I realized then that she's a completely self-centered woman, lives in a world of her own, and that she had just brought me over to suit her needs. I realized freely then that I had a crazy lady on my hands, and I had my own emotional sickness to cope with.

It erupted one day, when I said that I wanted to go back to New York. Actually, I had given up my apartment and had quit my job, but I just had the feeling that I had to get away from the situation. I was sunk in depression. I was immobile, I couldn't even walk. All the old shit came out, you know, and I felt trapped. Then one day I burst into tears and I said, "I don't know what's going to become of me. I get the feeling that someday I'll just have to kill myself. I feel I can't cope with all these feelings anymore, and I will have to be committed."

The reaction I got from her was a stony silence; she walked out of the room. The next morning she said, "I don't ever want you to upset me like that again." She had taken it as a threat to her. I decided to return to New York immediately.

When I got back to New York, my depressions were even more intense. I went back to the psychotherapist I had been seeing in group therapy and he said, "Well, look, I guess you realize that you do need some professional help, and I think we should start in terms of your seeing me several times a week." Which I did. I saw him, I guess, two or three times a week. He was, I guess, a Freudian. I also returned to the group.

That was really a rough period, as far as my private psychotherapy was concerned. I did all the talking and he would just say, "Hmmm." I mean, I didn't even get a good morning out of him, and I was climbing the walls. And the only person I still had whom I felt close to was this actress-cousin, and then, about a year after I'd gotten back from Europe, she unfortunately died.

I went through a few years where all the turmoil, everything, was brought up, and I was feeling suicidal. In psychotherapy I had become aware of all of my problems, my shortcomings, neurosis, my dependency on my mother—in spite of the fact that she was a very cold mother—but I just was unable to change. I was so frightened of my feelings.

I'd really think I was going insane after a session with the therapist. It was like throwing a stone into a pond, stirring up all that water—you've got all that mess, then what do you do with it? But I just kept going. I trusted him. I believed he was going to find a way for me to help myself and that it was going to be rough. I stayed with it for several years.

All this time I wanted to act, but I guess I was too sick. I just needed a job to keep going and to pay for my therapy. That was about the way my life had become.

B.B.: How did you eventually get into Recovery?

CARL: Well, I lost my hotel job, and I was really frightened. So I went to the Community Church where they had some kind of a counseling on jobs; they also had something like a therapy group, and I met a lot of people there; they spoke of being members of Recovery. I asked about it, and they said that it's an aftercare program for people who've been hospitalized or in therapy.

I finally went to a meeting—this was probably nine or ten years ago.

Of course I still hadn't fully acknowledged to myself—in spite of the fact that I'd been depressed and suicidal and in therapy—that I was very sick. But I went in, and I saw a lot of sick people; many of them had been hospitalized, and I'd never taken a tranquilizer in my life. I'd just been under the care of a psychologist.

B.B.: You're not on any therapeutic drugs?

CARL: None at all, I never have been. Which I'm sort of glad about in a way, because I feel I've coped this well without them so far.

Anyway, I realized that these people were very sick, and wondered what I was doing there; I thought I really didn't belong there, but the program seemed to have something for me right away. In other words, all those fears that I'd had in the years of therapy—this constant feeling of going insane, all the feelings of prejudice and the tenseness—I suddenly felt they were just, as they say in Recovery, an outpouring of the nervous imbalance. In other words, they were not dangerous, and I think from the minute I heard that, I felt at home in Recovery.

I kept going. Looking back now, I guess I was pretty sick, because I still had difficulty communicating with the people in the group. I seemed to latch onto rather sick people—well, let's put it this way: aggressive bitches, something like my mother was, and I would always get stuck with these kind of women. It frightened me, because I couldn't handle it.

And so I started staying away from Recovery. My therapy, of course, continued all along . . .

B.B.: Are you still in therapy?

CARL: Not at the moment, no. My therapist was kind of skeptical about Recovery. I don't know why. Maybe because he felt it was a lay organization or because it was something you didn't have to pay for. I don't know.

But I always disagreed with that, because I felt that in Recovery I learned to handle myself in my therapy sessions, that I no longer had to be afraid of my feelings. If I did run into a problem in the Recovery group with somebody, I could then use what I'd learned there in my private session with my therapist, so I always felt that the two worked very well together.

I still had the problem of expressing myself, as they say in Recovery, without anger. And I burst an ulcer, ended up in the hospital. I was in the hospital for three months. I was bleeding internally and they removed most of my stomach. I guess after that I finally came to realize that I had to learn how to handle my anger. There was an awful lot of anger, an awful lot of hostility, and it was after that, that I really got involved in Recovery. And I really started practicing. I attended meetings;

I became a leader in Recovery, and I found that I didn't have to lose my temper. I'm not saying that I don't have a temper, but I found that there is such a thing as discipline. We all get these feelings and we all have anger. And I also found that most of my depression was very suppressed anger.

B.B.: Inner anger.

CARL: Inner anger, yes. And that didn't necessarily solve that but at least it made me less afraid of my depressions. Whenever I got extremely depressed, I would say to myself, "Well, I must be very angry with something." It might take me days to find out what it was, but at least it was no longer that frightening. I didn't have to feel that I'm depressed, so I can't cope, I have to do away with myself.

B.B.: How often do you get depressed?

CARL: Well, now I've been going through a stage of depression, but again, I think of it realistically. I was in a play, my first in a long time—I had gone back into theater.

I think this is very important to bring out. I still, with Recovery and therapy, tried to get involved. I never admitted to myself that I wanted to act or could act. So I would get involved with backstage work, which I really didn't like very much. But I got on and I became a stage manager for a number of Broadway shows. Fortunately, having once been an actor, when occasionally they needed somebody to play a small role, they would cast me in it. Then I would immediately come alive. So I realized what I really wanted was to be an actor. My heart always was in acting, and finally, two years ago, I finally made the decision that I would just concentrate on acting.

I was asked to stage manage one show and I said no, that I would only work on it if I could be in it. I was given a part and I did very well. Since then I've gotten parts in several movies. I still had a lot of symptoms, a lot of anxieties, but with my Recovery training . . . well, Recovery helped me in this. I think it's important.

It was about this time that I went to Europe again to visit my family. I hadn't seen them in twelve years, and I felt that I was strong enough to visit. Now, what happened really unhinged me. I stepped off the plane and my relatives were there and they rushed toward me and hugged me and kissed me. All except my mother who was standing on the arm of her husband and just said, "Don't I look younger than ever? Don't I look gorgeous?" And, you know, I was longing for her to embrace me. When I went to kiss her, she offered me her cheek; she didn't want me to muss her hair.

So, I had to come face to face with the situation, really—that there was nothing for me in Europe. I guess I'd always had the idea that when I grew up my mother might change, but I realized then that that hadn't happened, that she was really a very vicious woman, very unkind, very cruel.

I came back to a situation in New York that I think would have thrown even a healthy person. I was living in an apartment in Brooklyn Heights, and they were trying to get me to move out because they wanted to remodel the house. But I knew they had no right to make me move. Before I left for Europe, I'd gone to the housing people for their help. They were reassuring, but when I returned after two weeks there was no longer an apartment. They had demolished it. They had completely torn out the walls, there was nothing, there were no windows, no doors, no stove. . . . It was an empty room, as if a bomb had been dropped.

My furniture was there and completely covered with dirt and dust. I slept there that night and, of course, I practiced my Recovery like I'd never practiced it before. I said this is a triviality compared to my mental health.

I also had lost my therapist. We had discontinued just prior to my going to Europe. He had left the city, so my one crutch, which I'd had all those years, was no longer there and I had nobody to turn to. I had no relatives.

Well, in the morning I called the hotel I'd been working for. I thought I'd get a room there for the night. Called them up and they connected me with personnel, and I said, "You misunderstood, I wanted to talk about getting a room." She said that they wanted to talk to me because they decided to lay me off, while I was in Europe. So I didn't have a job or a place to stay.

And then the final blow; I have a cat that I am so fond of, and I'd left it with someone and thought she was taking care of it. But apparently she had reacted violently to the cat, and there had been terrible fights. The cat supposedly had destroyed her whole apartment and the cat almost killed itself by getting caught in a mattress spring under the bed, so the poor cat was in very bad shape.

Added to all this was that I hadn't worked long enough to collect unemployment. So I had no money coming in.

But I said to myself, "I have to face all this, right here and now, no matter what else." I went to Recovery meetings every night of the week, and I kept giving an example every night. I said that everything—the apartment, the loss of a therapist, a sick cat, the loss of a job, no money coming in—they are trivialities compared to my mental health and I must never forget that. I guess I must have gone to meetings steadily for months. And I took any little job that came along, even if it paid me two dollars an hour for a couple of hours a day. I said that I'm not too proud. It's therapy just for me to be doing it. And I did it; I was on the job and they hired me to stay on permanently and I got back into acting. I finally did a Broadway show that closed recently. I found myself feeling depressed when the show closed.

B.B.: Are you going to another therapist?

CARL: I was in bioenergetic therapy for a while. They believe very much that the body and the mind are very closely associated. They work more on physical things rather than mental things—doing exercises. You do some yelling and screaming, you know, expressing your feelings, but you don't really go into your problems all that much. At this point, I guess, I've tried everything, all sorts of therapies—encounter groups, and so on. They've all helped in various areas, but I've always come back to Recovery. I found that that's very simple, very basic.

B.B.: What are your symptoms now when you're depressed?

CARL: Well, it's complex. I feel kind of hopeless, that I'll never act again, I'll never work again, I'll never make another cent; that I'm going to be at the mercy of somebody. But there ain't nobody. But then I try to view myself as a strong person.

B.B.: So you get up and go and look for jobs.

CARL: Well, I haven't looked for acting jobs very much because there isn't much around. I did the realistic thing this time when the show closed—I went to the unemployment office first thing. There always are other things besides acting that I can do.

B.B.: But you know you're a good actor.

CARL: I'm a good actor, but I also know that there are very few acting jobs, that there are thousands of unemployed actors. So, I no longer feel it as a personal rejection every time I don't get a job.

Right now, I feel a lot more confident. I feel I'm going to start doing auditions, maybe after the first of the year. I figure I'd give myself time to get organized. There were bills to be paid and letters to be answered. The holidays are coming up, and that always means a lot of activity. I cope one step at a time.

B.B.: What are your interests outside of acting?

CARL: I like to walk, I like to swim, I read. I never used to be a reader. I used to read the theater page and not much of anything else. But I'm getting very politically oriented. I never was until the Watergate thing. Having already lived through Europe's worst political period in this century, when so many people ignored Hitler, and enabled him to become so powerful, I realize that no one can really be an ostrich anymore.

B.B.: I agree.

CARL: I'm still neurotic in a lot of areas, but I feel that I'm strong enough to face my problems. The very fact that I was able to stay on Broadway with a man like Otto Preminger, who has shaken quite a few stars, is evidence of my own strength. Working with him I used to think, "I'll never live through another day of this." But I made up my mind I was going to stick with it. I wasn't going to walk out; and I had a contract, so if he was going to fire me, he was going to have to pay me for the run of the play and I was not about to give in. I not only coped with my feelings, but I was also able to give a good performance. Which proves that you can function, as they say in Recovery, with symptoms.

B.B.: I think you must have a very strong character not to have been hospitalized, and to have made it through without any therapeutic drugs.

CARL: I guess there's a certain strong survival need—that I'd always felt I didn't have—but I guess if you've survived all the years in Germany and the blitz and the bombings in London, and living with that terrible family of mine, you indeed have that survival sense.

You know, it hurts, even now, when I hear people talking about their family, at holiday time, especially, and I have to admit to myself that I really just ain't got a family. My mother now, of course, is very much playing the mother; you know, she has a son who's an actor. My son the actor. Now, all of a sudden, I'm somebody she can tell her neighbors about, make her look good, you know. But it's still not a family. It's nobody whom I feel you could ever talk to or confide in or run to for help or turn to, or even want to spend any of my time with. Yet, I've survived all that. Maybe, I don't know, maybe all that's made me stick with theater, because that's so much like the theater, which is a sort of crazy family. They pick you up one minute and they kick you down the next.

B.B.: But you don't mind being alone?

CARL: I think I've learned to live with it. Of course I get lonely. But I couldn't even live alone years ago. I always had roommates, and I had put up with the most impossible situations because I just didn't have the strength to live on my own. I tried it a couple of times. I would take a hotel room or stay at the Y, and the walls would cave in on me. I'd get so lonely and so frightened. But I enjoy living alone now. I have my independence, I can do as I please. I have to take care of my own place, and I do in a fashion. It's not the tidiest place in the world, but it's mine. And I enjoy going on trips on my own.

B.B.: You're not afraid to go on a trip?

CARL: No, not at all. In fact, I think that if I have any fears at all, it's close relationships. I have a problem there. In other words, if I'm in a situation with people, I don't get along too well. I still feel kind of uncomfortable. But as far as new places, no. Because I feel there I've started from scratch, and it's kind of fun.

B.B.: Carl, thank you for sharing your experiences.

CHAPTER EIGHTEEN

"A Poor Little Matchgirl Act"
Nancy Lintner

A member in one of Father James Lloyd's therapy groups, Nancy Lintner, like many women today, has learned to express herself as a person. She describes herself as a once timid and dependent woman, but with the help of group therapy and Recovery, of which she is also a member, she has developed an inner strength and independence.

Nancy is single and lives in New York; a practicing Catholic, she tells how group therapy has strengthened her faith, opened her mind to the real value of her religion, and helped her find and build on her own inner worth.

Nancy Lintner

B.B.: Would you tell me a bit about your background, Nancy?
NANCY: I was born in a small New England town—Boston is the nearest city. I came from an upper-middle class family. My father is self-employed—he has his own business, which he's maintained for the past forty years. I have two brothers. One is a year older, and one is ten years younger. They're both married. And the older one has three children and the younger one has two children.
B.B.: What kind of family life did you have?
NANCY: Well, despite the fact that I had all the material advan-

tages, my childhood for the most part was not a happy one, for the simple reason that I always felt pushed in the background on account of my brothers. It took me a long time before I finally found the knowledge that my own identity was more important than trying to imitate my brothers or going by their identity. I'm in group therapy right now. I'm under the care of Father James Lloyd, who is a priest and a psychologist. I attend group therapy every Tuesday night. This has given me a tremendous awareness, and it hasn't been without a lot of pain and a lot of stripping of the dishonesty which I have used in my dealings and my relationships with other people.

B.B.: Has there been any background of mental illness in your family?

NANCY: Yes, my mother had a nervous breakdown and was hospitalized for a while. She had shock treatments. She had trouble with a nervous stomach for a number of years and went from doctor to doctor, until finally they put her on antidepressants. The drugs worked, and she is much better now—she's able to really cope with life now.

B.B.: Nancy, what brought you to seeking professional help?

NANCY: Well, I've been seeking professional help since I was a teen-ager. I went to the hospital for a thyroid operation, but at the time, the doctor put me under psychiatric care 'cause he could see that there were some patterns of behavior there that were very infantile and very disturbing for a girl of my age. I was fourteen at the time, but somehow I wasn't developing emotionally as other fourteen-year-old girls do.

So from then until now—and I'm thirty-seven years old—I've been in the care of either a psychiatrist or a psychiatric social worker, and, presently, with Father Lloyd.

B.B.: But you've never been hospitalized specifically for emotional problems?

NANCY: I have been hospitalized, yes; I've been hospitalized twice. I was hospitalized at Payne Whitney, both times because of suicidal tendencies. It's good that it was a more or less positive experience—Payne Whitney is not run like a state hospital or a city hospital. You have easy access to your doctor; the first doctor I had was a woman doctor, and the second doctor I had, during my second hospitalization two years ago, was a man.

For my aftercare, Payne Whitney sent me to the Suicide Prevention Center, where I saw one of their psychiatric social workers regularly. But with the treatment with Father Lloyd, I find that I need private therapy less and less. I'm focusing more now on group aspects, because

I find that my social life—which is a sore point with me—is something that I have to straighten out.

B.B.: Do you make more friends by going to group therapy?

NANCY: Yes, I do, because it takes a lot of guts, it takes a lot of humility, and it takes a lot of time and pain to go through group. But each time I go through group I feel as though I'm not only a better person, I'm more of a woman. I'm more able to not only cope with life, but to really see myself as I am.

You see, the healthiest thing that I ever admitted in therapy, despite all the years of analysis and so on, I recently said in group. I'd never even mentioned this to a therapist, but I finally came out with it in group. I said, "You know, the trouble with me has been that inside, while physically I'm a woman, inside I feel like a kicking, screaming child who has been deprived."

And you know, as soon as I admitted that, the panic about feeling this way gradually began to dissipate. I had been in a panic over it for years; the feeling would come and I'd either give in to it, or I'd repress it. And in repressing it, I'd become more panicky. Now I just don't repress it anymore. I've brought it out into the open, and I trust the group enough so that I've come out and said to them, "Hey. look, this is how I am, and this is how I feel, and this is what I have to put up with and cope with in my everyday existence.

The more I cope with my feelings, the more I admit what my feelings are and face up to the fact that I have them, the less they build and overwhelm me and frighten me to the point to where I just can't cope with life anymore. You know, I just have days where I say to myself, "Oh boy, this has been another one great big fantastic day of feeling." And I feel just very much in touch with myself.

Well, when I first started group it was a very painful experience, but out of the pain came an inner strength that I didn't know I had—and also a tremendous joy, because I had finally found a vehicle where I could release what has overwhelmed me for so long and so many, many years. You see, intellectually I realized many things; it's just that I couldn't connect them with my emotions and this is where the trouble came in.

B.B.: Can you think of anything that triggers off a depression with you?

NANCY: Yes, I find if I am alone for any great length of time, if I don't make contact with other people, if I don't attempt to do something, some activity on my own—that will trigger a depression. I feel as though I'm alone again and I'm unrecognized and nobody cares.

But I recognize that these depressions come partly, anyway, because basically I'm going through a poor-little-matchgirl act, a poor-little-me act; it's just another way of screaming for attention. Evidently, when I was a child I just didn't get a whole lot of attention, and it's showing now.

I have gotten out of the habit of isolating myself. One of my friends, who is a member of the group, once said to me, "You know, the question you have to ask yourself when you feel this way is, 'What does this child want?' "

So I find more and more that when I do this, when I ask myself this: "What am I kicking and screaming about now?" I find that the depression decreases. Also, I am gradually decreasing my medication.

B.B.: What sort of medication do you take?

NANCY: Well, I am on an antidepressant, but my psychiatric social worker taught me how I could decrease it by eliminating it just very, very gradually, one pill at a time, until I feel that I can cope without it.

B.B.: Nancy, how do you cope with life from day to day?

NANCY: Well, I get up and I make up my mind that it's going to be a good day. This is going to sound real corny, but I'll get up and I'll look out the window, and I'll say, "Well, good morning, Lord. It's going to be a good day today." And I find that when I start the day like that there's less of a chance of me falling into a depression. I believe that Norman Vincent Peale had something like that in mind when he wrote in his book, *The Power of Positive Thinking*, that every time you wake up, just say to yourself that this is the day the Lord has made and rejoice and be glad in it. It's a similar kind of thing. I find that my faith is very comforting to me.

B.B.: You have a faith—do you go to church?

NANCY: Yes, I do. You see, I find that I have grown in my faith as I have grown psychologically. I know that a lot of people tend to put the two in separate boxes, but they're not, really, and as I advance in one direction I automatically advance in the other.

B.B.: What is your faith?

NANCY: I'm a Catholic. I try to attend Mass daily, but I don't go into a whole lot of hang-ups about what's proper to do at certain times. I'm very spontaneous, very relaxed in a relationship with God. It's much like my relationship with Father Lloyd. I sit down and I talk to him and, you know, if I have difficulty, my response is usually to go into a church and say, "Okay, what do you want from me?" And I'm much more honest and I'm very straightforward and I let Him know right off exactly what I want.

This has only been happening since I've grown so much psychologically. I used to feel safe with formal prayer, because it was a ritual that you could go through, but now I find that I'm very uncomfortable with rituals. Once in a while, I go through it, but usually it's the informal, spontaneous kind of thing that I use in my relationship with God. This is how I talk to Him.

B.B.: When you get depressed now, what are your symptoms?

NANCY: Well, when I get depressed now, I call it, in Recovery language, lowered feelings. That takes the big weight off the fact that you're in a depression; you know, the feelings are low and they'll be lifted eventually. I know that feelings will rise and fall and run their course, as long as you don't attach danger to them, and I'm not attaching danger to the symptoms once they come.

Before I was in Recovery I would attach danger to them. This is why my depressions would last and last, why I would go into such a panic that I would feel swallowed up by the whole thing, and I just couldn't cope with it.

B.B.: I know you attend Recovery meetings, because that's where I met you. What have they done for you?

NANCY: Yes, the Recovery has helped tremendously, too. Tremendously, in dealing with the panic from a depression.

I have my good days and bad days, but on the whole I would say my good days usually outnumber my bad days. I find that I'm able to handle new situations much better now, and I don't get as uptight about them.

B.B.: Does it worry you to travel, for instance, go to a strange place?

NANCY: Oh no, that doesn't bother me. My panics in any kind of situation have become less and less. Panics are extremely painful to go through; most of all, it's painful to face yourself and, well, just growing up is painful. You know, too often we think of growing up in terms of growing from a child into an adult. But emotionally, the adult can still remain the child. I'm coming into my own person now, a woman. I feel a lot better about myself, I feel more comfortable with myself.

B.B.: You don't mind being alone anymore?

NANCY: No, because having learned to ask what the child wants, well, if I can, I satisfy it—at least, I try to. If I don't, I say, "You know, it's just not possible for me to satisfy that need for this moment. But that doesn't mean it's the end of the world. There's always tomorrow and a brand-new day."

So I only live life one day at a time and I never look too far into the future. I don't review and preview the past and the future with self-blame.

We got on the subject of friendship the other night, after Father Lloyd's group met, and we realized that when you're a child you shed certain friends, and then you go through your teens and you shed another group of friends . . . well, this goes on all through life—as we grow psychologically, we shed certain friends. This is what I'm doing and it's very painful for me to realize that certain people are just extremely detrimental to me as a person.

B.B.: In what way?

NANCY: Well, for instance, I went around with a man for two years who kept making me feel as though I was helpless without him, that I wasn't worth two cents, that my family was turned off to me, and so on. I even got to believe him.

Now that I'm coming into my own self-worth, I don't even want to be with him. Instead I'm associating with people who will build me up, not tear me down. He spent two years with me, and in these two years, I do not feel that we got to know each other, because he was hiding behind a facade—right now his latest facade is religion. Before, he tried to be Mr. Cool, you know, Mr. Wealth of the business world. Now he's trying to be very religious. Always a facade. The healthy thing now is that I'm able to see the facade. And recognize that underneath is a very tormented person who is full of pain. He desperately wants me to need him and lean on him and depend on him. Right now, he is in torment because I have not called him and I have had nothing to do with him. I feel badly that he is in torment, but I have to protect myself. I recognize now that he's a very sick man.

You see, when you're in a group like Father Lloyd's you learn to be extremely honest, nothing but honest. If you're anything but that, you just defeat your own purpose for being in the group.

B.B.: Does the group help you and make suggestions?

NANCY: Yes. Because it's been through group that I've been able to shed this relationship. And of course, Father has been concerned, too, that I don't go back to hurting myself—we all tend to do this. He was most concerned that I don't drift back into the same pattern.

But now, he said, "I like the way you're operating this year. You're not as defensive and you lay it right out on the table, and you're not afraid to tell anybody what's what. You tell it like it is, and you're not afraid to do it."

That is in complete contrast to my first group experience, which took place in Payne Whitney, when I was extremely defensive. I was telling the doctors, the staff, and everybody else that they were all wrong. They were trying to help me, they were trying to reach out, and I'd say, "Will you leave me alone and get off my back?"

Now, I simply come out with how I feel about what a person has said, and in doing this I find more and more I'm able to cope just with me, just with Nancy. And that's a twenty-four-hour job.

B.B.: Yes, a full-time job, I know.

NANCY: You know, I got a lot of insight from reading your book, [*Prison of My Mind*]. In many ways, I identified with it—except I had never been in a bad hospital, I had always been in Payne Whitney. But, nevertheless, I have known what it's been like to be under the care of a very indifferent doctor, and I did have a doctor like that just before I went to Payne Whitney. And I gave him up. I tried to see him to talk, even about his indifference, and he wouldn't do this. I didn't understand and I felt . . . I just felt horrible. I felt rejected, I felt abandoned, lonely. I came to realize that he was not the right doctor for me. Then, in the hospital I started seeing the woman therapist I became so fond of.

Now, of course, I'm seeing Father Lloyd regularly, and I don't see the need so much for the individual therapy as I do the group therapy.

B.B.: That's a big gain.

NANCY: For me it is, because I was terrified by group at Payne Whitney. Every time we'd go to meet, I would go into a panic; I would be terrified, because I didn't know what they would come out and say about me or to me next.

Now, I go to group and if I have anything on my mind, I say, "Look, I want the floor tonight, everybody. Does anybody have any objections?" And, of course, Father Lloyd is pleased about that. He has encouraged each one of us to be our own chairman. In other words, if we have anything to bring up, to come out with it. He's encouraged us to grab the floor when the floor is open. Not to be timid about it, because being timid will get you nowhere.

As a matter of fact, there was one girl who would come into group, week after week, and say nothing. So, finally, I got so mad at her; I looked at her one night and said, "You know something, I'm angry as hell at you." She looked at me, and I said, "Why the hell do you come here, week after week? You're just sitting there, saying nothing. You're contributing nothing. You just sit there like a prima donna and you don't come out with anything. So why the hell are you wasting my time and Father's time and everybody else's?"

And with that, well, the poor kid burst into tears, and she said, "You know, it's getting harder and harder to come to group week after week and be so frightened of being able to talk."

I felt guilty then, but afterward she thanked me, and now she's coming out of her shell and she talks more. I feel as though, somehow, I have helped this girl.

B.B.: How would you compare the way Recovery has helped you with the way your group has helped?

NANCY: Well, Recovery has helped me in the area of being independent, of being self-sufficient, both emotionally as well as physically. It has not helped me with some personal things, like the source of my panics, my fears, my anger. I have to work these things out in Father's group, which is a very personal thing and informal thing. I need the informal atmosphere.

Recovery is disciplined, formal, structured, and rigid. I don't mind it, but while I don't mind it, at the same time it wasn't helping me in certain areas I needed help in.

B.B.: I had the same reaction. It was, by itself, not enough help. How did you meet Father Lloyd?

NANCY: The way I met Father Lloyd, by the way, was a miracle. I went on a Day of Recollection to Mary Reparatrix, and there he was. He was giving conferences, so in between conferences, I met him and he invited me down to his group. He said that he runs the Institute for Self-Awareness, and the nuns had told me that he was a priest-psychologist. As soon as I met him, I said, "Something tells me we are going to have a lot of contact in the future." That's how it turned out.

B.B.: I've wondered if, as a Catholic, your faith would be enough to sustain you.

NANCY: Well, this is a very hard point to drive home to many Catholics, because a lot of them feel you only need religion. Religion, religion, and God help you if you mention anything about psychiatry or psychology or growing or learning or expanding, or anything else. These are the areas that are pertinent to me right now—growing, learning, feeling, expanding. Just being joyful and hopeful.

But there's this sole concern with rituals among many Catholics—did I do this right, and did I do that right. I'm relaxed. I'm spontaneous. Nothing bothers me in church. But these people are so tense—and I'm speaking for the majority of Catholics that I've met. It's a sad state, and, thank God, the Church has men like Father Lloyd.

I have a more realistic relationship with the Blessed Mother now. Yet, I still meet people who regard her with fear.

I try to tell these people that there comes a time in your life when you need something else besides faith. God has many people who work as his instruments. He has people like Father Lloyd. He has people like my two doctors at Payne Whitney. He has people like your doctor. He has people in Recovery. He's got so much that he's working through, and the thing is to utilize what comes our way. If we don't, well, we just never grow and we just never learn.

B.B.: Nancy, did it take you a long time to come to your own self-understanding, to be able to deal with your depressions and panics?

NANCY: Well, it took time, Barbara. Time is the greatest cure of all —I know that sounds trite, but it's true. You cannot expect to apply what you've learned in Recovery perfectly all at once. It took me at least two years before I was able to really start applying what I learned once I recognized that I had an emotional illness. I was going around for years, not even recognizing that I had a mental illness. I wanted to bury it.

Father and I talked about this and he said that once you recognize you have the illness, it takes the pressure off on one level and you expand onto another level—the level of growth.

I think the best of his theory is in facing your feelings connected with the panic. Once you learn to realize that inside you're screaming for help, once you learn to see yourself objectively, the panics decrease. And it's a good thing not to think about them too much. You know, try to take your mind off the fact that you have panics at all.

B.B.: Thank you, Nancy, for sharing your insights, and for your friendship.

PART FIVE

Biochemical Therapy

PSYCHIATRY HAS always treated the problems we have functioning on an emotional or mental level; medicine has always treated the bodily, or organic, problems we have. But aren't the two related? Everything we do —whether walking or thinking, eating or crying—involves a chemical reaction somewhere in our bodies. And if our bodies aren't producing the right chemicals, or if our body's chemicals are reacting in faulty ways, the consequence can be emotional illness.

Biochemical therapy—sometimes called psychochemical therapy— looks for physical causes of emotional disturbances. This isn't a revolutionary idea in psychotherapy, but it has been a long-neglected one. None other than Sigmund Freud said that an essential first step in psychoanalysis was a medical examination; but the idea of organic causes of mental illness seemed to have been lost in the field of psychiatry for a while. Ripples of change were felt in 1913 when a bacteriologist, Hideyo Noguchi, announced that the mentally disturbed behavior of syphilitic patients was caused by a specific bacteria that attacked one's nervous system; until that time, no one had any idea why people with advanced cases of syphilis "went mad." At about the same time, Paul Ehrlich, another bacteriologist, discovered a cure for this apparent mental disorder: a drug called Salvarsan, which destroyed the culprit bacteria.

This was one of the most dramatic advances for psychiatry, because it proved that psychiatry could treat people on a medical model, and it completely eliminated one form of mental illness which had plagued mankind for centuries. A drug put postsyphilitic insanity in the same history book as the bubonic plague.

Is it possible to do the same with other types of emotional disorders? Yes, according to therapists who specialize in the biochemical approach to emotional illness. Some encouraging developments to this point:

1. Early in this century, one Sir Victor Horsley discovered that certain kinds of mental retardation was caused by the thyroid gland not functioning up to par; today, medication can stimulate the thyroid gland and cure those kinds of retardation.

2. In the late 1950s, Jean Delay discovered the phenothiazines and their ability to help diagnosed schizophrenics lead normal lives; the phenothiazines include drugs such as Thorazine and Stelazine, which seem to reduce schizophrenic reactions.

3. The discovery of the therapeutic effects of Lithium on diagnosed manic-depressives. Lithium is one of the light metal elements, and for reasons not fully understood at this writing, if a manic-depressive maintains a certain level of the element in his bloodstream, the symptoms of the manic-depressive illness disappear.

In this section the biochemical approach to emotional illness is discussed by some of the leading doctors in the field; and some patients who are under biochemical care tell the effects of such treatment. With more and more being discovered about how our body chemistry—especially the chemistry of our brain—affects us emotionally, there is increasingly greater hope for real cures and real prevention of emotional illness.

CHAPTER NINETEEN

Psychopharmaceutical Agents
Ronald Fieve, M.D.

Dr. Ronald Fieve, one of the country's foremost researchers in drug therapy, is associated with the Columbia-Presbyterian Medical Center (Columbia University College of Physicians and Surgeons, New York City) and the New York Psychiatric Institute. He received his medical training at Harvard Medical School. Later he trained as an internist at New York Hospital as a psychiatrist and psychoanalyst at Columbia.

Through the Psychiatric Institute, Dr. Fieve treats several hundred outpatients for various mood disorders. He is also in charge of an eight-bed metabolism unit in the Institute's hospital, where he treats moderate to severe depressives. In his research and practice, Dr. Fieve has found that illnesses such as recurrent depression and manic-depression are often due to disorders in body chemistry that can be corrected with a carefully prescribed regimen of psychopharmaceutical agents. His outstanding contribution has been pioneering the use of Lithium in the treatment of manic-depression.

Dr. Fieve's patients are primarily from the metropolitan New York area, although some come from all over the world. Patients who are treated both in his free clinic and in his private practice represent nearly every economic and social background.

Moodswing, Dr. Fieve's definitive book about his research and clinical experience with psychopharmaceutical agents, has been published by Morrow and Co., $8.95.

In this chapter, adapted from my conversation with Dr. Fieve, he discusses the types of illnesses he treats, the results with psychopharmaceutical treatment, and the reasons;drug therapy may fail in some cases.

Ronald Fieve, M.D.

Unlike the majority of psychiatrists in the country, I tend to treat people who represent a very special cross-section of patients: manic-depressives, unipolar or recurrent depressives, and chronic depressives. Using modern psychopharmaceutical agents, we are able to treat people in each of these categories quite successfully.

For manic-depressives—people who suffer from alternating extremes of highs and lows—we prescribe Lithium both as a therapeutic agent for a manic attack and as a preventive for future highs and lows. Lithium, perhaps the single most effective psychopharmaceutical agent today, is effective in 80 to 85 percent of the cases we treat.

There have been five recent studies, which suggest that Lithium is also an effective prophylactic antidepressant for unipolar recurrent depression as well. However, we do not as yet know definitely if Lithium will always turn out to be the preferred prophylaxis for recurrent depression since antidepressants may be equally effective in some cases. We do know that this group of patients does not respond as quickly and as completely as manic-depressives to Lithium treatment.

In certain cases of periodic depression, we first preprescribe an antidepressant such as Tofranil, Elavil, Nardil, or Parnate, to alleviate the deep depression. Then we add Lithium to help prevent future recurrences of the depressed mood. Most of the psychopharmacological agents we use are less effective for people who suffer from chronic depressions—people who have been depressed continuously for a number of years. We try the classic antidepressants from the tricyclic group, which I just mentioned, and later we try the M.A.O. inhibitors such as Nardil and Parnate. These drugs created a revolution in the treatment of depression when they came into use in the late 1950s. Although the major tranquilizers such as Thorazine and Haldol are effective in schizophrenia, their use in chronic depression is not very successful.

The prognosis for someone who suffers from a chronic depression, who feels down over long periods of time with no interval of normal mood between episodes, is not nearly so good as the prognosis for someone who experiences alternating highs and lows. Nevertheless, antidepressant treatment can definitely improve many cases of chronic depression.

True depression should not be confused with a grief reaction. Grief may last several months, but then it goes away. In a grief reaction psychopharmacologic agents may not be needed at all. Time will pass, the patient will work out the loss—or the grief from whatever he is reacting to may be helped through different kinds of psychotherapy. Most grief reactions disappear on their own, but if such a state lasts over three or four months, I would suspect that the person may have another form of depression, possibly biochemical in origin that may be drug responsive.

Psychopharmaceutical agents are not panaceas. Although tremendous strides have been made in medicine toward treating certain biochemical depressions, these agents are for specific illnesses. Not everyone can be helped by them. Some people cannot tolerate drug therapy as well as others; some people are more sensitive to the same dosage of a drug that other people can take effectively. If a patient is extremely sensitive to drugs and suffers from side effects, we have to resort to other psychotherapeutic modes, particularly milieu therapy and behavioral therapy.

Whether or not a person will respond to drug therapy often depends on personality characteristics. For instance, patients who respond to the medical model and the *idea* of drug therapy often tend to be more trusting. They see the doctor as a helpful authority figure and they believe the doctor can and will benefit them. Other people are more doubting, more skeptical of physicians in authority; they do not think they will be helped. Such a patient may go through the motions of coming in for drug treatment, but through fear and doubt sees the drug treatment as potentially harmful. Often, in a situation like this, the patient will not take his medication and I will have no way of knowing unless he is on Lithium treatment, in which case a blood test can verify if he has been taking the pills.

Studies have been conducted that show that 30 to 70 percent of patients being treated with medications on an outpatient basis do not follow their prescribed drug regimen. They do not take the proper amount of medication at the proper time, or sometimes they take their own medications. Therefore, in analyzing the lack of responsiveness in some patients to drug therapy, we must take into account not only an individual's idiosyncratic biochemical reaction to a drug, but certain personality factors as well. A person may have an inordinate fear of being controlled by a pill: What will the drug do to him? Will he do things he cannot control as a consequence of taking the drug?

Another type of adverse psychological reaction to drug therapy is characterized by certain hysterical features. For example, I might give an aspirin or a placebo to a patient, yet he will suffer a variety of bizarre side effects. The placebo appears to actually make him ill. He may get a reaction to what he believes is a psychopharmaceutical agent, although it is not a drug at all, since a placebo is an inert substance. This is not a conscious reaction; such patients actually do develop side effects. This type of person is usually not as responsive to actual drug therapy. However, it is possible to condition the hysterical person through behavioral techniques so that he may benefit from medications without developing hysterical symptoms.

Among manic-depressives there is a small group who do not like to take Lithium because they do not want to lose their highs, a state in which some great minds can only create. I would estimate that this group comprises 10 to 15 percent of manic-depressives, and their manic states are relatively mild. These patients will drop in and out of treatment, coming for help only during their depressive cycles and staying away—and off Lithium—during their highs. They don't want the doctor to take away the good feeling of a high, but because it is only one part of their cycle, they fall into a depression and return for help.

Why are psychopharmaceutical agents used in the treatment of certain emotional disorders? The answer can be found in the very solid studies done by geneticists and psychiatrists, which show that some emotional illnesses have a strong genetic base with a presumed biochemical origin. Manic-depressive disorders, schizophrenia, alcoholism, and hyperactivity in children are thought to reflect disorders of the body's biochemistry. Studies conducted with monozygotic (identical) twins show that if one twin suffers from one of these genetic illnesses, the likelihood of the other twin having the same disorder is considerable. The incidence of both twins having the disorder is much higher among identical twins (developed from the same egg) than among fraternal twins (developed from separate eggs) if the first suffers from the illness. In other words, identical twins, who have the same genetic programming, are more likely to have the same disorder than fraternal twins, whose genetic programming is no more alike than two siblings who are not twins. Other studies done with families also show that the incidence of these disorders is higher among family members than it is among the general population. Studies have amassed a great deal of evidence that genetic programming for biochemical disorders is at the root of the above-mentioned major mental illnesses. This, of course, contradicts the earlier ideas that mental illness was caused by purely environmental factors. No doubt environment is involved, but to a lesser extent than we have thought in the past.

It is now accepted that genetic and environmental factors interplay to contribute to a person's illness. But when we get to the treatment of these illnesses, we find that the most effective therapy is the use of psychopharmaceutical agents. Among the schizophrenic population, for instance, the most positive results are achieved by prescribing one of the phenothiazines—the major tranquilizers such as Thorazine, Haldoperidol, Trilafon, or Stelazine. (In the past, these agents were given to manics as well, but since the development of Lithium, the biochemical imbalance can be corrected with Lithium alone.)

These drugs improve the emotional status of severely disturbed patients who don't respond to psychotherapy. In many cases they improve the patient's condition to the point that supportive psychotherapy can work as an adjunct toward solving a person's psychological problems of living.

In the past, before the introduction of the phenothiazines into psychiatric treatment for schizophrenics, these acute disorders were dealt with in an almost haphazard way: shock treatments, insulin coma, wetpacks, Metrazol therapy, as well as various types of psychotherapy. In the late 1950s, Jean Delay, a French psychiatrist, discovered that phenothiazines suppressed the acute schizophrenic attack, thus enabling patients to live in the community as constructive individuals.

Another illness, which seems to have a basis in the individual's genetic programming, is alcoholism. There are no drugs that correct this disorder. For many, Alcoholics Anonymous seems to be the most positive treatment thus far. It's an extremely supportive organization. The mutual support the members have for each other allows a psychological recognition of their common illness, which leads to a group interaction that is therapeutic. For other alcoholics, AA is unacceptable. Very recently it has been suggested that certain types of alcoholism may respond to Lithium.

Once a person's biochemical imbalance is corrected with the appropriate psychopharmaceutical agent, psychotherapy can be employed if the patient wants it and needs it. Manic-depressives are not freed of all of their problems by Lithium alone. Like anyone else, a manic-depressive may suffer from any of a variety of neuroses that can be approached with psychotherapy. However, very few of my Lithium patients are in psychotherapy, and I feel that once Lithium corrects the specific biochemical problem the person's difficulties by and large disappear; most patients of mine feel they don't need psychotherapy.

In addition to our Lithium clinic, which treats several hundred patients on a once-a-month basis, I have an eight-bed metabolic depression unit in the hospital, where milieu therapy is practiced as an adjunct to the drug therapy. Milieu therapy, I have found, is perhaps the most effective new development in psychotherapy for the illnesses we treat. An attempt is made to give the patient a task that he can finish and from which he receives gratification. Social workers, occupational therapists, and psychologists work with the patients on the ward. The patients are organized and have an active part in the day-to-day life on the ward with their own government. Drug therapy is not used in isolation, either in the clinic or in the hospital. If an outpatient needs psychotherapy, we will refer him to an appropriate doctor, although we find that this is rarely needed with manic-depressives on Lithium.

Patients on psychopharmaceutical agents are checked carefully for side effects. Lithium patients have to return monthly for monitoring of the Lithium level in their blood to be sure it is not toxic or too low. In this way we can be sure that they are taking their medication. Of course, when a manic-depressive stops taking Lithium he will experience a "relapse," a mild to extreme high or a depression.

Side effects from the major tranquilizers are often similar to symptoms of Parkinson's Disease. The main effects are dry mouth, constipation, and some rigidity of the forearms and legs. These side effects are counteracted with Artane and anti-Parkinson agents. The antidepressants—Tofranil, Elavil, Parnate, and Nardil—will sometimes produce a high. Most often they produce such a reaction in manic-depressives who are given the agent during a depression before it has been determined that the patient is a true manic-depressive.

In the last five to ten years, very few of my patients have been hospitalized. Now, this is very interesting, because technically I'm treating one of the most severe types of disorders: manic-depression. This group has the highest suicide rate (15 percent) when the disorder is not treated, or treated incorrectly. I think that this low hospitalization rate indicates that treatment of this illness with Lithium has resulted in major advances. Prior to the development of antidepressants and Lithium, these people would have been hospitalized, treated with multiple drugs and shock treatments off and on for years.

CHAPTER TWENTY

Nutrition:
Megavitamin and DietTherapy

When psychiatrists use megavitamins and improved diet as a part of therapy, they are acknowledging a fundamental piece of information that has been with us since ancient Greece: the home of our psyche is a physical organ, the brain.

Like all physical organs, the brain needs energy to perform its function, and it gets that energy from the nutrients our digestive system manufactures from the food we eat. The cells that make up our brain and nervous system need specific quantities of the different nutrients, and shortages of them will result in impaired functioning of those organs —which means impaired mental health.

Massive doses of specific vitamins that are necessary for the brain to produce energy became a therapeutic method in the early 1950s, when two Canadian psychiatrists found that treating schizophrenics with Vitamin B_3 seemed to help them. Though it should be pointed out that many excellent doctors consider very large doses of vitamins hazardous to the health, today more and more psychiatrists are looking into this therapeutic mode, known as *orthomolecular psychiatry*.

The orthomolecular psychiatrist aims at treating and preventing emotional disorders by giving patients the proper balance of necessary vitamins and minerals, through improved diet, and through vitamin pills and injections.

Although everything is not known about just what vitamins *do*—how they act in the chemical process in our bodies—we do know what apparently results from a lack of certain vitamins and minerals. The B vitamins, which comprise the mainstay of megavitamin therapy, play roles in a wide variety of bodily processes. It has been found that schizophrenics are deficient in Vitamin B$_3$ (niacin), and that people who exhibit signs of senility are deficient in several of the B vitamins. Low levels of Vitamin A can either result in or be the result of stress. Depression, hallucinations, and muscle spasms are associated with low level of magnesium, according to a study published in the *Journal of the American Medical Association* (June 25, 1973: R.C.W. Hall and J. R. Joffe). In the fall of 1972, the *Los Angeles Times* ran a series of articles about orthomolecular psychiatry, and gave evidence that a shortage of potassium in the body is associated with restlessness and perhaps insomnia.

Vitamins and minerals must also be present in the proper ratios to each other, because they act and react together in the body. For example, when Vitamins A and E are in a proper ratio to each other, the E helps keep the A from being burned up too rapidly, so that it may be stored in the body for later use, and not depleted.

Blood sugar, or glucose, is the brain's most important source of fuel; the brain cells use it—or, a form of it—to metabolize nutrients. A shortage of glucose in the bloodstream, known as hypoglycemia, means that the brain cells are not able to break down nutrients into the chemicals they need for energy. Hypoglycemia shows up psychologically as depression or anxiety neurosis. Dr. A. Allan Cott, a practicing orthomolecular psychiatrist in New York City, told me:

> I have found, as many of my colleagues have, that one of the major findings in depression is a disturbance in glucose metabolism, and low levels of glucose in the bloodstream do produce depression. . . .
>
> I see a great many people who suffer from some disturbance in glucose metabolism and other biochemical disorders, who might be diagnosed elsewhere as suffering from anxiety neurosis. The symptoms of anxiety neurosis are recurring bouts of depression and irritability; many of these people also suffer from additional physical symptoms, and together, they are the signs and symptoms of most of the patients who have a metabolic disorder.

Orthomolecular psychiatrists such as Dr. Cott may give their patients a five-hour test to detect hypoglycemia if they exhibit the psychological signs of low blood sugar. If the results of this test, known as the Glucose

Tolerance Test, are positive, the patient will be put on a therapeutic regimen to correct the condition and put an end to the related psychological symptoms. The exact form of the therapeutic regimen may vary from doctor to doctor, and according to a patient's previous diet. For instance, many doctors have found that a low carbohydrate diet can contribute to reversing the effects of hypoglycemia. But what if a patient has been on one of the low-carbohydrate reducing diets, and has been taking in almost no carbohydrates previous to showing the psychological signs of low blood sugar? Then, of course, he will have to increase the amount of carbohydrates he takes in his food.

The level of blood sugar is maintained primarily through two types of food you eat: carbohydrates, or starches and sugars, and protein, or fish, meat, some grains, eggs, and different dairy products. The carbohydrates convert to glucose in the body very quickly, and the protein undergoes chemical changes to become a type of sugar that is stored in the liver, to be converted into glucose when the supply from the carbohydrates becomes low. (Approximately half of the protein we eat is transformed into blood sugar, but all the carbohydrates undergo this transformation.) But the protein-based sugar cannot become glucose unless our body's cells are burning glucose already; carbohydrates have to be present for the cells to do the work of drawing on the reserve supply of sugar we get from protein.

The important thing here is that although some people may have a predisposition to hypoglycemia because of an inborn, or genetic, programming for a faulty metabolism, others may become hypoglycemic because of a faulty diet; the therapy will, in many cases, depend upon whether a poor metabolism of blood sugar is "natural" to the individual, or whether his diet created it.

Since the early 1950s when Drs. Humphrey Osmond and Abram Hoffer began treating schizophrenics with massive doses of niacin and Vitamin C, orthomolecular psychiatrists have been using megavitamin therapy quite successfully to arrest the symptoms of schizophrenia. It has been one of the most puzzling mental disorders, and is one of the most debilitating to its victim. Although its symptoms vary from individual to individual, all schizophrenics have one thing in common: distortions in perception. The brain seems to translate what they see or hear improperly. This seems to indicate that the brain isn't working right, perhaps because of a disorder in the way its cells metabolize nutrients.

The 1950s saw the development of several antischizophrenic medications—drugs called the phenothiazines—which helped arrest many of the symptoms of schizophrenia. Today, in the orthomolecular treatment of schizophrenia, both megavitamins and the antischizophrenic drugs are used. When I interviewed Dr. Cott on the subject of schizophrenia he said:

> In examining schizophrenic adults some years ago, I found that about 75 to 80 percent of them had some gross disorder of glucose metabolism. By altering their diets, adding large doses of vitamins to their regimen, and using psychotropic drugs such as Thorazine, Stelazine, and Prolixin, I found that their conditions improved. These drugs have the potential to alter a person's thinking and to alter psychic states. For a schizophrenic, this is a positive alteration, because schizophrenics suffer from distortions of perception; any or all of their senses can be distorted so that they receive improper messages from their environment. With these medications, the distortions can be dispelled.
>
> In treating adult schizophrenics with megavitamins, I focus on niacin and niacinimide, two forms of Vitamin B_3. . . . I think that if the average person took larger doses of vitamins, particularly B vitamins, he would feel better.

Why the B vitamins? Research on the body chemistry of schizophrenics shows that one of the chemical disorders in the brain tissue is the way a schizophrenic's brain converts certain substances. One substance in the brain is a hormone called adrenochrome, which can be changed into other chemicals; the schizophrenic's brain cells convert it to a poisonous substance known as adrenolutin. Although we all have adrenolutin, we also have enough of the other harmless substances made from adrenochrome to balance it out. But the schizophrenic has too much, and this seems to be one of the causes of the psychological disorders in schizophrenics. Niacin retards the production of this poisonous substance, helping to make a normal balance of the chemicals manufactured from adrenochrome. Vitamin C helps in this process as well, for it interacts with adrenochrome to produce the nontoxic substances needed in the brain. Schizophrenics suffer a shortage of Vitamin C in the brain cells, because this vitamin is rapidly depleted by the chemical transformation of adrenochrome, so massive doses appear to aid in the therapeutic effects.

"Schizophrenics," Dr. Cott told me, "very often present depression as a major symptom."

How do B vitamins affect low blood sugar? One of the forms that glucose takes in the brain cells is acetate, and it is this form of sugar that provides the majority of the brain's energy. One of the main components of acetate is a chemical known as pantothenic acid, one of the B vitamins. If this B vitamin is missing or if there is a shortage of it, the acetate level in the brain's cells drops drastically; the individual isn't functioning at his best, because he is low on "fuel" for his brain cells. The result can be depression, listlessness, and psychological disorientation. Replacing the pantothenic acid with large doses of B vitamins can reverse the effects.

Orthomolecular therapy can be practiced only by a psychiatrist or a physician. The treatment program does not usually include supportive psychotherapy, but relies exclusively on a biochemical approach. Often, an orthomolecular psychiatrist will refer a patient to a therapist for additional or adjunctive psychological therapy. As Dr. Cott told me:

> I no longer (I did for 25 years) practice supportive psychotherapy, but I often refer patients to doctors who do. Good supportive psychotherapy is valuable for many schizophrenics. If they have been ill a long time, particularly during the important formative years of their lives, they will have missed much in their social development. When their illness is arrested through a biochemical treatment program, they may be emotionally lost—they've lost a number of years out of their lives when they would have been developing social skills.

For too many years the biochemical origins of mental illness were overlooked, but today, new developments in this area are pointing to relief and possibly cures for thousands of people. The mind-body dichotomy that has posed a seemingly endless question in Western thought might finally be resolved.

Another aspect of nutritional therapy is based in the research of such doctors as Theron G. Randolph in Chicago, who has taken what he terms an ecologic approach to mental illness. Different people, he says, are addicted to certain foods in much the same way as a drug addict is "hooked" on a specific drug. If you are addicted to a food, you must have it, even though it produces any number of psychological and emotional problems; because *not* eating it results in other emotional symptoms—withdrawal symptoms.

If you are addicted to a certain food, you are actually allergic to it, but the form the allergy takes is different from the more well-known, specific allergic reaction. According to Dr. Randolph:

Specific intolerance to foods, with immediate acute reactions following the occasional ingestion of shrimp, buckwheat, cashew or other foods taken only rarely or intermittently, has been known since the days of Greek medicine. Everyone knows about these reactions, although they may be referred to by various names. Nevertheless, this is *food sensitization as it is ordinarily considered*.[1]

But there is another type of allergic reaction that one may have to a food to which he is sensitive if he eats it regularly and often. Unlike ordinary allergic reactions, the allergic effects of the food tend to decrease after eating the food, and then to disappear when more of the food is eaten:

> The cumulative use of such a food is either not followed by a reaction or the subject reports that he feels better after than before eating it.
>
> This *pick-up* or actual improvement in symptoms following the oft-repeated ingestion of a particular food, as contrasted to an immediate post-meal reaction when it is consumed occasionally, is one of the characteristic features of *food addiction*. . . .
>
> In contrast to the narcotic addict who knows when he is "hooked," the food addict usually does not know of any food acting in this manner. He is only aware that eating in general is pleasant, relaxing, and seems to agree particularly well with him. Because this process usually involves the commonly eaten foods such as corn, wheat, coffee, milk, eggs, and others, the person addicted to one of these is likely to include some form of it in each feeding.[2]

In other words, the culprit foods are foods we eat almost every day, sometimes twice or three times a day. Because food addiction involves a completely different kind of allergic reaction from the ordinary immediate reaction, it is often difficult to detect. If you are addicted to a food to which you are allergic, the reaction is actually timed to your mealtimes. Let us say that you're allergic to wheat; you eat toast for breakfast, but before your body has recovered from the allergic effects of the wheat in the toast for breakfast, you are having lunch—a sandwich on whole wheat bread. You again have bread for dinner.

1. "The Descriptive Features of Food Addiction: Addictive Eating and Drinking," *Quarterly Journal of Studies on Alcohol*, Vol. 17, No. 2, pp. 198-224. Reprinted here by permission.

2. Ibid.

What is happening is that you are adapting to wheat; when you first adapt to a food this way, you may feel quite well after eating it; there is nothing really wrong with you, but as time goes on, and you become more and more "hooked" on a specific food, changes begin to take place.

The active, happy, "good" feeling doesn't last as long. Dr. Randolph calls this the *stimulatory phase* in the cycle of food addiction. You will actually have to eat more wheat-based foods to maintain an "up" feeling. But the "up" feeling goes beyond just feeling well. You become jittery after you eat, hyperactive; you can eventually lose physical and mental control.

What should you do if you realize that it's bread that sets you off balance? Do you merely stop eating everything with wheat in it? No. No more than a narcotic addict simply stops taking the drug to which he's addicted.

In food addiction, as in drug addiction, there are also withdrawal symptoms. If you're addicted to wheat, you may feel these withdrawal effects when you wake up in the morning, since you haven't eaten anything for eight to ten hours, and your usual "addiction schedule" keeps you away from wheat for only four hours at a time—between meals. You may wake up feeling low, perhaps your nose will be stuffy; you may feel achy, depressed, confused. But you're also craving breakfast—and you eat whole wheat toast. If you are severely addicted, you "pick up" almost immediately, and the greater your addiction, the sooner you will need bread or some other form of wheat to overcome withdrawal and return to the "stimulatory," up half of the cycle. According to Dr. Randolph:

> In progressive food addiction these delayed *withdrawal effects* or hangovers persist for increasingly greater portions of a day, being dispelled only temporarily and sometimes only partially immediately following ingestion of the evocative food. Thus, the course of events in food addiction associated with the oft-repeated ingestion of a specific foodstuff . . . consists of an initial relative respite in symptoms followed by a delayed recurrence. . . .[3]

Over time, then, you can develop a severe addiction to a food to which you are allergic. You must have it more and more often, until your diet becomes monotonous for containing more and more of the ad-

3. Ibid.

dictive food; since you can't eat twenty-four hours a day, the withdrawal symptoms come on more and more frequently.

Dr. Randolph and his colleagues describe the different phases of addicted life as food addiction advances in its severity to the point where it has to be treated. We all have a base, or normal, level of behavior. When one is first adapting (in an addictive way) to an allergic food, eating it makes him feel "up." He is a bit overactive, but happy. The withdrawal symptom, which occurs before he eats the culprit food in this stage of the addiction, can be a runny nose, wheezing, itching—many of the less serious reactions we normally have as specific allergic reactions. At this point, the person is not in serious trouble. But the addiction becomes worse with time. He finds that after eating the offending food, his overactivity increases; he becomes jittery, brash, supercharged until the withdrawal symptoms in this phase begin. Now, without the food, or just before he eats, he is tired, he has headaches, chest pains; he isn't thinking very clearly, and physically, he feels puffy and stiff.

At this stage, the food addict is still able to function in everyday affairs, but not for long. The next phase of addiction makes him more manic, egocentric, aggressive; uncontrolled fits of laughter may bring some people to conclude that something is definitely wrong. Then the withdrawal, which at this point is becoming increasingly frequent: he gets depressed; he's unable to make decisions; he may withdraw socially, and even suffer blackouts, until he returns to his addictive food. And if he does, he soon will become intensely hyperactive, out of control. His mental and physical control will be severely impaired and he may exhibit signs of "altered" consciousness—faulty logic, poor and distorted perception. This alternates rapidly with the withdrawal phase, for at this point he would have to eat almost constantly to maintain the manic part of the cycle. He also becomes severely depressed, stuporous, disoriented. Amnesia, at least sometimes, may result; he may feel paranoid and may hallucinate.

In any stage of food addiction, the "up" phase is merely the other side of the "down" phase; both symptom patterns will trouble the addict. It is during the later stages of addiction that people go for help. If one truly is addicted to a food, then the addiction must be broken.

Dr. Randolph's treatment procedure involves a stay in his hospital, where patients are fasted under carefully controlled conditions. Because he has found evidence that certain pollutants in the air and water, as well as certain synthetic fabrics, may also cause allergic reactions and are potential addictants, the air and water in the hospital are purified, and only natural fabrics are used for patients' clothing and bedding:

Patients are fasted preliminarily, drinking only relatively less contaminated water, avoiding the use of all drugs, tobacco, cosmetics, and synthetically derived clothing. The duration of the fast averages 4½ days, the range is between 4 and 6 days, only occasionally 7 days or slightly longer. . . .[4]

During this fasting period, of course, the patient suffers from withdrawal symptoms, which begin to stop. When they do, the patient is given common foods (which have not been "processed" with chemicals), one type of food a meal for three meals a day. If a patient has an allergic response to one of those foods, it is flushed from his system. Once a person has completely withdrawn from the addictive food, he will react to it if he eats it, for he is no longer "adapted": his allergic reaction will be immediate and severe.

When all the common foods have been tested for a patient, he is given foods taken from the commercial market, that is, foods that have been "processed" with different chemicals. Perhaps the patient is not actually addicted to the food itself, but to either the processed form of the food, or the chemicals.

When all the foods have been tested, the culprit foods are taken from the patient's diet:

Incriminated foods and/or chemical additives and contaminants of the diet as a group are avoided as patients return to their homes, still adhering to other avoidance programs as in the hospital. A recurrence of reactive symptoms the first few days there suggests the presence of reactions to some home exposure.[5]

One may have allergic reactions to pollutants in the air at home, and Dr. Randolph puts utility gas (such as the type we use in our kitchen stoves) high on the list of home pollutants. Although food addiction is a primary cause of ecologic mental illness, other things in the environment may also produce adverse mental reactions:

As knowledge of the relationships of chemical environmental exposures to mental illness increased, it soon became apparent that air contaminants were of primary importance, especially indoor or domiciliary chemical air pollutants.[6]

4. Theron G. Randolph, M.D.: "Demonstrable Role of Foods and Environmental Chemicals in Mental Illness." Paper presented at the Annual meeting of the Japanese Society of Allergology in November, 1973.
5. Ibid.
6. Ibid.

Because patients in the ecologic ward of the hospital have lived in a pollution-free environment, returning to an environment where the air is polluted can result in an immediate reaction to the specific chemical to which one is allergic. As in the case of withdrawing from food addiction, the patient has lost his "adaptation" to the pollutant and now has an allergic reaction to it immediately.

The answer is to avoid exposure to substances that produce an allergic reaction, for if the patient continues to be exposed, he will readapt; he will again become "addicted," and the cycle will start all over again.

"Ecology" is formally defined as biology dealing with the mutual relations between organisms and their environment. Our own personal "ecologies," according to this definition, is the way we are affected by (and adjust to) our physical environment—the air we breathe, the water we drink, the things we touch, and the food we eat. The ecologic approach to mental illness looks at these aspects of our environment to find out the causes of emotional disturbances.

Like megavitamin therapy, ecologic therapy recalls that fundamental principle established by the physicians of ancient Greece: the seat of our mind, and our mental activity, is the brain, which is a physical organ. "Healthy body, healthy mind" is turning an old adage around, but it makes just as much sense this way.

CHAPTER TWENTY-ONE

"Taking Off in a Big Balloon"
Elsie Dunsmore

For a manic-depressive, the cycles of ups and downs become a way of life. Before Elsie Dunsmore began Lithium treatment, her cycles had not only become a way of life, but a cause for shock treatment and hospitalizations and a seemingly endless search for the right psychotherapist. Nothing helped until she was put on Lithium.

Today, at fifty-nine, Elsie's manic and depressive cycles have been arrested and she leads a normal, happy life. This is her story.

Elsie Dunsmore

B.B.: How old are you, Elsie?
ELSIE: Fifty-nine.
B.B.: Where were you born and what kind of family life did you have?
ELSIE: I was born on Long Island. My father was German—born in Germany, but he was an American citizen. He was a boilermaker, a very well-paying trade at that time. My mother was born in New York City.

I didn't have much of a family life. My folks had lost a son when he was five years old, and I was born as a replacement. But being a girl, I wasn't a satisfactory replacement.

My father was a very arrogant man. We were considered well-to-do for that time, propertywise, moneywise. I didn't give much thought to this as a child, but since I've grown up I realize that my father's biggest thing in life was to show what he had accomplished in this country. For instance, when I was in the seventh grade I had a raccoon coat. Now, we lived out on Long Island, which was quite country then, and I went to public school. There wasn't another child on Long Island, I'm sure, who owned a raccoon coat, unless they had millionaires for parents. I realize now that the coat was extremely important to him, and I hated it, oh I hated it with such a vengeance. But that was part of his attitude toward my mother and myself. My mother was a very pretty, tiny woman, and the amount of money she spent for clothes never bothered my father, as long as she was the outstanding woman when they went out and had the clothes no one else had gotten yet.

B.B.: Would you consider you were neglected, that you didn't get enough love and affection?

ELSIE: As I look back now, well, I have two definite feelings toward my parents. My mother was an alcoholic. If I had been mature when her drinking had started, there was so much I could have done, but I didn't know. I was an only child and we really had very few relatives who could help. I always thought she was just sick. Even when I was a teenager, I still didn't know—what did I know about alcoholism?

And my father, I absolutely can't tolerate him. I refuse to use the special words I have for him on tape. They are simply my words for him and they are contemptible.

When I got older, I met and married a wonderful man, and had my own family. And I finally realized my mother's problems. She and I saw one another every day then, and the fact that she was an alcoholic was much, much too obvious. I knew what was wrong with her, but it was too late to do anything, and my father wouldn't cooperate at all. My husband and I had to take her into our home, six months at a time, and with us she was marvelous. And then my father would stampede in: No, thank you for it. "She's my wife, I want her home." And the moment she walked in the door, the first thing he handed her was a drink. It was like banging your head against a stone wall.

B.B.: Do you think there was any background of mental illness in your family?

ELSIE: Aside from my mother being an alcoholic, no.

B.B.: Now, what brought you to seek psychiatric help?

ELSIE: Well, it was this manic depression, that's what first started it I was thirty-nine. There was no particular problem of any kind. It was something over which I had absolutely no control. I would either be higher than a kite or just as low on the ground as you could be, and for no apparent reason.

I had lived in Pennsylvania when it first started, and the psychiatrist I went to kept trying to find out what it was that preceded it. Well, it got to the point where I was trying to think so hard of what was causing it that I was even making a list of things, ridiculous things: "These things certainly make me feel that way," I'd say, and he agreed.

B.B.: What treatment did your doctor prescribe?

ELSIE: I had been taking shock treatments over an extended period of time from this doctor, in his office. It wasn't helping. I would imagine that I had twenty-five, thirty shock treatments in his office.

I remember those first shock treatments. My husband and I were so green about things like that—we were looking for help for me, and this doctor said, "Shock treatment." What did we know about shock treatment? Nothing. So we agreed. After all, he was the doctor. I had no idea what was going to be done to me. I remember sitting in his office, waiting my turn, and I kept getting more nervous. They were simply bringing patients out from treatment unconscious, no stretcher or anything. I was sitting there, watching people go in; when they went in they looked perfectly normal, and then they'd be carted out, unconscious, hauled into a taxicab with a member of the family to help them. I was terrified. Fortunately, no one operates like that anymore.

B.B.: Were you hospitalized?

ELSIE: Yes, several times. Three hospitals in New York City. In two of those, I also received shock treatments. Then, in the last hospital, New York University Hospital, I met the psychiatrist I'm with now. And he stopped all the shock treatments. He realized I'm a manic-depressive, and he put me on Lithium.

I have always felt that shock treatment was not for me, because I never saw that it did much good. When I would come home after being hospitalized and getting shock treatment, I'd fight every inch of the way to do what I had to do to make myself go out, to try to apply what I had been taught, if I could remember it. I think I had had twenty or twenty-two shock treatments in hospitals when I first saw the doctor I'm seeing now. I had tried to tell any doctor that I wasn't getting any better, I was getting worse. I was getting to the point where it was an effort every day to get my clothes on, and that doesn't happen to be my natural disposition. When I told my present doctor about it he stopped the shock treatments. It was a long haul but we made it. A year ago he put me on Lithium.

B.B.: Since you've been on Lithium, have you ever gotten depressed?

ELSIE: Well, I may get down for a day or two, but everybody gets down for a day or two. This is perfectly natural. Depressed, such as I have known depression? Not within the past year. Absolutely not. I almost ran into my doctor's office and threw my arms around him. For years, my cycle from the manic phase to the depressive would change, exactly on the twenty-sixth of June. On the twenty-fifth of June, I would be fine; on the twenty-sixth of June, there it would be, just like a cement block, and from there on it was down all the way. This year, on the twenty-sixth of June, I saw him. I said, "Hey, do you know what date it is? And I'm laughing, can you believe this?"

B.B.: In the past, what were your symptoms when you were in your manic and depressive phases?

ELSIE: Well, manic was wonderful—gay, happy, the world was just there to pick the biggest plum from, and to have a ball in. But the depression—all I wanted to do was to die. The last depression I had lasted nine months. That left me three good months, and I remember thinking, "You can't do that much living in three months." I vowed I'd never go through another depression. I told that to my doctor—and about that time he started the Lithium.

I'm just too old to be bothered by those depressions now. I can't keep that kind of life up—I just can't keep fighting to get up in the morning, fighting to get dressed, going out when I don't want to. I'd hate everybody and if somebody would smile I wouldn't be able to stand him: "What do other people have to smile about when I'm so damned miserable?"

Of course, I realized that it was all a part of the depression, that that's the way it goes. But that last time, I said to my doctor, "Pretty soon I'm going to hit one of these depressions, and it's going to be the worst one. And I'm just going to call it quits." At first he was hoping that when my menopause was over, things would get better. But they got worse, so he put me on Lithium.

B.B.: And there was never anything that used to trigger these episodes of manic depression?

ELSIE: No. I think it's biochemical. My first doctor really tried to find what would trigger it off. He really worked at it, but never came up with anything.

I used to get a little angry with myself, because when I was manic, I would have such a ball. That's the only word I can think of; everything was fine and there was so much to do that I could barely take the time to take an extra breath. Everything was just so exciting, and I used to say, "Well, why don't I feel something, why isn't there anything that I can point to and say, "This is making me feel so high?" You feel as if you could set the world on fire one day and the next day, it starts to get down, and it was nothing but down, down, all the way down, for four, five, six, seven months. No, I can honestly say I have never found anything that triggered an episode.

B.B.: Do you feel that Lithium is definitely responsible for your cure?

ELSIE: Yes. Well, I don't know whether this is considered a *cure* for the condition, or whether it's just an arresting medication. I know that now a manic-depressive condition is considered a biochemical problem. I don't know whether that means that they will be able to do something else to totally cure the condition so that Lithium wouldn't be necessary.

B.B.: Elsie, you haven't been hospitalized in how long now?

ELSIE: Six years. Isn't that fantastic?

B.B.: That's wonderful. What are your interests in your life now? Do you find that you have added dimensions?

ELSIE: Well, my husband will be retiring in about a year and a half and we have a little place up in Pennsylvania, a couple of acres. We go there almost every weekend, and last year I became interested in gardening. I find it absolutely fascinating. All these years I was never one for putting my hands in the dirt, but all of a sudden I have become quite enthused about it.

And then—I wouldn't say this has been an exciting development—but I was working up until a year ago, and now I'm not. This is the first time I have ever been home and been a lady. Neither of my children live nearby, so they are not in the picture at all. I may see them once a year, sometimes I don't see them for three, it just depends on where they go. But just the thought of the simple things. I like to keep house. I hate to cook, but I like to read. I seem to keep busy. I am very happy with the situation.

B.B.: Do you think you've gained insights into yourself?

ELSIE: Oh, yes, thanks to my doctor. I think I know a lot more about myself now than I did six or seven years ago, when I started going to him. He has been excellent for me. He is the finest young man anyone could have as a doctor. I have nothing but praise for him. When he got me I wasn't very much to get. I was in some shape, but I find that he has been good to me. I have been to maybe five or six psychiatrists during my life, and I really feel that he has been the best for me. Other psychiatrists have spent an awful lot of time probing for what triggers this, what triggers the depression off, and in all the time, they never came up with even one thing.

B.B.: Well, then Lithium, for you, has been a lifesaver, hasn't it?

ELSIE: Well, with the manic part, before, I never realized how fantastically high this high was. I see that when I was up there, it was like taking off in a big balloon. Now there seems to be more of a level. So I am hoping that Lithium will continue to help. My doctor said that there would be some rough spots, but they are nothing, so far, compared to real depression, just nothing.

I am very grateful, I'll be truthful. I am too old to keep pushing and pushing and pushing. The last time I was depressed, before Lithium, I thought, "This was all right when I was thirty-one, but look at how old I am now." I don't have the energy to scrape, scrape for every damned step I take. I am just too old. I don't have that kind of fight anymore. Yes, Lithium has been a lifesaver.

You know, it's surprising how many people do suffer, but they go to work and so forth. I don't know how they manage. I went to work every day. I don't know how, and I often wonder, didn't somebody notice what was the matter, how bad I was?

CHAPTER TWENTY-TWO

"I Just Felt Free"
Anne Forsythe

Anne Forsythe is a twenty-year-old college student who suffered from severe depressions; standard psychotherapy didn't seem to help. There just didn't seem to be any reason why a young college student, apparently with everything going for her, could suffer such acute depressions.

Her family had heard of the work being done in food addiction, and thought it was just possible that this was Anne's problem. She underwent therapy in Dr. Theron Randolph's hospital with dramatic results: Today, instead of a psychiatrist, she consults a diet schedule.

Anne Forsythe

B.B.: Tell me Anne, how old were you when you went to see Dr. Randolph?

ANNE: Seventeen.

B.B.: What sort of problems had you been experiencing?

ANNE: Mostly depression. Also stomach problems, headaches, and other aches and pains; and allergies.

B.B.: Had you been seeing a psychiatrist?

ANNE: Yes, I'd been seeing different psychiatrists, but no one really seemed to have an answer; they all said there was nothing wrong with me that they could find out; that it was just a personality thing—and

I had always had trouble in school. I was hyperactive, always getting into trouble and not really wanting to, but just finding an outlet for a lot of pent-up anger and frustrations.

B.B.: And anger turned in makes for depression.

ANNE: A very bad depression.

B.B.: Tell me, what was Dr. Randolph's approach to you when you went—exactly what did he do?

ANNE: He took me off all medication. I was on tranquilizers and sleeping pills. He put me in a "chemically free" environment, which means that the hospital itself, all the windows and everything were closed. There were no foreign odors allowed in. I was not allowed to wear clothes made from synthetic material, or to use toothpaste or deodorant or shampoo—except baby shampoo—and only the mildest pure soaps. I was only allowed to wear wool and cotton, and the mattresses and pillows and linen—everything was made from wool or horsehair or cotton. I guess it was a cotton mattress.

And then, I was taken off food when I first got there for four days. I wasn't allowed to eat. I was given a laxative to clear out my system the first day, and then I was put on this fast for four days. I couldn't eat anything.

I started feeling really bad. My symptoms got worse the first two days without eating: I would go into rages and I would cry. I would cry a lot and I couldn't sleep, and I had aches in my stomach. The problem came back, the aches and everything.

Then, I think it was the fourth morning, I woke up and I just felt fantastic, really happy. I felt as if something had been lifted off my back. I just felt free, wonderful.

I went in and I talked to Dr. Randolph, because I had to see him every morning. At first, he'd say, "How do you feel?" And I'd say, "Terrible, I want to leave, I don't want to stay here. I want my parents to come and get me." He'd say, "Well, just try it a little longer," and the fourth morning when I woke up he said, "How do you feel?" and I said, "Fantastic." He said, "Good, now you can start eating." So he started allowing me to have different foods, and kept watching my reactions.

B.B.: Your allergic reactions?

ANNE: Yes. If I ate something that disagreed . . . well, I was taught how to read my pulse, and if something disagreed with me, I'd know it right away. If I had something like tea for breakfast and it disagreed with me, I would notice it immediately. My pulse would be much faster and I would start getting the aches and pains back, and then

I would start getting depressed. Someone would come in and say something and I would burst into tears or start throwing things and go into a rage. But soon I realized myself that it was a reaction—not just something that was going on in my own mind. When I'd have a reaction, I was given a laxative—milk of magnesia is what he used to clear out my system. When it was all out of my system I would be okay again. And then he kept testing me with each food.

B.B.: *He introduced one food at a time?*

ANNE: Yes.

B.B.: *How long did it take?*

ANNE: About two weeks. At the end of that time, I had tried just about everything that I would be in contact with as far as foods went. I also was given a shot of hydrocarbon to test and see if I was allergic to gas and petroleum fumes or synthetic materials and things like that, but I wasn't. That didn't affect me.

B.B.: *Have you had any trouble since you've seen him?*

ANNE: The only trouble I've had is when I'm in contact with something I know I shouldn't eat.

B.B.: *Yes. How many years ago is this?*

ANNE: Well, I'm twenty now, it's three years.

B.B.: *Three years. Do you really stick to his regimen?*

ANNE: It works. And I can't afford not to, because—well, for instance: I have an apartment off campus, a roommate of mine brought a cat back after this past Christmas vacation. I didn't realize that I was allergic to cats. I'd never been tested for cats. Anyway, she brought the cat back, and immediately, within a day or two, I started getting headaches. My stomach was a mess, and I was throwing up and was really sick. And then I got depressed and disoriented. I remember falling down the stairs; my speech was really slurred as if I was drunk or something. Finally, I went to the hospital, which is near my apartment, and told them that I had been having an allergic reaction. They gave me a solution of what I was given in the hospital when I'd had reactions before. That cleared me out, but we had to get rid of the cat.

B.B.: *What did they give you in the hospital for an allergic reaction?*

ANNE: Oh, it's a mixture of bicarbonate of soda and potassium.

B.B.: *And your stomach problem took the form, not of an ulcer, but of nausea.*

ANNE: Yes. And I had aches in my joints.

And the old fears really started to come back because of my allergic reaction to the cat. You see, I had a fear of things when I first left home, when I was seventeen. Sometimes I couldn't go to classes, and I was afraid of getting up and meeting people and just doing simple things. I was in my room all the time with the shades drawn. It was awful. When I went back home I went to see a psychiatrist, because I just couldn't go on like that at school. It took me a long time to get the courage to go and see a psychiatrist. But it was just fear of all these things, and I didn't know what was causing it.

B.B.: *You just withdrew inside yourself.*

ANNE: Yes, exactly. And then I started taking drugs, too, because—well, then I'd have done anything to get out of my depression. Drugs would help for a while, and then I would get much lower again.

B.B.: *Anne, how did you hear of Dr. Randolph's work?*

ANNE: Well, my uncle had arthritis. He was so thin. He was dying from it. He'd been to all kinds of specialists, he had been taking all kinds of medications, and nothing helped. Then he went to Dr. Randolph and now he's fine.

When I went, there were different kinds of patients. I was sort of the depression case, and then there was a lady with arthritis, and a little boy with asthma, really acute asthma. People had different rashes and things like that, and all of them were cured. It was amazing. The lady who had arthritis in her fingers—when she would eat something she was allergic to, her fingers would get all swollen, the joints would get all swollen. She had her own doctor come down and see her before she went into the clinic, and then when she was fine and symptom-free after the fast, he wouldn't believe it. He'd just say, "I don't believe it," and would walk out.

B.B.: *What were the things he found that harmed you? What can't you have?*

ANNE: Well, tea was probably my worst. Wheat—wheat flour—beef, onions, and tomatoes. That's about it.

B.B.: *Wheat flour. That means you can't eat any bread of any sort.*

ANNE: No, it doesn't, because I can make my own. I make it with rice flour or soy flour. I just don't eat commercially made bread, or cake. And I don't miss it. When I first heard that I thought: "Oh, I can't possibly live like that." But it really wasn't so bad. You know, once you know you can't eat a certain thing, you just don't.

B.B.: *Were you in Dr. Randolph's hospital?*

ANNE: Yeah: Henratin Hospital. You're in there for two weeks, a little over two weeks.

He checks you every day and you have a physical while you are in the hospital every couple of days to see that you're okay. He has assistants who go around and check your symptoms—they see you every morning after you have slept and after you have eaten. They check you, and you learn how to read your pulse, and he's always there to sort of help you understand it better.

B.B.: And what happens if you are allergic to a food? You said before that your pulse goes up?

ANNE: Yes, or it gets erratic.

B.B.: Irregular?

ANNE: Yes. But a reaction can take any form for me actually. Sometimes I just get violent nausea, or I get headaches, really bad migraine headaches, or backaches or a depression. I just cry for a long time. When I was depressed, I'd think, "I can't do anything about that." And then after a while it would get worse and I would get more and more depressed, and then I would realize that it was a reaction. But he doesn't give you anything until you realize that it is a reaction. You know, he doesn't want to just say, "You are reacting to this negatively."

B.B.: So at the end of two weeks he really sizes up everything you've had?

ANNE: Yeah, and he lists it in order from the most severe symptoms to the least severe symptoms. You know, maybe you would just get a headache, but if you constantly eat whatever is causing it, it would lead up to something worse. That's a cycle, you know. If you get a bad stomachache, that doesn't make you feel very well mentally either . . . so it just goes 'round in circles.

B.B.: Were you comfortable in the hospital?

ANNE: Except for my problems—my reactions—yes. It's a comfortable place. And Mrs. Randolph helps out. She is an amazing woman, a really strong person. She is always there with books for you—because you can't really do anything while you are in the hospital except watch TV. You are not allowed to go outside for a walk because of the air. She is always around with books, and she will come in and talk to you and she will show you—say, if you are really a sensitive person and can't wear synthetic clothes, she will bring in catalogues from places where you could buy just cotton and wool. And if you have problems with your furnishings—a lot of people are allergic to foam rubber in cushions and things like that—she will tell you where you can get synthetic-free cushions. If you are allergic to wheat, she tells you all the products that have wheat in them in some small quantity. She is just amazing, they all are. They do their best to make you comfortable.

B.B.: Did you find the four-day fast pretty rugged?

ANNE: The first time I did, yes. I really did. Well, I didn't understand it. I was so depressed and upset when I got there. I thought I was being sent off somewhere and I didn't know if I was ever going to see my parents again. I was such a mess; really upset mentally and physically. I guess I had been eating pretty badly. Because when you are allergic to something you eat more of it. It is sort of like taking a drug. For instance, I'm really allergic to wheat, and I can remember before I went in the hospital, I would wake up in the morning and eat English muffins. I would wake up feeling terrible, but after breakfast I would feel a little better, and toward evening I'd feel worse. Then, for dinner, I would have steak, which is beef—and I can't have that, either—and something else, with onions or something. It would pick me up a little and then by the next morning, I'd be down again.

But the fast really wasn't hard. The first two days are the worst, because you can't smoke and you can't have any coffee.

B.B.: Just water?

ANNE: Just water. And spring water, too, not just any old water. But it is worth it when you wake up that last morning—you just feel fantastic. I couldn't believe it. I really couldn't.

B.B.: Would you recommend this kind of therapy?

ANNE: I do, but the thing is that few people will actually go through it unless they are really sick. It's sort of a last straw, because no one wants to give up his own doctor. And a lot of physicians or specialists say, "Don't listen to him, that's crazy." My psychiatrist was really funny. I told him that I was going for the treatment and I said that I might get help, but that I didn't really understand what it was. And he said, "Well, if your parents want to do it, okay," but he was really negative about it.

When I came back, I bounced into his office and I said, "I feel great, I don't need you anymore." And he said, "I don't believe it."

PART SIX

Some Newer Therapies

IN RECENT YEARS, many psychotherapists have taken another look at the ideas that have dominated their field. We have already seen one of the results; the growing practice of drug, vitamin, and nutritional therapy. Another consequence of this professional reevaluation has been the emergence of humanist psychology.

The traditional approaches, psychoanalysis and behavior therapy, are two forces in the field of emotional health: Freudianism and behaviorism. Humanist psychology might be called another force and it is the basis for many of today's newer therapies. A psychotherapist who views himself as a humanist psychologist has probably been influenced by the writings of Abraham H. Maslow, whose classic book, *Toward a Psychology of Being*, caused a stir in the psychoanalytic community with its publication in 1962. Maslow never rejected psychoanalysis or behavior therapy, but his contribution, rather, was to add that the therapist should pay as much attention to the *subjective* and *creative* sides of people, as well as trying to find the symptoms and causes of their problems. Psychotherapists influenced by Maslow are more diverse in their approaches, and if it is possible to summarize their optimistic views on human behavior, it would be to say that they look at the healthy side of people—at what comprises mental health, rather than mental illness.

The newer therapies now have as many theorists, subdivisions, and methods as psychoanalysis had in its early years. There are the existential analysts who look to R. D. Laing, Rollo May, and Victor Frankl; there are the Gestalt therapists who look to Frederick S. Perls; there are the bioenergeticists and Rolfers whose body exercises are based in the works of Alexander Lowen and Ida Rolfe; and the scream therapists who draw from the clinical work and writings of Arthur Janov.

There are sensitivity training groups, which come from the encounter movement based to a large extent in the Esalen Institute in Big Sur, California. It was at the Esalen Institute that many of the newer therapies were developed. The Institute is run as an open community, a place where people may go to delve deeper into themselves and their relationships with other people, and where newer therapists may bring their methods and ideas. Esalen—named for the Indian tribe who once lived in the area—has seen the growth of Frederick Perls's Gestalt therapy, Lowen's and Rolfe's body therapies, and a number of encounter group methods. Growth centers such as the one in Big Sur have sprung up around the country since Esalen's birth in 1962.

A thorough investigation of all the new therapeutic methods would, of course, be the subject of another book; but because there is growing evidence that some of these third force therapies are, indeed, helping people to deal effectively with their emotional lives, I would be remiss in not including at least some of them in a book of this kind.

I have spoken with therapists who are practicing treatment methods that I feel are representative of recent trends, and which are available in ongoing programs. Many of these newer approaches are being incorporated into public and private facilities, and many are being used as adjuncts to the more traditional psychotherapies.

A rapidly changing world demands the sort of reevaluation that psychotherapists have been making. Quite possibly, the newer therapies may offer hope for people who are in psychological pain—and do so more quickly in the future than has been the case in the past.

CHAPTER TWENTY-THREE

Scream Therapy:
The Casriel Institute of Group Dynamics
Daniel Casriel, M.D.

Dr. Casriel founded and directs the Casriel Institute of Group Dynamics, which is active in New York City. A 1949 graduate of the University of Cincinnati, College of Medicine, and a former president of the American Society of Psychoanalytic Physicians, Dr. Casriel was the first psychiatrist in the country to introduce encounter group therapy into private practice. His current innovative work with scream therapy for both severely and mildly disturbed patients puts him in the forefront of doctors practicing the newer therapies.

The therapeutic aspect of the Casriel Institute is called AREBA (Accelerated Re-education of Emotional Behavior and Attitudes) and enlists the use of New Identity Scream Therapy,[1] a treatment method, which he himself developed: "It is an evolutionary outgrowth of an amalgamation of my psychoanalytic training and experience, and my

---

1. Dr. Daniel Casriel's book, *A Scream Away from Happiness* (New York: Grossett & Dunlap) 1972, details this new approach to scream therapy.

experience with encounter groups such as Synanon[2] and later, Daytop."[3] (Dr. Casriel started Daytop and was its medical psychiatric supervisor for seven years.)

"The process has been evolving gradually," says Dr. Casriel of his new work. "In March, 1970, I started AREBA—my third generation of therapeutic communities (after Synanon and Daytop). This new therapeutic community is based on a treatment concept, which we term Accelerated Re-education of Emotional Behavior and Attitudes, and uses my scream therapy techniques."

His scream therapy techniques are intended to "enable a person to experience his full feelings and to use these newfound feelings as a tool to re-educate his attitudes and behavior."

At the Casriel Institute a person can receive treatment through a once-a-week consultation, either privately or within a group, or he may become part of the residential facility—actually living within the Institute. "AREBA residents," explains Dr. Casriel, "include several categories. There are people who need total rehabilitation. The ex-addict is a good example: someone who never functioned constructively in life. They spend a year in intensive educative treatment.

"A second group are those who need a reeducation more than an education. These are problem people who have functioned in the past, but who have broken down; generally, this group is older than the first group. They are either the severe alcoholic or severely depressed or anxiety-ridden persons.

"We also have day care and night care at AREBA. A third group who enter the therapeutic process need intensive treatment; these people spend perhaps eight to nine hours a day at work, school, or home, and live in the AREBA facility for the rest of the day. This sort of arrangement enables a resident to remove himself from a possibly pathologi-

2. Synanon began in 1958 when a group of ex-alcoholics began meeting regularly for "talk sessions." The group grew to include drug addicts, who were able to give up their habits with the help of the group. Synanon today is a residential community in Ocean Beach, California, and is open to both addicts and nonaddicts who can benefit from the dynamic, often heated group interaction. The books, *Synanon: The Tunnel Back*, by Lewis Yablonsky (New York: Macmillan), 1965, and *So Fair a House*, by Dr. Daniel Casriel (Englewood Cliffs, N.J.: Prentice-Hall), 1963, give the complete story of Synanon's development.

3. Daytop Village and Daytop Lodge are also self-help therapeutic communities, based on the same lines as Synanon. Dr. Daniel Casriel's book, *Daytop: Three Addicts and Their Cure*, written with Grover Amis (New York: Hill and Wang), 1971, is considered the definitive work on the theory of treatment for addicts in such a community setting.

cal environment and freely go into a therapeutic environment for the greater parts of the day during their period of treatment here. Some of the people in this category come in for the day, returning home at night; others come in to stay at night, going to work or school during the day.

"In addition to these groups of residents, we have several hundred at the Institute who come in for a three-hour group, and are not residents."

Most of the people who receive either resident, partial resident, or outpatient therapy through the Casriel Institute are, of course, from the metropolitan New York area; however, people from all over the country receive treatment and training here. "There are people from Europe," Dr. Casriel told me. "Italian, French, Dutch, Spanish, and German psychiatrists have been trained here; and patients from Venezuela, the Virgin Islands, France, Israel, Australia, and Canada have received treatment here, as well as people from around the United States."

The majority of residents at the Institute are from middle- and upper-middle-class backgrounds. As Dr. Casriel explains, "AREBA is not a 'mental hospital,' and therefore has not been eligible for third-party payment such as Blue Cross and Blue Shield. It's for people who can afford it. Although the cost here is about a third of the cost of a hospital per day, a year's treatment for a full-time resident can run to about twenty thousand dollars."

A large number of people who attend AREBA have been in hospitals and emerged from their hospitalization in need of further treatment; people come to AREBA from an enormous variety of previous experiences: "I guess that many of the people who have been here for a prolonged period have had previous institutionalizations in hospitals, jails, fancy boarding schools, which were a little bit more than a cross between a jail and a hospital. People here have had all kinds of previous treatments, from shock therapy to drug therapy to insulin treatment, from imprisonment to changing their environment with a trip to Europe or wherever a family could send someone.

"We can help many of these people here. Of those who come in for prolonged, intensive therapy/study, we graduate about seventy percent. When they leave, they're healthier than the average person on the outside: Not *as good as*, but *healthier*, able to function better than the average. The AREBA graduate functions better, vocationally and socially, than other members of his peer group."

There are fifty-six beds available at the Institute for permanent residents. Residents must sign in and out, but they can leave at any time they want to. Dr. Casriel emphasizes that this is not a "locked" hospital situation. As a matter of fact, he says, "It's harder to get back in; a lot of these youngsters have broken out of all kinds of hospitals and jails. Here, you don't have to break out, you can just leave, and it's difficult to get back *in*."

With a standard treatment period that extends over about one year, Dr. Casriel estimates that 30 percent of the patients receiving this treatment leave before they are ready to "graduate." He divides this group roughly into three categories: 10 percent who have to be discharged because they are too ill or beyond the Institute's means for help; 10 percent who simply refuse to cooperate, or who leave against advice; and 10 percent who have to be withdrawn because their families cannot financially maintain a resident for the entire year.

One of the unique aspects of AREBA is its adaptability to a variety of emotional problems—problems that range over the entire spectrum of human dealings. "Upstairs, in the resident section of AREBA, are people with more serious problems, both drug- and nondrug-related. Downstairs at the Institute are people who face the more common personal problems—close human relationships, marital problems, work-related problems, feelings of depression and anxiety."

A classical situation from which an AREBA patient comes would be a family in which, as Dr. Casriel explained to me, "the father is very alienated—turned off. He feels his only role is to provide money and nothing else. That's exactly what he provides—money and nothing else. The mother becomes depressed, and either overprotective of the child or distant and hostile toward him. The child becomes a symptom of the bad relationship between the parents. If the child takes drugs, the parents cannot possibly understand why he has turned to dope. If the child is old enough, we have to get him out of that family environment so he doesn't go back. If he's young and he has to go back to his family, then we try to engage the family in treatment; if the family refuses to engage in treatment, and the child is too young to be on his own, then we suggest residential schooling away from the family. To put a child back into a pathological situation is going to bring back the old pathology."

During my interview with Daniel Casriel, he addressed my questions about his therapeutic methods and the process of therapy at the Institute; the following is based on that conversation.

Daniel H. Casriel, M.D.

The psychiatric conditions of the residents, or group members, of AREBA are more a maladaptation to life than "mental illness." I think of "mental illness" as "chemical illness": organic schizophrenia, organic depression. AREBA treats the nonmetabolically ill person through an educational process. In the program we've now adapted, we reeducate residents emotionally, behaviorally, and attitudinally.

We do not use shock treatment, nor do we use drugs in therapy. Occasionally, when a person first arrives as a resident, he or she may need sleeping pills, and in that case they will receive them, but only initially and not as a part of treatment. Otherwise, there are no ups, no downs.

Residents live in a dormitory situation, rather than in individual rooms; there is no isolation, no way to withdraw.

The nature of the therapeutic process at the Institute is entirely psychological, aimed at getting a person's feelings out very quickly. AREBA's New Identity Scream Therapy differs from Arthur Janov's scream therapy and treatment process in significant ways.[4]

Briefly, Janov's treatment is a one-to-one process that involves isolating a person from the world, in a motel room, for instance. He sees the patient once a day for a few hours, and in this time the patient expresses his thinking and feelings. Janov encourages the patient to scream; the purpose is to get the patient to experience his "primal pool of pain"— that reservoir of early emotional deprivation.

Janov feels that when a person has arrived at this level, discharging the primal pool of pain, the treatment is complete. At some point during this period of intensive one-to-one therapy, he puts his patients in a room of other people who are also in the process of primal therapy. But this is not actually a group; rather, it is a situation wherein each person does his own "thing" separately. Therapists go from person to person, helping each individual get to what Janov terms "primal feelings."

I am often asked how our type of process compares with bioenergetics, as established by Dr. Alexander Lowen.[5] Lowen treats his patients on an even more one-to-one analytical basis than does Janov. Like us, he tries to get his patients to *feel* as soon as possible, but unlike us he does not use the scream method: he encourages deep breathing, or actually inflicting physical pain to get at the feelings.

I differ from Janov and Lowen in that I primarily use a group pro-

4. Arthur Janov's primal scream therapy created a revolution among psychiatric circles when he published *The Primal Scream* (New York: G.P. Putnam's Son), 1970.

5. Alexander Lowen began much of what we now call "body-oriented" therapy; among his writings that detail his concepts of bioenergetics are: *The Betrayal of the Body* (New York: Macmillan), 1969, and *Language of the Body* (New York: Collier), 1971.

cess. I never isolate people as they do, and even at the first stage of getting at the feelings, people here are in a group. I find it much more efficient and effective. First of all, in a group situation people are less afraid of their feelings; they see other people expressing themselves and become aware that if they get angry, they don't go crazy; if they let their pain out, they won't die; if they show their fear, they won't be helpless.

The first steps in my treatment process involve using the scream as a vehicle for getting at the feelings. We encourage the person to say something louder and louder until he's screaming it. Very often, after screams come out, emotions will come out.

Not every scream ends up in a feeling, but the scream is an exercise to get at the feelings; once a person gets at his emotions, he doesn't have to scream. It works very quickly.

Actually, we teach group members the logic of emotions. It's not the same logic as you would associate with the intellect, but one has to understand the logic of emotions or he is going to be in trouble. For example, emotions don't know right from wrong, good from bad, ethical from unethical, moral from immoral. Emotions distinguish only between pain and pleasure—that is all they know. You go to things that give you pleasure and you try to avoid things that give you pain. You'll love things from which you anticipate pleasure; but you'll avoid things that are painful, with a running fear or a withdrawal fear, or with fighting, anger, a coiled wire ready to spring combatted anger.

These are the emotions we try to deal with: pain and pleasure, fear, love, and anger.

I do not mention such emotions as depression, shame, or guilt here, because these are secondary emotions. Depression is not an emotion; it is a symptom of an underlying feeling, an inability to express pain or anger, or an inability to express a need. When basic emotions are fully expressed, a person no longer feels depressed.

Consequently, I can frequently break through a severe depression in one group. As soon as the pain is out, or the anger is out, or the need is out, the depression ends. It's as if you have a spear in your belly; when you pull it out, it hurts. But once you get it out, you feel better and start to see that you're going to live.

We do not take group members through an extended period before they reach the point where they can scream. Rather, we simply explain the technique to them, teaching them how to do it: if you have a feeling, say it. Say it louder and louder and louder. The scream will come, then the feeling, and with it a feeling of strength, a certain self-dignity, a feeling of well-being.

The groups at AREBA are very different from the type of group experience known as an encounter group. The encounter group is a provocative, hostile interchange, but my groups are involved in a different process; they are much more introspective in getting at their feelings. Occasionally, group members will confront each other, but much of the time is spent getting at one's own introspective feelings and learning to understand those feelings, to express them, and to share them. Your emotional needs cannot be met if you cannot express them to others; the nonverbal attitude of "guess what I'm feeling" will never get a person's needs fulfilled. We teach a person how to share his feelings.

Emotions are for communication. The only reason we have them is to help other people to understand us. Most of us have been taught to repress our emotions, and therefore we lose three-quarters of our ability to communicate with people on significant human levels. For instance, it is a simple matter to communicate something like, "Pass the salt," or, "Turn on the radio." Emotions are not a part of that type of message. But as for your personal human needs, you can't effectively communicate them without feelings. And this is the basis of almost everyone's problems.

The process of getting to those feelings, as I've said, works very quickly. Group members who are in the process of dealing with their emotions either sit in chairs or lie back on mats, depending upon whether they are dealing with current situations or with historical feelings. You feel differently sitting up than you do lying down; when a person is sitting on a chair, one thing happens; when one is lying down, something altogether different is going on. When you lie down, you're in a more helpless position, and a lot of feelings, especially historical feelings, can come out. When you are sitting up and facing people, you are more apt to deal with the emotions of the current situation. Both are necessary, and both are used in the group very effectively.

When a group member gets to those feelings, especially the feelings that have a deep root in his or her past, that person is going to be faced with a whole kaleidoscope of his or her history. At the end of it all, the person will give us the core of his or her awareness that is coming out with the screams.

When this happens we talk to the person; at the point where a person is screaming out all these emotions, we can begin the process of educating or reeducating someone toward changing attitudes and behavior. You can't change feelings—the pure feelings of fear, anger, love, pain, and pleasure. But you can change the attitudes and behavior, which are fed by, and give rise to, peripheral feelings.

Why can a person learn new attitudes and behavior at the point when the screams are coming out? We have no conclusive proof yet, but very important physiological research that we've done points to chemical changes in a person's body that go on as a result of those emotions expressed in a scream. There are changes in the urine and trace changes in the blood. There seems to be what is called a steroid change: a type of chemical, secreted by the adrenal glands, can be measured in the blood; it is relatively unstable, that is, it is quickly utilized by the body and disappears from the blood. In other words, these substances in the body break down very quickly during this highly emotional scream; they break down within a few hours. The people who are conducting these studies hypothesize that the unstable chemical in the blood that is liberated by the scream may unlock programming in the brain and help change the way a person thinks and learns.

If this is true (I'm not saying at this time that it is, of course), then the whole nature of education will be changed. Instead of teaching a child that one and one is two in the way we all learned it, the child would scream that lesson out. He would learn it differently, more quickly and more effectively. If a child responds emotionally, he'll learn. Any mother who has ever screamed at her child knows this: the child learns whatever it is she's screaming (and hence, he's responding to her emotionally) very quickly. There seems, then, to be a direct relationship between education and emotionality. And that is an entirely new aspect, which I never anticipated when I began this type of therapy.

Of course, in many children's educational programs today, educators are discovering that for the children to concentrate, they have to be emotionally involved in some way. What we do here is to get the utmost emotional involvement, and we've found that a person can learn or relearn behavior and attitudes toward situations that he could not handle previously.

Again, we cannot prevent pain or fear or anger from imposing themselves on a person in his life pursuit of pleasure. But we do teach people how to avoid pain if possible. And we teach them how to deal with unavoidable painful situations most effectively and most efficiently in order to minimize the pain and maximize the pleasure.

To illustrate with a very simple analogy: if you go through life crossing streets with your eyes closed, you're going to keep getting hit by cars, and your life is going to be full of pain simply because you have your eyes closed. You can learn the simple fact that by opening your eyes a lot of pain can be avoided—you avoid getting hit by a car when you see it coming. Many people go through life, symbolically, with their eyes closed.

Carrying this analogy further: now that you've learned to open your eyes so you can avoid getting hit by a car, the possibility is still there that one day, through no fault of your own, a car might come out of nowhere, aimed right at you. Now you have to have learned more than just to open your eyes to avoid pain. You have to know whether to stand still, to run to the corner where you started from, or to take a chance and run to the corner where you were originally headed.

The same is true with life in general, with human relationships. Through no fault of your own, and even though you are taking all the precautions you've learned in order to avoid whatever pained you in the past, that type of experience can suddenly appear again. And you have at least to have an idea of alternative ways of dealing with it.

So, we teach people how to avoid potentially dangerous situations, as well as what to do if, because of circumstances they cannot control, they are suddenly confronted by a painful situation.

We help people to restructure the patterns of their lives so that, when they leave us, they have a much better chance to stay healthy. Actually, *happy* is a better word. If they tend to fall back, they now know what it is that has pushed them back—they know what causes their feelings.

We had one young woman who had been in and out of hospitals for years because of self-mutilation. She didn't simply cut her wrists—she inflicted serious wounds on herself, some requiring surgery. After experiencing the scream therapy and learning how to avoid pain, she began to change considerably. Today, this woman is healthy; she is a happy person who has learned to deal with her feelings and to express them in nondestructive ways.

Not long ago a man arrived who was on his way to a hospital for shock treatment; I interviewed him and put him in a group. This man is a professor, married, and the father of five children. He was depressed, and for his first two days at AREBA, he was quite upset. Then, I put him in a nine-hour group, and the following day he was no longer suffering from depression; he'd started to express his real feelings and needs. This was the first time in twenty years that he'd been on a sabbatical, and it was the first time in twenty years that he'd become depressed, because he felt guilty about not working. He is an overconscientious person, overreligious, guilt-ridden, and he felt that he was not entitled to the freedom that his sabbatical gave him. These feelings were let out to me and the other therapists here, and today this man is a different person.

Over all, we've had about seventy graduates; two have slipped— they've stumbled. We've straightened them out and they do okay. The only people on whom we keep long-term records are former drug addicts with severe problems.

Former group members, when they leave, change their lifestyles, socially, vocationally, professionally. As I have pointed out, they leave their families if they are old enough; if they're young, we have a family change, too. Otherwise, we encourage the young person to move someplace else—out of town. Divorces often occur in this lifestyle change. People know what to do with their feelings; they know that if they're starting to feel upset, something is happening, and their feelings aren't sick, but an expression that something is going on—a person's body is telling him that its needs are not being met. The ability to get out your pain or anger isn't available in certain circumstances, or the ability to have your needs of love, closeness, or warmth met is not possible in a given situation. Some people learn very quickly that they are not sick.

Group members stop treatment when they are doing well and feeling well. If, after a week or a month or a year, they feel that something is wrong, they can return. I don't think that when this happens it is an indication of failure in the treatment process; part of the process is the idea that if you are feeling bad, you have to see what it is that is making you feel that way; if this involves returning here for additional treatment, one should do so without seeing it as failure.

There are certain aspects of life that just are not dealt with when a person is first in treatment, because he is not in that aspect of life at the time. For instance, let us say that someone comes here for treatment because she is fearful of closed spaces; she is claustrophobic. She goes through treatment and learns how to deal with and understand the symbolic meaning of her phobia: those feelings of fear in close spaces were symbolic of early fears in her childhood. She faces the fears gradually and resolves her phobia. Then, two years after she has left, she forms a relationship with someone and her feelings of being closed in—trapped —begin to surface again. Though she may now have some understanding, she cannot deal effectively with the new situation. Her new feelings of being pressured or closed in may not cause fear, but they may cause her to turn off her positive feelings toward her lover; she stops feeling love for him. Her inability to feel love for her lover is really due to the same symptom as her previous phobia, but now it is a situation with a person rather than a space situation. But her feelings still represent those earlier fears of being controlled. If she returns to AREBA, we deal with this new aspect of her life, which we hadn't dealt with before because it hadn't existed. We extend the learning process to a higher level of social interaction.

We are now opening new branches of AREBA; in addition, this type of treatment process is being utilized in seven different countries. I estimate that 10,000 people a week are being treated along the lines we developed and practice here. I hope that it will filter into some public institutions, and that eventually, this sort of identity process appears in the school system. I envision it as a course in communications—two additional R's to add to the educators' "three R's"—Relationship and Responsibility.

It is time to stop thinking of emotional depression and anxiety as sicknesses, and to see them as adaptation problems that can be altered through emotional, behavioral, and attitudinal reeducation.

CHAPTER TWENTY-FOUR

Esalen-oriented Therapy
Dan Sullivan

Dan Sullivan, a Gestalt psychotherapist, trained in existential therapy with R.D. Laing in London, and later studied the humanist therapies at Esalen Institute in Big Sur, California: Gestalt, bioenergetics, and Rolfing. He has led weekend Gestalt groups at Esalen and other growth centers, and he presently practices individual and group therapy through the program of the Princeton Gestalt Center, of which he is the director.

In his practice, Mr. Sullivan employs both Gestalt therapy and his own methods, which grew out of his experiences with Laing and the Esalen Institute, and his background in existential philosophy.

He is currently completing his Ph.D. in philosophy at the Sorbonne under Paul Ricoeur and finishing his book, *Eros and the Ironic Vision*.

In this selection, which is based on my interview with him, Mr. Sullivan discusses his experiences with the Esalen Institute and some of the theoretical views on which he bases his therapeutic approach.

Dan Sullivan

Before I began practicing therapy I was in existential analysis for three years, chiefly with R.D. Laing in London. Mainly as a consequence of his recommendation, I went to the Esalen Institute in Big Sur, California, to explore "body therapies" and the areas that Laing himself felt as an analyst he was not sufficiently versed in. For the past seven years I have had my own practice, which has been influenced by Laingian thought, Esalen techniques, and Eastern spirituality.

Laing saw that for therapy to be truly effective, more was needed than the traditional verbal analysis. At Esalen, the emphasis was on *affect*, on getting one's emotions out, which seemed at once to me to be infinitely deeper than other approaches to therapy, even existential analysis. To speak very superficially, the therapist at Esalen pays attention to body language and to whatever discrepancies there may be between what you are saying and what your body is saying. For example, if you are speaking very calmly, but your jaw is tense, your fingers fidgeting, or your eyes are not focusing on anyone, the Gestalt therapist will ask you to concentrate on your eyes, your tight throat, your fingers; to go into them, *becoming* and expressing your eyes or your tight throat or your tears, staying with whatever parts of your body are belying what you are saying with words.

You are then asked, possibly, to verbalize what your eyes feel, to enter into conversation with your throat, until the affects—the tears and anger—erupt, and you see every part of your body as a reservoir of you. Your tears *are* you, as much as your intellect or dreams are you. The awareness, responsibility, and joy that may occur here are tremendous.

Esalen uses several approaches, most of them involving groups. When I was studying there, the method I just described took place usually in a group of twenty to twenty-five people, and was enhanced enormously by the group action. But many Esalen leaders have incorporated the ideas of Gestalt group work into other types of therapy. Bob Hall, for instance, a psychiatrist-turned-Gestaltist with whom I often worked, has gone into diet, Rolfing, and meditation to supplement his therapy. Another great therapist, Betty Fuller, has gone into the EST (Erhard Seminar Training) program.

Eastern religion has been very influential, generally, at Esalen; Reichian theory, bioenergentics, and Rolfing are other major influences.

Laing had talked about negative energy becoming trapped in the body, but he had no tool for working it out. The developments of bioenergetics and Rolfing now seem to be effective first-step therapeutic methods for releasing these energies, touching specific memories otherwise lost in the body, and eliciting acknowledgment in the patient for his feelings. I will not dwell on the techniques here as I do not practice them myself, but briefly, they involve deep muscle massage to get rid of physically blocked knots of negative energy in the chest, legs, stomach, throat, shoulders, and other sensitive parts of the body; bioenergetics includes rapid-breathing, gymnastic exercise, and deep contortions of the body, as well as massage, to work out body tensions.

In my own practice, I have incorporated what I learned with Laing and some of the Esalen approaches to psychotherapy. I have had Esalen-trained masseurs who are qualified to give certain massage techniques work with me if it is advisable for a patient. And if I see a patient whom I believe would benefit from Rolfing, I will recommend it, although it is difficult to find good, qualified Rolfers. Cognitive awareness is necessary in psychotherapy, certainly, but a therapist must work on many fronts, always checking and challenging his own assumptions. A person's body as well as his mind is tortured, and if one is to be fully relieved, the other must be, too. Therapy now is seldom complete and often replaces one repression with another.

Another element to psychotherapy, which complements the work with an individual's mind and body, could be called the social or interpersonal element. Just as the structured morality of Freud's Viennese society profoundly influenced his theory, especially his views of woman's sexuality, so modern therapists are influenced by their society and often fail to question their experience or to push beyond it. The social structure and its biases determine, in a sense, what sort of therapy a psychotherapist will practice and what sort of goals he will set for his patients.

While most contemporary psychotherapists recognize the sexual influence of society on their therapy and goals, I don't think that many acknowledge their own individual sex history and the influence their dealing with Eros has in their practices. This is especially critical in the area of their *wives'* (if they're men) liberation or lack of it. Any therapist who colludes with woman's exploitation in his personal life must inevitably resent the sexual "nigger" he has helped to create. His consequent "ironic" attitude to his own bedroom and its occupant must then pass on to his theory and to his patients. Freud's own wife and his misogyny, and his elaborate theory of the impersonal "id," are causally related. In the same way, the therapist who personally colludes at home in woman's dehumanization will naturally have disenchanted and depersonalized theories and attitudes about the importance of intimate interpersonal relationships for his patients.

There is now a broad frontal attack in many contemporary therapies against a dependency on the other for one's own "ground." I suspect a very subtle and nearly universal self-repression stemming from misogyny is working here. It is almost inevitable for a therapist to adopt a tempered, semi-Buddhistic approach in his therapy to love, since he is always dealing with his own repressions of Erotic hope. His own sexual experience with women generally makes the therapist aim at some sort of independence, invulnerability, and detachment for his patient, guiding him or her away from any sort of ontological dependence on another person.

My suspicion of this was reaffirmed when I was at Esalen. Here I saw a lot of people talking about their smashed personal lives, their romances that had eroded disastrously. Usually, I heard men talking about how their wives were not enough, and women talking about being left by their husbands or lovers. There was a lot of this kind of personal anguish: people were in pain from the failures of their relationships. The Gestalt therapist, however, instead of following them into their grief, would try to interpret a person's broken interpersonal life as a reflection of something purely intrapsychic, something *inside the individual*— something that had been going on for a long time. He would telescope the person's grief into an individual mess-up that was only being mirrored in the smashed relationship; although this is often obviously the case, more is happening than the individual's intrapsychic problems.

It was at this point, when I saw what I thought was a distortion of what people were saying and what their therapists were saying, that I broke from Perls and most Eastern-oriented therapists. I had begun to see a pattern, not only in therapy, but in religion as well, wherein the goal becomes one of inoculating a person against any kind of emotional need for another person, primarily against sexual need or dependence— passion, desire, anything that comes near the cutting edge of vulnerable personal relationships. The paradoxical result at Esalen (at least, when I was there) was a lot of people going onto a celibate track, whittling away at their former dependencies with a machete.

The insight, however, that puts people into this celibacy is valid: many of our dependencies upon a loved one—man or woman—are symptomatic of our own noisy emptiness, things that we are not willing to fulfill and satisfy within ourselves. In other words, if I fall in love with someone who has a great sense of humor, it may be at least partially because I'm not willing to risk being funny myself, to fulfill that part of myself for myself. But it also seems to me that you can appreciate a rare quality or an extraordinary degree of a gift in someone else; it may be a quality or gift that you already possess in yourself, so it can be an appreciation without that attempt to "fill in" your own holes. It's possible to fall in love with someone without the neurotic needs, without trying to make up for what's missing in yourself. And if your relationship breaks up, you must be ready to admit feeling you have lost a lot of "you." This, of course, is a basic problem in any philosophy or psychology, the *reality* of the object, the other, the outside.

It's this sort of schizophrenic gap that I try to work out with a patient, allowing him first to find his own space, and then to acknowledge his need for a beloved.

I allow patients to talk about their broken hearts, to accept their own estimate of what love may mean to them. I use the ideas inherent to feminism, and try to get both men and women into the feminist awareness. For it is certain to me that only *equal* partners can make satisfying, enjoyable human sex possible. This approach is, of course, Gestalt in the fullest sense, including the "irrational" heart.

I try to allow patients to make a distinction between those parts of their lives that they could and really should be fulfilling themselves, and those parts that they are never going to fulfill for themselves. I believe that human beings need other people and that many aspects of life and self cannot be developed alone. Masturbation will never take the place of orgasm with a loved one; God will never take the place of a good intimate relationship with a loved one. One may believe in God, but he or she cannot pin Him or Her down here on earth and call that a love object. Contemporary gurus and classic mystics would deny this, but only because they gave up their bodies.

I try to help people get in touch with where they are, with what they are experiencing; this involves guiding people, though not directing them, toward understanding that the grounds of their neuroses are tied up with being out of touch with their feeling, with running away from pain or fear or whatever it is, just running away from the experience. If you can be in touch with your now-experience, especially your emotions, you can get your self-roots firmly planted. But one must realize that his or her biggest emotion is in the heart, and that is where the greatest repression and denial is.

Again, this depends on straightening out a person's messed up sexuality—messed up largely through social conditioning. It depends on recognizing and working toward *total* equality between men and women. I think that it is possible for people to have life partnerships, but first, equality in the home must be worked out. Until you have that kind of complete equality, you can't even talk about having human sexuality. Most of the world has never known human sex because of that lack. All books on sexuality are based from the start on an inequality that largely precludes spiritual and intellectual coexistence and friendship.

Normally in my practice, I see patients in individual therapy for six months to a year. I will employ some Gestalt therapy, some analytic psychotherapy, and with the help of a qualified masseur, I may use some bioenergetic therapy. In my groups, the type of therapy will be much different; the group is an encounter format, and the members work in a context of Gestalt therapy. The group experience, as Perls saw, is much quicker and often deeper than the individual experience.

My patients run the gamut from people in search of developing their true human potential, to deeply distressed, sometimes suicidal people. We often see people who are violent toward others, but violence is more often inner-directed.

Whether patients are turned inward or outward, my experience is that their problems come from not being in touch with themselves in the *now*. They are not in their bodies—in their eyes, their throats, their muscles, not even in their words. They are not in the living moment. They are not experiencing what is happening to them, because they spend all their time in some kind of historical search, trying to go back to find out why they are the way they are. Or, they are spending their time projecting their problems on the outside world, playing guessing games with the future. Fritz Perls used to say that people dwell on the future in order not to have it, in order that nothing will happen. They stay in the tomorrow in order to avoid having tomorrow. They are simply out of touch. Their starting point in therapy is to accept this hiding-from-self about themselves; that is enough to start.

On rare occasions I will refer a severely depressed patient to an M.D. for antidepressant medications. But unless a patient is in immediate and real danger of harming himself, I think that it's better for him to stay with the depression rather than escaping from it. Most drugs, by numbing you, are helping to defeat your sense of being, undermining your bedrock source of responsibility.

In therapy, I do not go directly into the origins and the "whys" of a patient's problem: I don't say, "This happened—*why* did it happen?" I rarely ask *why* in Gestalt therapy—"Why are you doing this," or: "Why were you the underdog?" The therapist lets the patient just be the underdog, and his own growing awareness that one of his "rackets" is to be the underdog will eventually change his state.

As an example of a dramatic change in Gestalt therapy: I had a patient who was left-handed. His father had tried to "cure" his left-handedness, tried to force him to be right-handed. When this patient talked, he did a lot of wringing and battling with his hands. When he spoke about his father, his hands would tangle with each other. I let him have his left hand-right hand battle, identifying and exposing himself (left hand) versus his father (right hand), and then let him symbolically pound his father to death with his left hand, the focus of his own loss and torture. After that, his entire personality underwent a dramatic change, which has been permanent. He, exorcised himself of his father's "ghost," which was a mixture of love and hate, approval and despair. But the physical outburst was an essential ingredient to his cure. The symbolic killing of a parent in such physical outbursts can lead to the deeper layers, past anger, hate, grief, to, possibly, forgiveness from the gut.

I do not set a goal in therapy that says, "This is the promised land, over there." It doesn't exist. The promised land, in a sense, is right here and now. Many nonhumanistic psychotherapists try to divert the patient's attention to some kind of future goal—coping with one's work or household—but I don't think that there is a goal, except what you are right now. If you are really in touch with where and how you are right now, the awareness is going to make you richer and stronger, and it will lead you to incredible joy in the moment.

But, as I said, the present moment includes your heart's ongoing desire for a sexual union of equals that will create a lasting, ecstatic intimacy transcending inner division. Therapy must begin by noticing this human intentionality and acknowledging, rather than repressing, it in bogus spiritualities and self-autonomy.

CHAPTER TWENTY-FIVE

Transactional Analysis and Gestalt Therapy
Richard Abell, M.D.

According to the needs of his patients, Dr. Richard Abell employs transactional analysis, Gestalt therapy, psychoanalysis, and nonverbal communication methods in his private practice. He was certified as a psychoanalyst by the William Alanson White Psychoanalytic Institute in New York, and as a transactional analyst by the International Transactional Analysis Association; he has studied a variety of therapeutic approaches over twenty-five years, including Gestalt therapy, and has been prominent in the field of group therapy for some twenty years. He is presently Director of the Transactional Analysis Institute of New York and Connecticut.

Of his approach to therapy, Dr. Abell told me during our interview: "I use my therapeutic methods eclectically but consistently, and where they are indicated. Transactional analysis concepts might be appropriate at one place, Gestalt therapy at another.

Dr. Abell sees patients both individually and in groups. In addition to his New York City office practice, he conducts one-day and weekend marathons and five-day workshops in Connecticut.

In this adaptation of my interview with him, Dr. Abell addresses my questions about his practice and the ways in which he combines his different therapeutic approaches.

Richard G. Abell, M.D., Ph.D.

The majority of my patients are working to improve their potential and to use their abilities better. Generally speaking, they enter therapy because they're unhappy, displeased with something in their lives, and want to make a qualitative change. The basic difficulties that make people dissatisfied or unhappy are based on early responses to negative ways in which they were treated by their parents or other key figures in their early lives. They respond by making an internal decision to be "adapted" as a child—that is, to do what their parents want—and they continue this syndrome into adulthood, where it doesn't work, doesn't satisfy them. They want to learn how to be autonomous.

In working with patients, I employ the methods of transactional analysis, Gestalt therapy, psychoanalysis, and nonverbal communication. The last technique involves, of course, nonverbal methods of communicating—sound, sight, touch. The sound of the voice is often a better indicator of what is going on than words. The appearance (physical appearance) of the face and body are valuable indicators of corresponding psychological states. Feelings are often better communicated by touch than by words. Nevertheless, words are crucial.

I reeducate my patients; most patients lack information that is crucial to their welfare, and I supply such basic information to them—and the framework that makes it possible for them to understand and integrate it. I explain the concepts of transactional analysis, Gestalt therapy, psychoanalysis, and nonverbal communication, and as I work with patients it becomes clear to them how they can apply these concepts to themselves, at first with my help and later independently.

Transactional analysis is an excellent method for facilitating intellectual orientation. The concepts are simple, direct, and summarized by certain key words. These are: ego states, transactions, injunctions, counterinjunctions, early decision, script, games, rackets, stamps, strokes, contracts, redecision, and time-structuring. There are others, but these are the key ones. If a patient learns these key words and their meanings, he is in possession of important information with which to help himself.

The same is true for Gestalt therapy, with its emphasis on the "here and now," and psychoanalysis, which stresses the importance of "transference" reactions and their resolution by "working through."

None of these methods need to exclude the other, and there is today, among many forward-looking therapists, a desire to incorporate what is best in other methods than their own specialties. This bodes well for them and for the future of psychotherapy.

Transactional analysis—TA—is a method of psychotherapy based on the concept that the personality is composed of *ego states*: Parent, Adult, and Child. By understanding the *transactions* that go on between these ego states and the ego states of other people, and between the ego states within the person himself, this person learns to understand his relationships with others better and to understand himself better. He finds that his behavior often involves *games*, which are played outside his awareness, in order to structure his time and gain *strokes* (recognition), even though most of the strokes he gains are negative ones. He learns that he made *early decisions* in response to *injunctions* and *counterinjunctions* from his parents. He then makes *redecisions* about how he wants to live now—in the "here and now"—he gives up game playing as a way of getting strokes; he learns to get strokes in more constructive ways. He also gives up his *rackets*, which are the emotional feelings he had as a kid and which no longer apply to his life situation. He learns to give up collecting *brown stamps* (grudges) and using them against people.

The games patients play before they learn to give them up have the following formula: *Con plus gimmick produces response*; then there is a *switch*, a *cross-up*, and a *payoff*.

As an example, a patient of mine, a thirty-six-year-old woman, says to me: "Doctor, do you think I'm going to get better?" The *con* is what the game-player does to gain the "respondent's" interest. In this instance, she appeals to my interest in her welfare. The *gimmick* is, in this instance, my receptivity to the con. I am interested because I am her doctor, so I respond by saying, "Yes, you will, if you stay in therapy." Then she says: "What makes you think you know so much about me?" This is the *switch*, and it is a *discount* of me. That produces the *cross-up*, which is, "How did I get myself in this spot?" And this leads to the *payoff*, which is bad feelings for me. For her, the feelings may be false elation that she has put me down and feels good about it. It is a payoff which is ultimately unsatisfying.

As I said before, the game is played outside the person's awareness, and is a way of getting strokes in an undesirable way.

In his book, *Games People Play*, Eric Berne has identified an entire series of games people play and which, when you pick them up in group therapy, enable the therapist to help the person. When the games can be identified they can be gotten rid of. The importance of getting rid of them is that they never produce good feelings. I use game analysis, which, however, is only one small part of the whole therapeutic process.

I also use Gestalt therapy, which was developed by Frederick Perls.

The term *Gestalt* means configuration; a Gestalt is composed of *figure* and *ground*. As a very simple example: The ground in the Gestalt of a room is made up of the room's walls, the furniture, and the people in it, as well as where everything is in a certain relation to everything else. The figure in the Gestalt of the room is what satisfies an immediate need. If someone wants to catch a train, for instance, he looks around the room for a clock. The clock in this case is the figure, and everything else in the room is the ground. In this example, the person is looking at the clock in order to know the time. Not knowing the time is a situation we term an *open Gestalt*. When he sees what time it is then this Gestalt becomes *closed*—he has satisfied his immediate need.

As another example: A person is walking on a road on a hot day; he's thirsty. His Gestalt consists of the sky, the trees, the dusty road, himself, etc. At first there is no figure. Then he sees a spring, and because he is thirsty, the spring becomes the figure. The Gestalt is unclosed if he does not drink the water. It is closed when the person quenches his thirst.

Closing the Gestalt in Frederick Perls's sense is satisfying a need. What causes the most emotional damage to the personality is a lot of long, unclosed Gestalts relating primarily to early key figures in one's life, mainly parents.

To illustrate:

> My father did not pay much attention to me when I was a child; he was involved in astronomy, in apple trees, in violins, in anything that interested him. But *I* didn't especially interest him. I was kind of in the way. He gave me a "don't exist" message. So I had feelings of resentment toward him. I couldn't rid myself of them and they hurt.
>
> I didn't really get rid of them until I got into Gestalt therapy. What I discovered was that when I talked to my father in fantasy, I began to say things like, "I wanted you to pay more attention to me, why didn't you?" And, "All the time I was growing up, you ignored me and were more concerned with yourself and your violins and things that you were interested in. You weren't concerned with me, and I hate you for that." I yelled and screamed it out until my throat was sore. Getting out such previously repressed feelings in such an instance was closing a Gestalt; afterward I felt better.
>
> The interesting thing is that when you get the screams and yells and the anger out—sometimes facilitated by hitting pillows, for example—the love that is underneath is exposed. Then you may say, "But, you know, I love you."

Ultimately, I said goodbye to my father in a fantasized experience; he was dead then, but it didn't make any difference. You bring a person back in fantasy and say goodbye to him just as if he were alive. I went through a very deep experience, getting in contact with all the negative and then the positive things my father did for me. He was fond of sailing and had taught me to sail, but I had forgotten about that. In closing the Gestalt, I remembered. I like to sail and I have a sloop. When saying goodbye, I imagined my father and I were on the foredeck of my sailboat. When I said goodbye to him in fantasy, I broke down and cried. After that, everything was different. I never think of my father with anger or resentment anymore; now the feelings are always good. This came about by closing the Gestalt, getting the angry feelings out and uncovering the love. Then I could say goodbye to him and be free to lead my own life.

When transactional analysis is supplemented by Gestalt therapy, it produces amazing results. With Gestalt therapy, the person gets in contact with his deeper feelings and usually makes a new decision to be different. In TA this is called the "redecision." He implements this redecision with assignments to do specific things in the direction of what he wants for himself.

One of the therapeutic methods I use is the double chair technique developed by Perls, wherein I suggest to the patient that he imagine one of his parents (about whom he has strong repressed feelings) is sitting in a chair in front of him. "Tell this parent whatever you want to tell him; be whatever age you want to be, and talk in the present tense." After I have directed him in that way, the patient usually knows exactly what age he wants to be. He imagines himself at that age and says those feelings in this fantasized encounter. After he has expressed his feelings to the fantasized parent, I ask him to "play the role of that parent, *be* that parent, and reply." Then I ask him to be himself again and to answer back, and so on. In doing this, the patient gets more deeply into his feelings and releases more emotions than he otherwise would.

One of the problems with the psychoanalytic method is that patients do not get deeply enough into their emotions, since psychoanalysis is largely an intellectual "talking-about" method. Using the double chair technique, patients very quickly get deeply into their "gut" feelings, and release them with consequent relief.

Frequently, during such a fantasized encounter, the patient decides he no longer wants to behave the way he did as a child and makes a *redecision* to live his present life differently. He may say such things to a fantasized parent as, "I'm sick of you being on my back. I'm going to do what I want for *me* from now on." That is a redecision. Then I suggest that he specify ways of following through on that decision in his everyday life.

I use the methods I have described above (as well as others) in my groups to create an environment for personal growth, to bring out people's potentials. I set up circumstances in which they can be free to go through growth-promoting experiences, exercises that enable them to release their feelings about their childhood experiences—feelings of loneliness, grief, anger, feelings about having been rejected by their parents —which they have not previously expressed.

Another technique I employ for achieving this involves using five chairs for the different *ego states*: the *Adapted Child*, the *Nurturing Parent*, the *Free Child*, the *Critical Parent*, and the *Adult*. The patient moves from one chair to another as he assumes the different roles.

In an abbreviated form the interchange between the ego states must go as follows: The Adapted Child asks the Critical Parent for what he wants. The Critical Parent says he is not going to give it to him, that he is stupid, and why should he give him anything? The Adapted Child says he's upset and doesn't like it. The Critical Parent says, "Well, it's just too bad." The Adapted Child says, "I'm gonna get you, I'm gonna kill you, I'm not going to let you get away with it. How do you feel about that?" The Critical Parent says he doesn't like it very much. Is he willing to give some? Well, maybe he would give him a little freedom. How do you like that? I like it . . .

In the process of the dialogue, the patient moves from the Adapted Child, gets into the Free Child, and begins to experience some freedom and enjoyment. His Nurturing Parent says this is fine, and his Adult approves, also.

The process rests on the idea that, as an adult, a person has Parent, Adult, and Child ego states inside him. The person's Parent ego state consists of the messages given to him by the Parent ego state of his own parents when he was small. These he incorporates and remembers. Examples of such messages are: "Be perfect"; "please me"; "hurry up"; "be strong" (don't show feelings).

All those messages make up a patient's internal Parent, and make him feel that if he doesn't hurry, if he isn't strong enough, or if he isn't perfect or doesn't please others, he is no good. He becomes *adapted* and tries to do these things, but never feels he succeeds.

Other, even more powerful irrational messages come from the Irrational Child ego state of the real parent and go to the Child ego state of the child. These messages are termed *injunctions*, or *stoppers*; an example of such a message is "don't exist." The parent usually gives such a message indirectly, for example, by saying something like, "If it weren't for you, I'd be an opera singer." This gives the child the feeling that he's standing in his parent's way; this "don't exist" message is given outside of the parent's awareness, but it produces in the child the feeling that he shouldn't be alive, and it enters into his life *script* as: "I'll show you I deserve to be alive if it kills me." His response is to work, work, work, so his parents will see how good he is. But the parents don't see this and he may end up a suicide unless the pattern is interrupted, because the goal is unattainable and simply leads to more frustration.

Another injunction is "don't be you—be my fantasy." Another is "don't grow up—let me do those things for you, I know better." Another is "don't belong." The person who receives such an injunction feels he doesn't belong in the family, or any other group, for that matter. Another injunction is "don't show your feelings," and, even worse, "don't have your feelings," where you are not only *not* allowed to show feelings, you can't even *have* them. For instance, a child falls and hurts his knee and his mother tells him, "Oh, that doesn't hurt." And he learns not to trust his own feelings. After a while, with many such repetitions in various ways, he no longer knows what his feelings are.

"Don't make any demands." "Don't think." "Don't be spontaneous." "Don't enjoy." These are other messages that produce people's life scripts. With a "don't be sane" message (well, you are just like your Uncle Frank who was in a state hospital since he was twenty), the child accepts the idea that he is just like his Uncle Frank, and that he's going to be insane. And he may become insane: That's his life script.

Usually the child responds to the injunctions by following them. He does this for fear of not being taken care of and not being *stroked* (recognized) if he doesn't. He adapts himself, again, to the parents' demands. The adapted person is always overconcerned about the other person: If I'm adapted, I can't be myself with you, because I'm afraid I won't please you. The feeling of the adapted child is that if he doesn't please others, he can't survive. His position makes his life very uncomfortable.

The double chair fantasy technique is one way to help a person out of his uncomfortable position by facilitating the expression of feeling toward key figures. It works very well, but needs to be supplemented by other methods. The person has to see how he got to be adapted, and he needs to make a redecision about being autonomous. He needs to see that he doesn't have to stay in such an unsatisfactory position. In addition, he needs permission to change from the therapist, and protection from him if he does. The effects of injunctions are powerful, but they are reversible.

Some therapy groups are critical, but mine are not. They support each other and get feelings of warmth, of being with each other. After a patient has worked out something crucial, he makes contact with the other group members: "How did you feel when I was yelling at my mother?" "Great. I felt like doing the same thing." A group member gets that kind of positive feedback over and over. It gives him the strength he didn't have in the beginning, and he begins to make up for what he missed as a child. As that occurs, his ego becomes stronger and he feels better about himself. He gets in the "I'm okay" position of transactional analysis.

The use of videotape in therapy is a new and very useful innovation in the hands of a skilled therapist. I have video equipment in my office and use it in some of my individual therapy sessions. As an example of one of the ways in which the videotape technique is used: I had a patient who was rigidly entrenched into a series of patterns, all of which had to be changed. I videotaped her during sessions and she told me everything that was bothering her. She was in a "don't make it," "don't be you," "whatever I do will fail," and "if something good happens, something bad will follow" series of patterns. We played the tape back over and over; she listened to and watched herself, and finally said, "I'm fed up," and dropped most of these unsatisfactory patterns. She is now a very different person. (After we play the tapes back, of course, I erase them.)

Videotape technique helps the patient get to the point where he really sees what he is doing, until he becomes fed up with it and is willing to make a redecision.

I see most of my patients twice a week, once in private and once in a group, but of course, that can vary. The length of treatment varies according to a person's degree of difficulties. In general, significant permanent change is not produced in less than a year, in spite of everything that is said by behavior therapists and others who believe they can shorten the time taken for therapy. People can be relieved of symptoms more quickly, but I doubt very much whether there are character changes that stick. The person slips back after a while if he doesn't go through enough therapy to produce a permanent change. In order to get real change, he has to be convinced that he doesn't have to be the way he is: I'm okay, I can be different, and I will be. He begins to have a different kind of life script and follows it out. That will stick and he will stay with it.

Simply getting rid of a phobia doesn't necessarily produce that kind of change. I believe behavior therapy is great, but one needs to do more.

A final word, and that is about drugs. I usually don't use drugs in the treatment process, because my patients are not the type who require drugs. Drugs *are* important in the treatment of many types of patients— schizophrenics, manic-depressives, senile psychotics, and so on. But for the most part these are not the kind of patients I treat. If I did use drugs with my patients, that would not produce character changes. Psychotherapy does. I do use drugs to facilitate psychotherapy when they are needed. Permanent change, however, is not produced by the drugs. It is produced by the psychotherapy.

CHAPTER *TWENTY-SIX*

Transcendental
Meditation
Michael Grossman, M.D.

Not long ago, meditation was the realm of Eastern mystics and a hand-ful of their Western followers. Today, according to Michael Grossman of the International Meditation Society, more than 900,000 people throughout the world are trained in the Transcendental Meditation pro-grams, many at the suggestion of their doctors.

The claim of Indian Yogis and Zen Buddhists, that meditation can reduce psychological stress and anxiety by controlling certain "involun-tary" bodily functions, no longer causes Western eyebrows to raise. Indeed, since 1966, when the Transcendental Meditation Program—TM —was introduced in this country, people from every walk of life have learned to meditate through more than 200 centers. Behind the tech-nique is an Indian physicist who, after receiving his university degree, studied under the guidance of the Shankaracharya of Northern India, a religious leader. He learned transcendental meditation from his teacher, and innocently began making it available to Indians. After teaching it for a few years in India, he realized that its benefits could be made available in the West, as well. His regular teacher-training sessions in the United States began in 1966; Dr. Grossman estimates that today there are approximately 8,000 instructors trained in Maharishi Mahesh Yogi's method.

The International Meditation Society, also known as the Student International Meditation Society, is a nonprofit organization, incorporated in the state of California, with offices in every major city in the country.

Michael Grossman, a medical doctor in private practice, is also an instructor at the International Meditation Society in New York City. He has used TM in his own work and has conducted research into the physiological changes brought about through meditation. In this adaptation of my interview with him, Dr. Grossman addresses the TM technique and discusses various researches into its effectiveness.

Michael Grossman, M.D.

Ever since the Industrial Revolution, modern man has been changing his environment with his technology. The complexity of our world changes with almost incredible rapidity and requires enormous physical and mental efforts to adjust and adapt to those rapid technological and social changes. What sorts of psychological and physical effects do our efforts to cope with a constantly changing environment have on us?

As medical doctors, we see the consequences of the tensions and stresses which individuals face every day. In my practice, at least three-quarters of my patients suffer from illnesses that are directly related to psychological stress and tension. High blood pressure, premature ventricular contractions (irregular heartbeat), heart disease, peptic ulcers, gastrointestinal complaints, asthma, eczema (inflamation of the skin), headaches, muscle aches and pains, and menstrual disorders are caused primarily by accumulations of psychological stress. Diabetes, arthritis, lowered resistance to infections, obesity, and many other diseases, are often aggravated or partially caused by accumulated psychological stress, as well.

Anxiety, stress, tension: psychologically, a person becomes easily fatigued and irritable; it becomes difficult for him to concentrate and to think clearly.

We can treat each problem, each symptom, at its own level as it arises, taking either a medical or a psychological approach. Or we can approach the mind and body as a unit that is capable of developing its own resources to cope with the vicissitudes of a complex world on a very fundamental level. The latter is the approach we take in TM. Transcendental Meditation is not a treatment program for a specific problem, nor is it an intellectual analysis of a person's psyche. Rather, it is a means of reaching one's inner area of energy, the area we call the "source of our thinking." From the evidence of recent research, I do not think we would be wrong in assuming that this inner area we experience through meditation is the area of union between our psychological and physiological beings.

What is this inner area and how can we experience it in ourselves? To understand what it is, we must first understand what *consciousness* is. All our thoughts are impulses that emanate from a source, and that source—the basis of all our thinking—is our consciousness. Every action we take is supported by a thought; physically, this thought becomes an electric impulse in the brain. So we have an impulse emanating from the consciousness, setting off brain activity, and as the thought rises to the surface it becomes more concrete and is finally translated as an action that we take. In other words, everything we think and everything we do can be traced back to our consciousness; if we have no consciousness, we can have no thoughts and no experiences.

If our contact with our inner area of consciousness is strengthened, then all the outer areas of our life improve; our thoughts, our actions, all improve quite naturally and effortlessly.

There are different theories about how to contact this inner area of consciousness through meditation, and most techniques require years of training and discipline. Transcendental Meditation, which was developed and introduced to the West by Maharishi Mahesh Yogi, is comparatively simple to learn and requires a short period of training. Unlike certain forms of meditation, it does not require a particular lifestyle of its practitioners. TM consists of two sessions daily, each for fifteen to twenty minutes.

Sitting comfortably in a chair with his eyes closed, the individual learns how to think an appropriate sound—a "mantra"—that has been assigned him by his instructor. The "mantra" serves as a direction for the mind; the technique works in such a way that the mind naturally enjoys experiencing the sound of the "mantra" in progressively more quiet, refined, creative levels, until all thinking has disappeared. The individual is left awake inside, but without any thought. It is an experience of consciousness itself—the source of thought.

When one is in this state of meditation, the body is experiencing the most profound rest it has ever experienced; yet the mind is alert. In this "state of restful alertness," the body is eliminating all the accumulated anxiety, fatigue, and deeply rooted stresses, much more so than it does during a regular night's sleep.

The mind quiets down, and with the mind quieting down, the body quiets down. How do we know this objectively?

In recent years, a great deal of research has been conducted to verify the effects of meditation on certain bodily functions, especially those related to psychological stress and tension: lactate levels in the blood, breathing rate (or oxygen consumption), heartbeat (or cardiac output), electrical resistance of the skin (or GSR, the response that is measured in "lie-detector" tests), and brain wave activity.

One of the substances that our bloodstream carries to different parts of our body is lactate, or lactic acid. Some years ago researchers found that people who were suffering from anxiety neurosis had very high levels of lactate in their blood, and that people with hypertension also showed higher lactate levels than the normal individual. When Drs. Robert Wallace and Herbert Benson of the Harvard Medical School examined transcendental meditators in the state of "restful alertness," they found that the amount of lactate in their bloodstreams decreased remarkably during meditation. It not only decreased, but it did so *four times faster* than it normally does when people are in a normal state of sleep. They also discovered that the anxiety-producing lactate stayed at a lower level after people stopped meditating.

When a person is nervous, his body is using more of its energy; for your body to get the energy, it burns calories and nutrients in your bloodstream, and to do that it needs oxygen. The faster you breathe, the more energy your body is using, and the faster it burns up its nutrients. When you're in a nervous state, you need more energy, so you breathe faster to take in the oxygen that helps speed up your metabolism. Wallace and Benson measured the amount of oxygen that people take in when they are meditating, and they discovered that meditators consume far less oxygen—about 17 percent less. For each minute that a person is meditating, he takes in 40 cubic centimeters of oxygen less than he does when he isn't meditating, and this reflects that he is in about twice as deep a resting state than he is during a usual night's sleep.

Another study of transcendental meditators that was reported in England showed that when people are in the state of "restful alertness," the number of breaths they take a minute decreases. Before one goes into meditation, he may take as many as fifteen to sixteen breaths a minute; during meditation, the rate can fall to as low as four breaths per minute, physical evidence, again, of a resting state of the nervous system.

Another finding by Wallace and Benson of the Harvard Medical School was the decreased cardiac output of people in meditation—fewer heartbeats per minute: an average reduction of 25 percent, which means a lessened work load for the heart.

When a person is under stress and anxiety, his skin has a lowered resistance to an electric current; in technical terms, this is known as a decrease in the Galvanic Skin Response (GSR). People suffering from certain emotional disturbances also show a lowered GSR, as well as a highly unstable skin resistance. The meditators studied showed a much higher skin resistance to electric current while they were in the restful state, as well as a more stable GSR after meditation. Their higher GSR indicates a reduction in anxiety, and the more stable GSR indicates increased stability of the nervous system.

All these technical findings point to the same conclusion that meditators themselves have reported: they feel better, more relaxed, free of tension. Yet, when the brain waves of meditators were measured, the results showed a unique pattern of quiet, orderly, synchronized brain-wave activity, indicating mental alertness without anxiety. So our term "restful alertness" is grounded in hard scientific fact.

How do these changes we experience during meditation affect our day-to-day lives? More research has been done in this area with regular TM practitioners. Without lingering on all the details, let's take a look at the results of some of those experiments.

Regular TM practitioners have faster reaction times; they are better able to concentrate on their work; they are more stable emotionally; they can recover from stress more quickly; and they can adapt to changing situations more easily. Someone who meditates twice each day improves his mental and physical senses of coordination. A study at the University of California at Berkeley showed that regular meditators had improved their memories; another study in Cologne, Germany, showed that meditation improves one's personal psychology: transcendental meditators are less aggressive, less nervous, less depressive, less inhibited, and not as temperamental or irritable as nonmeditators; and they are more self-confident without having to dominate others; they had more staying-power at a task and performed it more efficiently; they were more sociable and more friendly than nonmeditators.

The deep relaxation and psychological improvements that people obtain through TM should, logically, mean that practitioners need fewer tranquilizers and stimulants to cope with their lives. At least one study indicates this. The Stanford Research Center found that the number of people using tranquilizers, pain killers, and amphetamines (stimulants) before being trained in TM dropped drastically after TM training and practice; in some cases, over half the people who had been taking a particular drug stopped when they began practicing meditation.

The number of people who stop using nonprescribed drugs such as marijuana and hallucinogens after learning to meditate drops even more dramatically.

Training for transcendental meditation is very systematic, and is the same for everyone. After one hears one or two introductory lectures explaining the basis of TM, he begins the actual course, which lasts four days, for approximately two hours a session. The first day, the person in training receives an hour of individual instruction; at this time he is assigned his "mantra," which is personally given him by his teacher. The other sessions are with the group of trainees—which can be from ten to fifty people—and consists of practicing the meditation technique, as well as discussions with the instructor. There are additional, advanced meetings, which people are invited to come back to attend. After the four-day training session, people are required to come back in one week for an individual check-up session, and then once a month for a year for similar meetings.

The cost of the training is $125 for adults, and is scaled downward for students.

With thousands of people throughout the country beginning TM each month, the need for qualified instructors is great, and we encourage people who have completed the initial training to continue and become instructors. It takes a minimum of four months' training to qualify one to teach the technique to others.

Most of our new trainees have heard of the International Meditation Society through word-of-mouth; there are no specific "types" of people who come into TM training—we train stockbrokers and workers, housewives and models, psychiatrists and patients, and professors and students. Different people will begin to feel the effects of Transcendental Meditation at different times; it will take some people longer than others to lose nervousness and anxiety, but ultimately the effect is the same for everyone: full use of mental and physical capacity for enjoying life. If the regular practice is stopped for a period of time, the individual will begin to feel less alert and less energetic. When he realizes that he is not growing in energy, clarity, and happiness as he did when he meditated twice a day, he'll probably return to the practice. The contrast between the alertness one feels as a regular meditator, and the "fogginess" and fatigue one feels as a nonmeditator becomes readily apparent when one stops the practice. And very few do.

PART SEVEN

The Patient vs. the Law

PEOPLE DIAGNOSED AS emotionally ill are as affected by the latest developments in psychiatric law as they are by the latest innovations in psychotherapy. The term "psychotic" is more than a purely psychiatric label; for anyone who has ever worn it, it becomes a barrier to equal employment opportunity and social acceptance; it takes on a legal significance in a court of law during a "commitment proceeding"—the legal process of confining someone to a mental hospital against his or her will. And until recently, a person who has been involuntarily committed to a mental hospital had no legal right to psychiatric treatment. All of his civil rights, in fact, will be ignored in practice, whether it is legal to do so or not.

More and more attention is being given to the inhuman conditions of public, tax-supported mental hospitals. But correcting the abuses of the system is not the sole answer to banishing the "snakepit" and its associations from society. The answer lies to a great extent in challenging the outdated statutes that govern the administration of mental health to the public; it lies in returning the mental patient's constitutional rights as an American citizen,to him.

Some very fundamental questions are being raised today in psychiatric law: Should mental illness be allowed as a defense in a criminal trial? Do patients—involuntary or voluntary—have a right to choose their own type of treatment? How often has involuntary commitment to a mental institution been used by district attorneys and defense lawyers as a means to prevent people from coming to trial for a crime of which they have been accused? Should a person be helped by the state against his will? Is expert testimony from a psychiatrist in a court valid? Does a patient have the right to sue the court and the public hospital for being wrongly hospitalized against his will?

These are not meaningless questions for the nearly 750,000 people spending time in psychiatric hospitals, or for the thousands who are former psychiatric patients. They were not meaningless questions for Alfred Curt von Wolfersdorf, who spent twenty-one years in a state mental hospital because of a murder he said he did not commit—a murder for which the guilty party was finally arrested and convicted But the fact that Wolfersdorf was obviously innocent did not result in his release from the hospital; it took nineteen more years and a court suit filed by Bruce Ennis, American Civil Liberties Union attorney, to free him. And in twenty-one years, he saw a psychiatrist only seven times. Upon his release, doctors said there was nothing wrong with him emotionally. Indeed, his "wild story" that had led psychiatrists to judge him insane and unfit to stand trial twenty-one years before, had been proven quite true during the second year of his confinement.

Alfred Curt von Wolfersdorf's case is not, unfortunately, an isolated one. In the case of Peter Nelson, whose interview appears in Part Two of this book, the archaic laws that allow a child to be put in a mental hospital for his entire boyhood—a child who is not emotionally ill—again dramatize the need for changing laws.

Today, more and more lawyers are becoming involved in psychiatric law. The Mental Health Law Project, which has offices in New York and Washington, D.C., and ex-patient civil rights organizations such as the Mental Patients' Liberation Project in several states, are fighting for change. These groups have been responsible for new laws that state:

1. A mentally retarded person who has been found incompetent to stand trial can no longer be confined in an institution indefinitely.

2. Institutionalized mentally retarded children have a right to free public education.

3. A state hospital can be held liable for an act committed by one of its patients if that patient leaves the grounds of the hospital.

4. Patients who perform jobs in public mental hospitals must be paid for their work on the basis of the minimum wage laws.

5. A patient has the right to reject nonemergency treatment on the basis of religious grounds.

6. Psychiatric patients in hospital cannot be used in experimental brain surgery even at their "consent," because their consent is given in an atmosphere where coercion is highly possible.

7. If a person is hospitalized against his will (involuntarily), and is not given treatment, he can sue the hospital for damages.

Some steps have been made, and many may argue that we have come a long way from the time when, in Illinois, a woman could be confined to a mental hospital only on the advice of her husband, whether she was emotionally ill or not. But as far as we have come, we have much further to go. In this section, we look at the people who are helping in the struggle for humanizing the laws that control the lives of emotionally ill people. These are the people who are asking the very basic question: if the laws governing psychiatric institutions are inhumane, how can those public hospitals provide rehabilitative, therapeutic care?

CHAPTER TWENTY-SEVEN

The Mental Health
Law Project
Bruce Ennis

In 1968, Bruce Ennis left a Wall Street law firm to direct Civil Liberties and Mental Illness Litigation Project for the New York Civil Liberties Union. He was the first lawyer in the United States to work full time with test cases on behalf of mental patients.

A graduate of the University of Chicago Law School, Mr. Ennis has written two books on psychiatric law: *The Rights of Mental Patients* and *Prisoners of Psychiatry*. His most recent publication for a professional journal, "Psychiatry and the Presumption of Expertise: Flipping Coins in the Courtroom" (published in the *California Law Review* in May, 1974), challenges the idea of the psychiatrist as an expert witness in the courtroom.

Mr. Ennis was instrumental in organizing the Mental Health Law Project, whose goal is to instruct lawyers in psychiatric law and to bring test cases before the courts on behalf of mental patients. One of his most recent victories was the June 26, 1975, U.S. Supreme Court ruling in the case of his client Kenneth Donaldson, who had been involuntarily hospitalized without psychiatric treatment for fifteen years, and whose suit for damages reached the high courts. The decision in that case states that mental patients cannot be hospitalized against their will and without treatment, providing they are: 1) not harmful to themselves; 2) not harmful to others; and 3) are able to take care of themselves and not become public burdens. The hoped-for result should be the release from institutions of almost a quarter of a million involuntary patients throughout the country. Speaking of this recent decision, Mr. Ennis told the *New York Times* that as of June 26, 1975, "mental hospitals as we have known them can no longer exist in this country as dumping grounds for the old, the poor and the friendless. Such institutions will have to re-evaluate the status of each patient."

In my interview with him, Mr. Ennis discusses some of the changes that have been made in the courts, and many of the problems still confronting us.

Bruce Ennis

B.B.: Why are the rights of mental patients, both during commitment procedures and upon release from confinement, so flagrantly disregarded?

B.E.: You started off with a hard question. I think one of the principal reasons why the rights of allegedly mentally ill persons are frequently disregarded is that until very recently there has been no guidance from the United States Supreme Court. In fact, until very recently, the United States Supreme Court had not considered one case that involved the constitutional rights of a civilly committed mental patient. Without any leadership from the top, the lower federal courts have adopted what could be termed a hands-off policy; they have paid no attention to the numerous complaints raised by persons alleged to be mentally ill.

That situation is changing, however. During the last five years the federal courts at least have begun to pay attention to the complaints raised by mental patients. In the last three years the Supreme Court has taken about five different cases involving the constitutional rights of the mentally ill. This action makes it clear to the lower courts that they have some encouragement from the higher court. In fact, in the *Jackson* v. *Indiana* Supreme Court decision, the United States Supreme Court said in a unanimous opinion that it is remarkable that the substantive limitations of the power of states to commit patients to mental hospitals has not been more frequently litigated. In other words, they were asking why the considerable power now held by states to commit people to hospitals had not been challenged in courts more often.

B.B.: Are there other reasons why the rights of mental patients have been neglected?

B.E.: Another reason that mental patients' rights have not been looked into and more frequently litigated is that there were not many lawyers who were sufficiently acquainted with the area of psychiatry and law to do the litigating. As you know, most of the people in mental hospitals are not fortunate enough to find themselves in a private mental hospital or even in a decent facility. Most mental patients wind up in public mental hospitals, primarily because they don't have enough money to go anywhere else. And that same lack of money makes it impossible for them to hire lawyers to represent them, so they have to rely upon public-interest lawyers—salaried lawyers whose salaries are paid by an organization; until recently there have been none of those specializing in psychiatry and law.

When I started working in this area in 1968—and I say this to you not to pat myself on the back, but simply to illustrate the dimensions of the problem—I was the only salaried lawyer in the entire United States who was engaged full-time in bringing test-case litigation on behalf of the mentally handicapped. That is an astonishing statistic. There just weren't lawyers who knew enough about the area who were in a position to help.

B.B.: Is this situation changing?

B.E.: Yes, this is now changing very rapidly. Recently, a joint effort by the Mental Health Law Project and the Practicing Law Institute (an organization that gives continuing law education) resulted in four three-day seminars to train lawyers how to get involved in psychiatric law. Those four sessions, which were conducted in Dallas, Pittsburgh, New York, and San Francisco, reached over a thousand lawyers; 60 percent of them paid a hundred dollars to come. They were serious about the issue. Right now I think it's fair to say that in the United States there are probably not more than thirty major court cases on the constitutional rights of the mentally ill or the mentally retarded. If just a third of those thousand lawyers who were trained through those seminars filed one case in the next year we'd have three hundred cases appearing before the courts instead of thirty. You can see the impact that would have.

The new encouragement from the Supreme Court, and the recent beginning of lawyers' interest in the problem, I think, make it safe to say that in the next five years we are going to see three hundred times the attention paid to the legal rights of the mentally handicapped as we did in the past five.

B.B.: In your book, Prisoners of Psychiatry, *you mentioned the case of a woman who was committed to a mental hospital as a consequence of her somewhat eccentric behavior; she had done nothing wrong, really, but her neighbors thought her odd. Why would an eccentric old woman be sent to a mental hospital by the courts when she'd done nothing wrong, when there was no specific act to prompt commitment proceedings?*

B.E.: That's a good question. The reasons for this type of action are, again, complex. But the principal reason in my mind is the enormous difference between the way we deal with alleged mental patients on the one hand and alleged criminals on the other.

First, the criminals. Constitutionally, someone cannot be put in a prison because he is a criminal type. To be sentenced to prison, a person has to have committed robbery, or arson, or murder, or whatever—a specific act with specific ingredients. Merely being thought of as a criminal type is not enough.

Mental patients, on the other hand, are committed *not* because of any specific *acts* that they have performed, but because of their status—a mental patient *type*. And that's why it's possible for persons such as that woman to be committed to a hospital. The law does not require any specific act to have been perpetrated as grounds for commitment. In most states, for example, the law does not require any proof that the patient is dangerous to him- or herself or to others. It's very difficult to prevent that kind of commitment, because there's nothing concrete you can prove or disprove.

B.B.: Don't patients in all states have a right to a trial or a hearing before commitment? Very few patients are informed of this. Those rights get hidden someplace and you don't hear about them.

B.E.: Yes, that's still all too common in mental hospitals. Some mental hospitals are making an effort to change that. In New York State, for example, it used to be the law that hospitals were required merely to give patients written notice of their rights. Now, by Department of Mental Hygiene regulation, hospitals are not only required to give patients notice of their rights, but the patient is supposed to sign an acknowledgement that he or she was, indeed, given notice. However, it's one thing to know of your rights, and it's quite another thing to be able to exercise them.

For example, in public mental hospitals, where medication is used not so much for treatment as for behavior control, patients are often so heavily medicated that they cannot sign the request for a lawyer or a court hearing—though they may know of their rights. Or patients may be disoriented from having had electroshock therapy at the time they're informed of their rights, and their confusion prevents them from exercising those rights. For these and a number of other reasons, even if patients know of them, they are often not in a position to avail themselves of their rights. The result is mere paper rights.

B.B.: Is it still true that all it takes in New York to commit a patient is two physicians—not necessarily psychiatrists—and one relative?

B.E.: Yes, that's quite true. That's true in many states now. The two-physician law in New York State allows any two physicians to sign a certificate stating that a person is mentally ill and in need of care and treatment. They do not have to allege that the person is in any respect dangerous to himself or to others—simply mentally ill. That signed certificate authorizes involuntary hospitalization for a period of up to sixty days. At the end of sixty days, the hospital either has to release the patient, or has to apply for a court order authorizing the hospital to detain the patient for an additional period of six months. The court order does not require a court hearing at which the patient, or attorney for the patient, may challenge the commitment. The hospital simply sends a piece of paper to the court and the court stamps it and it's good for another six months.

At present, the only way the patient can get a court hearing is if the patient, affirmatively and in writing, demands a court hearing. If the patient just keeps quiet, he can be held for the rest of his life without ever going before a judge.

B.B.: What is the procedure for demanding a judicial review?

B.E.: Patients have the affirmative duty of initiating the process; they can write to the hospital director and say they demand a court hearing. The hospital is then required by statute to forward that request to a court. But it rarely happens because most patients are too confused or under too much pressure to actually begin that process.

I mentioned in my book that in Bellevue Hospital, in 1969, there were about twelve to fifteen thousand involuntary admissions. *Involuntary* admissions—people who did not want to be there. All those patients had a right to a court hearing, but only 531 of them actually demanded and got court hearings. That's evidence of the difference between a paper right, and a real right.

B.B.: Is there a law that patients must be informed of these rights at periodic intervals?

B.E.: Not at periodic intervals, no. Most states now have laws requiring that patients be informed of their rights upon admission to an institution, but very few states require patients to be informed of their rights at periodic intervals.

B.B.: In other words, when they are better and less confused, they can't be told again?

B.E.: They should be, but they're not. Generally, what happens is that a patient is brought into the admissions ward kicking and screaming, crying and very upset; somebody shoves a piece of paper in front of him and says, "Here are your rights." And the patient says, "Don't tell me about my rights. I just want to get out of here!" So he's taken up to the ward, and three days later he's calmer and better able to understand his rights. But he doesn't have that piece of paper anymore.

Some hospitals now are beginning to post notice of patients' rights in the hospital wards, but it's not required in most states.

B.B.: *You've called the larger institutions warehouses, where patients cannot possibly receive any therapy of any consequence. What proportion of the larger institutions are in this condition? What proportion of all mental patients in confinement are in these types of institutions?*

B.E.: Well, I've visited a lot of mental hospitals, but I certainly haven't seen a representative sample of all the psychiatric hospitals in this country, and I don't have the hard statistics to give you. My information comes from colleagues around the country and from my own experience with hospitals in different states. I would say, however, that a majority of mental hospitals in the country are, for most of their patients, custodial institutions.

Let me try to be more specific about that. The average period of hospitalization for newly admitted patients in New York State mental hospitals is now about six weeks. That's not a terribly long period of time if the patient spends it on an admissions ward or in intensive treatment. But if the hospitals don't release a patient in six weeks, they transfer him to the back wards, and the back wards are merely custodial wards. In New York State, it's still true that 78 percent of all patients in public hospitals have been there two years or longer, and about 60 percent have been there five years or longer. Those are the people in the back wards. Essentially, they've been written off; they're not getting active treatment.

I think it is reasonable to estimate that approximately three-fourths of the mental patients in the country's state hospitals are probably getting, at best, custodial care. The same food, clothing, and shelter that they would no doubt receive in prison.

B.B.: *What can be done about this?*

B.E.: It's a big task. We're talking about how to change that system around for several hundred thousand persons. This is not easy. There are some beginnings, such as the recent wave of right-to-treatment cases. One of my cases, *Donaldson* v. *O'Connor* (which I mentioned in *Prisoners of Psychiatry*) was ruled on, on April 26, 1974, by a Federal

Court of Appeals; the ruling states that involuntarily confined mental patients have a constitutional right to receive adequate psychiatric treatment. Mere custodial care is no longer sufficient. Under this decision— the first of its kind by any federal court—the hospital has a constitutional obligation to give the patient an active treatment program, and if it does not, it must release the patient. If the hospital does not release the patient, the hospital must pay damages for false imprisonment. Now that, I think, offers some hope toward transforming these custodial institutions into treatment institutions.

B.B.: Could we go to another point for a moment? You have said that it is easier for an ex-convict to get a job than for an ex-mental patient. Would you comment on that?

B.E.: Well, I would say that perhaps more than half of the requests for assistance that I receive in my office are not from patients, but are from *former* patients who are unable to get public employment or any kind of decent job, because they have been hospitalized.

There are glimmers of hope on the horizon, however. There are a few good programs that help some former patients to get employment, but it's quite common for a person to be denied a job as a garbage collector, a teacher, a bus driver, taxi driver, or in any kind of public employment, simply because at some time that person was a patient in a mental hospital. This is totally without regard to the person's current mental condition. I've had numerous cases wherein I offered to have my client submit to a psychiatric examination, and the public employer refused. They say they don't care what the person's current mental condition is. A few years ago he was a patient in a mental hospital and that's enough for them.

B.B.: In your book you have also said that prolonged hospitalization is antitherapeutic, and I agree. Would you expand on that a bit?

B.E.: I'm not the only person saying that. I think it's fair to say that the majority of all psychiatrists support that position. After a certain period of time, adjustment to the hospital routine can, in itself, be antitherapeutic. After all, to live in that kind of a structured shelter, where all your necessities are provided for you, is not to live in the normal environment. After a while, the patient who successfully adapts to the hospital is going to have a difficult time readapting to the real world. In other words, the hospital, in fact, trains people to be dependent citizens rather than independent citizens.

The Director of Bronx State Hospital, which has been one of the best public hospitals in the country, testified under oath in one of my cases that after a short period of time, it was really more difficult to treat the conditions caused by the hospital environment than it was to treat the condition which precipitated hospitalization.

B.B.: It's my impression that you believe most people who are mentally ill could be treated on an outpatient basis, rather than being hospitalized. I think you're right about a lot of them—people now in hospitals—but how about people who are suicidal and need self-protection?

B.E.: Well, I have not yet been persuaded that there's such a thing as "mental illness," but I do believe there are persons whose thought processes don't work the same way as my thought processes do. I do believe there are disturbed people. I don't know whether it's a learned pattern of maladaptive behavior or if its a physiological imbalance in their system—a chemical imbalance. But I don't think that matters. Whether it's a mental illness, or physiological illness, or whatever it is, it's certainly a problem to be dealt with. Now, how to deal with the problem of a suicidal person is, I think, the most difficult question facing us. How to deal with persons who are thought to be dangerous to others is relatively easy compared to how to deal with suicidal persons.

I think the way California approaches the problem makes a lot of sense. Under California law, if a person is suicidal, he or she can be committed involuntarily to a mental hospital for a fourteen-day period, at which time the patient can receive intensive treatment. At the end of the fourteen-day period, if the patient continues to be suicidal, he or she can be committed for an additional fourteen-day period, for a total of roughly twenty-eight days. In other words, in California, a suicidal person can be involuntarily hospitalized for a month. At the end of that month, if the patient is still suicidal, and he's not dangerous to others, he has to be released.

I think that probably makes some sense, because it has been established that many persons are suicidal because they are depressed; many persons are depressed because of chemical imbalances in their systems, and those chemical imbalances, in many cases, can be treated with specific medications. So, if the patient has a physiological problem that can be treated, it makes sense to give the state a month to try to treat it. If it's something different from that, if a person is responding to a real grievance, an environmental problem and not a chemically produced depression, then keeping the patient in the hospital is probably not going to make much difference. If he is truly set on committing suicide, he'll probably at least attempt it at some point in or out of a hospital.

I think the California law strikes a balance. It gives the state roughly thirty days for an intensive treatment program. If it doesn't work, on balance, you're probably better off letting the patients go. It's revealing that in practice, California has not been using the full thirty days. They have found that now the average rate of commitment in the state of California for suicidal persons is only thirteen days, and that the rate of suicide by persons who are discharged after thirteen days is lower than the rate of suicide of persons who were discharged under the old California law, after six months or a year in the hospital.

The short periods of treatment seem to help. And there's a good reason for that. You'll find that most persons attempt suicide, not while they're depressed, but a few weeks after they get over the worst episode of their depression; not all, but most persons commit suicide when they're relatively together. They look back and they see what was an abject, miserable human being; how they must have embarrassed themselves; they don't want to go through that again. While they're in a relatively lucid frame of mind, they say, "Now I'm going to kill myself so this doesn't happen again." This also relates to the problems inherent to a prolonged period of hospitalization, which is such a dehumanizing experience, that when the person gets out, he may very well look back and say, "Wow, I'll never go through six months in a mental hospital again." Short periods of hospitalization are probably better for suicidal persons than long periods.

B.B.: You say that mental institutions are governed, not by laws, but by men who make their own laws. Who makes those laws? Psychiatrists? The directors of the hospitals?

B.E.: Well, the director, the ward psychiatrist, and to probably an even larger extent, the ward attendant. In public mental hospitals, 90 percent of the contact between patients and staff is with nonprofessional staff, with the attendants. And the attendants really run mental hospitals.

For example, I have a client who was telling me that she wanted to watch a particular TV program in the ward of a mental hospital, and the attendants didn't want her to watch that program. The attendants wanted to watch the World Series Baseball Game, so they came in and turned on the baseball game. Things like that happen. Or the attendants may say to patients, "Now, look, if you mop up that dayroom area, we'll let you go down to the canteen and get some cigarettes." That kind of thing. In other words, in order to lessen their own work load, the attendants will induce patients to do things that they [the attendants] otherwise would have to do; in return, they give the patients little favors —ground privileges, or permission to go to the canteen.

In most public mental hospitals, in the back wards—not in the admissions wards, in the back wards—a very substantial number of patients are required to work at hospital maintenance and are paid nothing for it.

B.B.: So many of these problems, it seems, could be eliminated if there were fewer public hospitals and more good halfway houses and homes for the aged. Isn't it true that a significant number of mental patients are old people, hospitalized merely because nobody wants them?

B.E.: That's a very, very significant problem. I recently saw the most current statistics for New York and I believe that now about 45 percent of the patients in New York State mental hospitals are sixty years of age or older, and most of those patients are not psychotic. They're simply old people who may have been senile, but they're not mentally ill, they're not crazy. But nobody wants them, and there's no place for them to go, so they go to public mental hospitals.

What do we do about that? In my opinion, the most disgusting thing about this whole problem is that for the same amount of money we are now spending to maintain the public mental hospitals—in fact, for less money than we now spend on public mental hospitals—we could develop smaller, community-based facilities, geriatric facilities, nursing home facilities, decent, clean, small places where people would want to live. But we don't do it. And because we don't do it, there are no community alternatives for the elderly, and they are forced to remain in the public mental hospitals. It's either that or a sleazy welfare hotel.

B.B.: Do you think the American family has failed in some way? Years ago, the elderly lived with their families and were taken care of at home.

B.E.: That's an excellent point. In fact, in the Bellevue area, which services Chinatown, a lower percentage of Chinese are committed to Bellevue than any other population group, because the Chinese have maintained their cultural concept of a strong family unity.

The problem has a lot to do with the change in family structure in the United States. Nevertheless, it is a *fact* that the family structure is changing, and we're going to have to come up with alternatives.

B.B.: You say the fact is that large mental hospitals don't treat, they just degrade. I agree with you. How can this be changed?

B.E.: I don't see it changing drastically in the next year or two. It's going to be a long process. One thing that I think is going to be required is more give-and-take between patients and doctors about the patients' own lives. Simply being told what's wrong with them and what to do is not enough; the patient should participate in planning a treatment program. The patient should participate in figuring out what they want changed in their own lives—goals they want to set for themselves.

The first step in that process is to allow patients to look at their own hospital records. Most hospitals do not permit patients to look at their own records. They don't know what others think about them, what others are saying about them; therefore, it's not possible for patients to make a realistic adjustment. In so many hospital records, you read, "Insight nil, judgment impaired, poor reality testing." Well, of course there's poor reality testing if a person doesn't really know how others think about him and his behavior. Unless the patient knows what the husband thinks, or the next-door neighbor thinks, there's no way the patient is ever going to be able to make adjustments.

B.B.: Do you think the family sometimes is the source of the trouble? That the family and the friends ought to be drawn in to see if they can help?

B.E.: Absolutely, and that requires a lot of changes. In most public mental hospitals today, a relative, a wife, say, brings her husband to the hospital. The husband is admitted and the wife leaves. And that's the only contact the hospital has with the wife. It shouldn't be that way. It should be that, if the wife brings the husband to the hospital door, the doctor sits down with the wife at that time and tells her when she can expect her husband to return home. It's a matter of changing expectations. As the situation stands today, persons go into a mental hospital and think that perhaps they will get out and perhaps they will stay there forever. It shouldn't be that way. The hospital should tell the family, the neighborhood, the community, the landlords, everyone, that this is a short-term stay; that they are going to do a few things, which only a hospital can do, and then the patient is coming back home. Some hospitals are doing that.

B.B.: At the close of your book, you suggest the development of community-based outpatient facilities as an alternative to spending tax dollars on what you term "custodial warehouses." What are some of the problems and possible solutions toward that end?

B.E.: Well, a major problem in this area right now is that states are spending 90 percent of their allocated resources on building new, large public mental hospitals, and only 10 percent of their resources on building smaller, community-based outpatient treatment facilities. It should be exactly the other way around. We should be spending 90 percent of our budget on developing community treatment facilities, preventive programs, supportive programs, day-care programs, partial hospitalization programs—a whole range of programs that would provide people with more options than full-time hospitalization or nothing. But we're not doing that.

I don't think that much is going to happen to reverse those priorities for the tax dollar until taxpayers find out that doing the job right, treating patients in their communities primarily on an outpatient basis, is not only better for the patients, but a lot cheaper for the taxpayer. For example, it costs the taxpayer one hundred twenty dollars per day to keep a patient in Bellevue Psychiatric Hospital. For that amount of money you could get a suite in the Waldorf Astoria and take a trip to Bermuda and a lot of other things that would relieve much of the depression that many mental patients suffer. What I'm saying is that we could do the job better and cheaper than we are now doing it, and it's a terrible shame that we're not. There is really nothing to prevent it except a lack of leadership at the top.

B.B.: Yet there's an uproar in most communities if you say you're going to develop a halfway house there. People seem to think that mental patients are going to do something awful. It would seem that people's attitudes about mental illness have to change before these reforms can be made. Do you think this stigma will lessen in time?

B.E.: I think there's going to continue to be a stigma, but people are starting to realize now that the mentally ill are not more dangerous than the so-called mentally healthy. There have been several studies made, all of which show that the mentally ill, as a class, are no more dangerous and are probably less dangerous, than the average population. As more and more people become aware of that fact, I think a great deal of the stigma will go away.

A big part of the stigma, as far as bringing halfway houses into the community, is a fear of being injured by a mental patient. You know, we read in the newspapers, "Former Mental Patient Stabs Wife," or, "Former Mental Patient Kills College Co-ed." These headlines stick in people's minds. To give the full story, every day the papers carry one of those headlines, they should run another headline saying, "20,000 Former Mental Patients Did Nothing Dangerous Today." But that's not news.

B.B.: When a person is committed to a mental hospital, then, he will most likely lose his status as a first-class citizen for the rest of his life, even after his release. He'll always suffer the stigma of having been hospitalized. It seems that in a commitment proceeding, the people who are doing the committing have all the "expert testimony" on their side, and the patient has none.

B.E.: You're right. It is very difficult to get expert testimony for a patient's side of a case; first of all, it costs money and most patients in public hospitals don't have money to pay for a private psychiatrist.

B.B.: But why do judges give more credence to psychiatrists' testimony than to that of the patient?

B.E.: Well, judges don't want to take risks; they don't want to release a patient who may go out and hurt somebody—then it would be the judges' fault. If they do what the doctors say—release if the doctors say to release, or not release if the doctors say to commit—they can rest assured that they have followed the experts' advice. Most judges aren't very courageous.

I've been troubled for a long time with the problem of expert testimony in civil commitment cases. For the June, 1974, *California Law Review* a psychologist and I published a very long article in which we went through all the available studies involving the reliability and validity of psychiatric diagnoses, and we found a very astonishing thing: psychiatrists, when they conduct these studies, find they can't agree among themselves who's crazy and who's not. For example, psychiatrists agreed among themselves whether a given person fit a given diagnosis such as schizophrenia or manic-depressive, only 40 percent of the time. In other words, if Dr. A said this patient is schizophrenic, it's more likely that Dr. B will *disagree* with Dr. A's diagnosis than that he will agree. Now, how can we justify depriving people of liberty when the judgment being made is as iffy as that?

B.B.: Do you think psychiatrists should be used as expert witnesses?

B.E.: My coauthor and I raise the question of whether psychiatry is, at this time in history, sufficiently scientific and precise to justify treating psychiatrists as expert witnesses. It seems to me, with the available evidence, that psychiatrists should not be permitted to testify as experts in civil commitment proceedings. I don't think they should be able to testify at all. And that's what we're recommending in this part of the article. The decision should be made by judges and jurors, really, not by psychiatrists. It's really a social judgment at this point in time, not a medical judgment. Psychiatry is too imprecise.

B.B.: How do you feel about the future?

B.E.: On balance I'm reasonably optimistic about further expansion of the rights of mental patients. As I have said, in 1968 I was the only lawyer employed full time in this area. Now I'm employed in part by the Mental Health Law Project, where we have seven full-time lawyers, and we're going to hire two more. We've just trained a thousand lawyers. This is a sign of incredible progress to me; about three years ago, I tried to organize a meeting of lawyers who might be interested in this area, to train them. Only five lawyers showed up for that meeting. But now we've had over a thousand come for that training. Lawyers are finally getting involved in this area and that's going to make a big difference. For years the American Bar Association had no involvement to speak of in this area, except an occasional study. The American Bar Association has now appointed a special commission, the Commission on the Legal Rights of the Mentally Handicapped; they are actively involved in cases and are encouraging local bar associations to get involved in cases representing mental patients. These are very encouraging developments.

We have a great deal of momentum going now, and I think the professionals essentially agree with us. You see, I'm in the business where, unfortunately, I have to sue psychiatrists, but on the other hand, I've tried very hard not to get into an antagonistic position with psychiatry in general. For example, I now represent the American Psychiatric Association in three major lawsuits. And I do that, in part, because I want to show that most of the objectives that civil liberties lawyers are pursuing are exactly the same objectives that the top men and women in the psychiatric profession are also pursuing. We all agree that patients ought to be given more rights, that they ought to be given treatment, that they ought to be treated in the communities whenever possible. A lot of press has been given to the supposed great dispute between civil liberties lawyers and psychiatrists. That's so misleading. I've written a letter to the editor of the *Times* saying that I was upset about their articles in this area. The *New York Times* as well as the other news media are talking about a dispute between psychiatrists and lawyers when there really is no dispute. Both psychiatrists and lawyers agree on the general way things ought to be moving.

Lawyers are now getting interested for the first time; the top people in the psychiatric profession are interested and they care, and if we can somehow channel the concern coming from those two professions into action I think real progress is possible. That's one of the reasons we founded the Mental Health Law Project. The Board of Directors is comprised primarily of psychiatrists and psychologists; we want to make it a joint effort among professions, with a common goal, rather than lawyers suing psychiatrists and psychiatrists telling lawyers they don't know anything about treatment.

Finally, there is the growing movement of former mental patients' organizations, such as the Mental Patients' Liberation Project. I think that's an extremely important development. No matter what lawyers do, nothing ever happens until the client groups themselves become organized. For a long time lawyers tried to bring welfare cases to court, but nothing really happened until their clients themselves started organizing the Welfare Rights Organization. For a long time lawyers tried to do things to expand the rights of women. Nothing happened until women started getting together, raising women's consciousness about women. I think that's also true about mental patients. The patients are going to have to organize themselves.

The Mental Patients' Liberation Project, here in New York City, now has a twenty-four hour switchboard through which they offer advice and help to patients who are having problems. A person may call and say, "I'm going to freak out again, I'm thinking of committing suicide." Or, "I've got no place to stay." The MPLP responds: "Come on down. We'll talk about it. We've been through it before, we know what it's like. We'll give you a place to stay." They're a self-help organization. I've been working closely with those groups of former mental patients, because I think that's an essential development.

B.B.: Yes, so do I. They eventually will be more able to speak for themselves.

B.E.: Right, that's the goal. The ultimate goal.

CHAPTER TWENTY-EIGHT

The Mental Patients'
Liberation Project

"You must realize that the mental health experts have failed us for hundreds of years. They said we were witches or possessed, they cut into our brains, placed us in snake pit institutions, shocked us into zombie-like states, heavily medicated us with internal straight jackets, and now they send us into what they have the gall to call the community (bad conditions in a care and shelter program).

"And all this has been done in our best interests, they say. When in history were we ever asked? If you are not already aware of this, the fact is that all psychiatric patients are not mute, or mumbling, or timid, or withdrawn, or in contact or out of contact at the same time. When we do not fear reprisals, we can, almost without exception, relate stories of insults, indignities, and humiliations perpetrated by mental health experts."[1]

These are the words of a former mental patient, now an active member of the Mental Patients' Liberation Project (MPLP) in New York City. The MPLP is one of several activist organizations that have been growing up around the country, aimed at changing the laws and attitudes that have resulted in brutalization, forced hospitalization, and the stigmatization of psychiatric patients.

1. "Quotes from the Beginning: 18 Months Mental Patient Movement." Paper circulated by the Mental Patients' Liberation Project. Reprinted here by permission.

Shortly after the MPLP became a reality in New York, they issued this statement, explaining their position and their aims:

We, of the Mental Patients' Liberation Project, are former mental patients. We've all been labeled schizophrenic, manic-depressive, psychotic, and neurotic—labels that have degraded us, made us feel inferior. Now we're beginning to get together—beginning to see that these labels are not true but have been thrown at us because we have refused to conform—refused to adjust to a society where to be normal is to be an unquestioning robot, without emotion and creativity. As ex-mental patients we know what it's like to be locked up in mental institutions for this refusal; we know what it's like to be treated as an object—to be made to feel less of a person than "normal" people on the outside. We've all felt the boredom, the regimentation, the inhumane physical and psychological abuses of institutional life—life on the inside. We are now beginning to realize that we are no longer alone in these feelings—that we are all brothers and sisters. Now for the first time we're beginning to fight for ourselves—fight for our personal liberty. We, of the Mental Patients' Liberation Project, want to work to change the conditions we have experienced. We have drawn up a Bill of Rights for Mental Patients—rights that we unquestioningly should have but rights that have been refused to us. Because these rights are not now legally ours we are going to fight to make them a reality.

MENTAL PATIENTS' BILL OF RIGHTS

We are ex-mental patients. We have been subjected to brutalization in mental hospitals and by the psychiatric profession. In almost every state of the union, a mental patient has fewer *de facto* rights than a murderer condemned to die or to life imprisonment. As human beings, you are entitled to basic human rights that are taken for granted by the general population. You are entitled to protection by and recourse to the law. The purpose of the Mental Patients' Liberation Project is to help those who are still institutionalized. This Bill of Rights was prepared by those at the first meeting of MPLP held on June 13, 1971, at the Washington Square Methodist Church [New York City]. If you know someone in a mental hospital, give him/her a copy of these rights. If you are in a hospital and need legal help, try to find someone to call (us).

1. You are a human being and are entitled to be treated as such with as much decency and respect as is accorded to any other human being.

2. You are an American citizen and are entitled to every right established by the Declaration of Independence and guaranteed by the Constitution of the United States of America.

3. You have the right to the integrity of your own mind and the integrity of your own body.

4. Treatment and medication can be administered only with your consent, you have the right to demand to know all relevant information regarding said treatment and/or medication.

5. You have the right to have access to your own legal and medical counsel.

6. You have the right to refuse to work in a mental hospital and/or to choose what work you shall do and you have the right to receive the minimum wage for such work as is set by the state labor laws.

7. You have the right to decent medical attention when you feel you need it just as any other human being has that right.

8. You have the right to uncensored communication by phone, letter, and in person with whomever you wish and at any time you wish.

9. You have the right not to be treated like a criminal; not to be locked up against your will; not to be committed involuntarily; not to be fingerprinted or "mugged" (photographed).

10. You have the right to decent living conditions. You're paying for it and the taxpayers are paying for it.

11. You have the right to retain your own personal property. No one has the right to confiscate what is legally yours, no matter what reason is given. That is commonly known as theft.

12. You have the right to bring grievance against those who have mistreated you and the right to counsel and a court hearing. You are entitled to protection by law against retaliation.

13. You have the right to refuse to be a guinea pig for experimental drugs and treatments and to refuse to be used as learning material for students. You have the right to demand reimbursement if you are so used.

14. You have the right not to have your character questioned or defamed.

15. You have the right to request an alternative to legal commitment or incarceration in a mental hospital.[2]

The MPLP began in 1971 on the inspiration of a young man and his sister who had been visiting in Oregon. Both were former psychiatric patients; both were impressed by an organization in Oregon, formed by and for former mental patients, the "Insane Liberation Project." The ILP was working toward the same goals that the MPLP would come to work for. Returning to the East, the two young people began contacting former mental patients with an eye to forming a similar activist group. The result was MPLP.

Today, the New York chapter is located at 56 East Fourth Street, in a storefront office run exclusively by former mental patients. The MPLP Crisis Center is run out of the same office; the center was formed as an alternative to standard psychiatry for people who are in the midst of a crisis situation. Its purpose is to keep a person suffering a psychiatric crisis out of the hospital, to provide moral and, as much as possible, material assistance. If the caller is a recently released patient, for example, with no place to stay, he may be asked to stop by the storefront and may possibly be invited to spend the evening there; a member may offer him a place in his apartment. Each "case" is dealt with according to the immediate situation; there are no formulas except the humanitarian formula of helping one's brother or sister.

Leon Ross, currently in charge of public relations for the group, elaborated on several points brought up in the Mental Patients' Bill of Rights statement during our conversations. MPLP, he said, is made up of "about nine-tenths ex-patients. A very few exceptions are made. We are supported financially mainly through gifts and contributions, and monies paid for speaking engagements, film exhibits, and benefit shows. We're a nonprofit, tax-deductible organization."

The MPLP, and other such groups throughout the country, have been publicized through television and magazines in the past few years, and are gaining in visibility and public recognition. But to fulfill their goals, they must have access to and recognition by not only psychiatric hospitals, but hospitalized patients as well. How do they learn of hospital violations of patients' rights? According to Mr. Ross:

2. "The Mental Patients' Bill of Rights." Reprinted here by permission of the Mental Patients' Liberation Project.

"We hear of hospital violations through phone calls from patients themselves or from their friends or others who speak to us on behalf of the victimized person. When we go to a hospital to speak to people for whatever person (usually to work on getting them out), we may give out our Bill of Rights and meet other people who want some assistance in getting out. We are working for more access into hospitals to monitor procedures and practices."

Although the majority of MPLP members are former patients of public hospitals, people who have been patients in either private or public institutions come to them for help. I asked Mr. Ross if in his experience he found any significant differences in the grievances between public and private hospital patients:

"My guess, after hearing stories from people who've been in the different types of institutions, and after visits, is: one, that state hospitals are generally worse all the way around; two, that in certain public hospitals a specific practice (such as shock treatment) may be given much more frequently than in a private hospital.

"But whether a person is coming from a private or a public hospital, whether coming from voluntary or involuntary commitment, prolonged hospitalization results in 'hospitalitis'—institutional conditioning for total dependency. That's why some of us seem to act so strange. We've been crippled by the people who wanted to 'help' us, usually against our will."

Getting the Bill of Rights to hospitalized patients, working with lawyers to bring test cases to the courts on behalf of involuntarily committed patients, helping people handle situations in their lives during a crisis, conducting workshops and demonstrations to publicize the mental patient's plight, are only a few of the organization's activities. Once a patient is released from the hospital, he still must face a society that looks askance at people who have had psychiatric problems, at people who have been in a mental hospital, whether justifiably or not. Many of the people who come to the MPLP have never had a job, are not trained in a specific vocation, and do not have private family funds to draw on. They are, in fact, penniless. No one in the MPLP, indeed, is wealthy; their funds come from each other in many ways. Sharing apartments, sharing meals, finding a place for someone to stay is all an informal procedure. Finding jobs, especially at this time in our history, is no easy task for an organization that is without highly placed connections. However, the group has a steady, though informal, job recruitment activity. Its newsletter, *Free Expression*, runs a regular advertisement, calling upon local businesses to use its job referral service; members personally solicit help from area businessmen. And they help recently released patients tackle the bureaucratic red tape involved in applying for public assistance.

In making the adjustment to the outside world, new members are helped by belonging to a dynamic, active group. As Mr. Ross explains:

"Being part of a group that is strong, articulate, and proud is a good step. People have a place to work for something, to work for political change. It's important to meet people who will not stigmatize you because you've been branded by the powers that be as a maniac or emotional defective. We retranslate the definitions attached to us through communicating with each other.

"Living situations are sometimes set up—you could call them temporary extended families—that are supportive of our ideas of ourselves.

"By educating the public and working on legislation, we manage to slowly change the image of the mental patient and improve his opportunities, socially and economically."

Is the MPLP working toward establishing more formal day-care facilities through established channels? Mr. Ross comments, "Yes, but I wouldn't say that we're trying to do it through 'established channels.' Of course, we want to remain 'legal.' But we want patient-run facilities. This goes along with our convictions: less brutality, less destructiveness to the individual, more concern overall.

"Community psychiatry is something we don't approve of, although on one level it is better than an institutional brand of psychiatry. We are aiming for something that we feel is more important than community-establishment psychiatry versus institutional-establishment psychiatry. We aim for total self-help, where professionals, when and if they are called upon, are our servants, rather than we being their subjects."

The Mental Patients' Liberation Project does not harangue people into refusing treatment if it is desired by members. The underlying idea of the organization is freedom of choice: people should be able to choose. Their actions are aimed at stopping involuntary commitment. In a short-term sense, this means "liberating" those who have been put into hospitals against their will. In a long-term sense, it means using every means available to change the statutes that violate one's constitutional rights vis-a-vis institutional psychiatry. It is both an outward- and inward-aimed movement. Much like the women's movement, the mental patients' movement confronts personal and social attitudes as well as the traditions and laws that have grown from those attitudes.

In 1974, over Labor Day weekend, representatives of about sixteen mental patients' activist organizations met in Kansas for the National Conference on Human Rights and Psychiatric Oppression. Leon Ross, reporting on the conference for *Free Expression*, wrote:

> When a person went mad in ancient Greece, a trip to the temple was called for. There, the soul was soothed and the spirit mended with poetry and song, wine and rest. The Ashanti tribe of Africa, on the other hand, chained madmen to trees. If their relatives came to feed them, they lived; otherwise, they perished.
>
> The Second National Conference is a reaction against the contemporary situation in America in which "delinquent" young people, aggressive or depressed women, political radicals, homosexuals, militant minority group members, recalcitrant prisoners, and cantankerous senior citizens, among others, are finding psychiatric facilities used as weapons of control. Victimized also are those with harmless, non-ordinary belief systems.[3]

In New York, it is the Mental Patients' Liberation Project; in Oregon, it is the Insane Liberation Project; in Kansas, it is the Mental Patients' Support Committee; in California, it is the Network Against Psychiatric Assault. By whatever name these groups go, their aims are the same: recognition as human beings. In whatever part of the country their modest headquarters are located, their task is as great as their will to win.

3. "Has Anyone Heard about the Second National Mad People's Conference?", by Lee Ross. *Free Expression*, Vol. 1, No. 3. Reprinted here by permission.

CONCLUSION

From the material in this book, the reader can easily conclude that selecting an individual therapist is a highly personal endeavor; some psychotherapists are more geared to treating certain people than others. If you are in a position to choose your own psychotherapist it is important that you share a sense of empathy with him or her. The same is true of hospitals: some, both private and public, are more helpful for certain people than others. To remain in a hospital environment that is either unsympathetic or is not geared to treating a specific problem is more harmful than not.

Tax-supported, or public, hospitals were originally founded with only good intentions—that people who could not afford private care be able to receive adequate treatment. However, it requires only a cursory glance at the newspapers to see that the situation with most public hospitals is far from satisfactory. From the incredibly shocking disclosures about the Willowbrook State School for the Mentally Retarded, Staten Island, New York, to the more recent reports on New York State's program to release thousands of state hospital patients virtually onto the streets, the news is full of evidence of gross neglect and maltreatment of state hospital patients. Public reaction is most often indignant, but indignation must lead to action before anything can be improved.

The trend toward releasing state hospital patients results in a large part from the advances made in psychiatric medications and the rapid improvement these new medications have produced in patients who previously had been thought of as beyond help. But merely releasing patients is not sufficient. Thousands of these people have no place to go, no funds, and are relegated to proprietary homes often of dubious ethics. The *New York Times*, in a series of articles written by Murray Schumach last year, discussed the conditions of many proprietary homes that were built to house patients released from state hospitals. According to Mr. Schumach, many of these homes cheated patients out of their state-funded weekly spending allowance; patients received minimal if any care and lived in the most depressing, physically uninviting atmospheres. In one of the articles, the *Times* quoted state officials as saying that a great number of proprietary home operators are in the business for "the fast buck," and are "ghettoizing" released patients. The problem has been transferred from the state hospitals to the community.

This situation clearly illustrates the need for what is described in this book as aftercare, or day care, such as Fountain House. William Sherman of the New York *Daily News* wrote a series of reports on New York State's proposals for decentralizing state mental hospitals and putting funds allocated for hospitals into developing state-run halfway houses. In theory, it seems a good idea; what happens in practice can be disastrous unless additional funds are granted to develop progressive, humanitarian facilities where people can get the attention they need instead of ending up in a proprietary home situation, living out their days without hope, without futures.

Follow-up care for released patients—which in the future may greatly help not only those who have been hospitalized, but their families and society as well—is now often regarded as a burden; often there is great hostility in a community toward a proposed halfway house. Conjured images of uncontrollable and uncontrolled "criminally insane" persons in the midst of a neighborhood throw a community into panic, and a follow-up center never gets built; patients stay in proprietary homes or welfare hotels and the vicious cycle goes unbroken. Headlines scream about "alleged rapists and murderers" being released into the community from state hospitals, and nothing is ever said about the overwhelming majority of patients who are harmless, lost, and much more the victims than the victimizers.

The stigma of emotional illness, as I see it, stems from unnecessary guilt and fear. If understanding the issues involved in mental health is broadened, if every scare headline about an isolated "escapee" from a mental institution were substituted with an article about the thousands of patients who recover and confront their struggles, the basic problems could be faced and dealt with. Families of patients would be relieved of their guilt, communities of their fears of halfway houses, and people who have had severe problems would be free to become the often special contributors to society, which many have already become.

Yet, through all the problems, the available help for people who are currently suffering or who have emerged from a hospital situation, is expanding. Modern medical advances mean that people suffering from many previously "hopeless" problems no longer have to remain in treatment indefinitely; people who thought they were condemned to a chronic illness within or without hospitals need not feel that this must be so any longer.

Most important, I think, is that people who have known life's ups and downs in that uniquely profound way labeled as "mental illness" have begun to help each other—to point the way to others and to demonstrate that almost anyone can benefit from some form of therapy (even if it is only kindness); that we are not unalike and alone but can gain from each other. The road to recovery can be long and arduous. I hope the material in this book will make it easier for some.

GLOSSARY OF TERMS

Acute episode—Often referred to as a *psychotic episode*, a period during which the psychotic patient suffers a severe onset of symptoms peculiar to his or her mental illness. An example would be a manic-depressive patient feeling severe depression and disorientation, withdrawal, and fear at the time he or she descends into the depressive phase of the illness.

Affect—Emotionality; expressing, rather than discussing or relating, one's feelings.

Alpha waves—The brain emits a number of "waves" of fluctuations of voltages (electricity), which are measures of different brain functions and states of mental activity. The alpha wapes are the large waves (as they show up on recording devices) that accompany relaxed state of feeling. The greater the fluctuation in the alpha wave, the more relaxed the patient.

Analytic psychotherapy—Treatment of a mental or emotional disorder through the application of the therapeutic technique of analysis. A Freudian-based and lengthy form of treatment. (See *Psychoanalysis*.)

Antabuse—Trade name for the alchol-abstinence drug disulfram. Authorities agree that Antabuse is one of the most effective controls for alcoholism. If a patient with Antabuse in his bloodstream takes any alcohol, he will

271

suffer severe physical reactions and fever. This serves as an effective deterrent to drinking, when in conjunction with supportive psychotherapy.

Anxiety—Similar to fear, especially as it shows up in physical reactions—increased heartbeat, tensed muscles, dilating of pupils, rapid, deeper breathing, and loss of appetite. Anxiety is normally an automatic response to situations that are emotionally (or physically) dangerous. But abnormal anxiety is often a result of imaginary problems and dangers, or an overreaction to real problems and dangers. Directive and supportive psychotherapy and antianxiety drugs are most commonly used to alleviate above-normal anxiety.

Assertive training—A method in psychotherapy used primarily with patients who have a history of withdrawing from threatening or challenging situations—i.e., the overly passive patient whose passivity has proved to be a problem in relationships with others. Generally, the patient is "trained" through direct, supportive, or behavior modification therapy to "assert" himself in gradually more threatening situations.

Aversive therapy—A form of behavior modification therapy that conditions the patient to associate strong rejecting feelings toward his undesirable behavior, thereby eliminating it. This technique has limited applications. See *Behavior modification*.)

Behavior modification—A type of psychotherapy that does not delve into the patient's "unconscious" for motivations and repressed emotions, but regards the patient's inappropriate behavior as a "bad habit." Approval by the therapist, or other types of rewards, are given for appropriate behavior. Used in treating phobias, anxieties, passivity, overaggressiveness, smoking. The goal is to "extinct"—do away with—the faulty responses of a patient, which have been a source of distress for him. The therapist need not be a psychiatrist (M.D.) to practice behavior modification.

Biochemistry—The study of chemical reactions in living organisms. Our bodies have very specific chemicals, and the way they react with one another is important to good physical and mental health. Our bodies' chemicals can only react with one another if there are catalysts present; the necessary catalysts are enzymes (substances produced by our cells). There are perhaps several thousand different enzymes, and each one is responsible for a specific chemical reaction. In psychiatry, there is increasing evidence that mental illness might be caused by poor chemical reactions in the body: hence, the biochemical approach to mental illness.

Bioenergetics—A therapy mode established by Dr. Alexander Lowen, M.D., using physical exercise and massage to release tensions in the body that have been built up from emotional distress and anxiety. Bioenergetics is based on the assumption that "negative" emotional energy becomes trapped in the muscles and nerves of the body, and that releasing these physical tensions will result in releasing emotional pain.

Biofeedback—A method of controlling mental states and bodily processes once thought to be involuntary by the use of electronic monitoring devices which indicate when the desired state is active.

Cardiac output—Literally, heartbeat. The rate of cardiac output is based on the number of times your heart beats per minute.

Client-centered therapy—A psychotherapeutic mode established in the 1940s by Carl Rogers in which the therapist asks the patient questions to clarify the patient's problems. The therapist neither judges the patient nor directs him (tells him what to do), but allows the patient to arrive at his own solutions after talking his problems out. Known also as non-directive therapy.

Depression—In psychiatry, a morbid, uncontrollable sadness, dejection, and often an inability to move physically. A withdrawal from outside affairs and activities. Most people have depressive states normally—a lowering of feelings, a detachedness, often as a reaction to something that has happened to them. If this type of depression persists too long, it can become neurotic, and is then known as reactive depression. The other type of depression, found among more severely disturbed and possible psychotic people is called endogenous depression; it has no external cause and is not a reaction to something that has happened. The latter type of depression, many now believe, has a basis in the person's faulty biochemistry. (See also *Manic-depressive psychosis*.)

Directive therapy—A general term describing a psychotherapy in which the therapist advises the patient in specific areas of his or her life. (See also *Supportive psychotherapy*.)

Eclectic therapy—Drawing from many sources, the eclectic therapist selects what appears to be best for the patient from various modes of psychotherapy.

ECT—(See *Electroshock treatment*)

Elavil—(See *Psychotherapeutic drugs: antidepressant drugs*.)

Electroshock treatment—Known also as electroconvulsive therapy, a form of therapy used to treat schizophrenia, manic-depressive psychosis, and other severe mental disturbances. During treatment the patient is rendered unconscious by electric shock; a small electric current is passed through the patient's brain, producing a convulsion. Though authorities are uncertain exactly why or how electroshock therapy works, it does seem to reduce psychotic symptoms in the patient. Not in extensive use today, and illegal in some states.

Encounter group therapy—A "newer" mode of psychotherapy conducted in a group, usually over a short but intense period of time (one entire weekend—hence, weekend-marathon group). Based on the assumption that people will confront each other intimately, aggressively, hostilely, and through these intense encounters (which may or may not include physical interaction), become less fearful of others, and more open and honest emotionally. Not generally recommended as therapy for severely troubled people.

Esalen-based therapy—A form of encounter therapy that originated at the Esalen Institute. (See Gestalt therapy.)

EST—Initials for Erhard Seminar Training, a "newer" therapy developed by Jack Rosenberg, who changed his name to Werner Erhard. EST was founded in 1972 by Rosenberg/Erhard, and is a self-help group technique employing a westernized version of Zen, some authoritarianism, and aspects of Transactional Analysis in two marathon-weekend sessions. The goal is apparently to enable people to shed their inappropriate and self-defeating behavior and beliefs. Seriously troubled people are not advised or encouraged to participate.

Existential analysis—Known also as existential psychoanalysis, this therapeutic mode was developed by R. D. Laing of London and his colleague David Cooper. In very general terms, the existential analyst denies the concept of insanity or mental illness and tries to help the patient overcome his or her fear of the judgments of others, and to live in the present for him/herself.

Galvanic Skin Response (GSR)—The amount of resistance the skin has to a current of electricity. The less electricity that can pass through your skin, the more emotionally stable you are. When a person is under stress, is nervous and anxious, his GSR decreases—that is, more electricity can be conducted by the skin. Used as a measurement in lie-dector tests; if a person is lying, it is assumed his skin resistance will go down, and this can be measured by instruments.

Genetic psychiatry—The doctrine that mental, emotional, or behavioral disorders are based on hereditary factors and are not the result of traumatic experience.

Gestalt therapy—A therapeutic method developed and made popular by Frederick S. Perls, formerly of Esalen in Big Sur, California. The basic idea behind Gestalt therapy is to help the patient "close his/her Gestalt"—that is, to resolve an early trauma that has continued to upset the patient throughout his/her life. Very often, this is brought about by acting out childhood scenes in a group with other patients. The word Gestalt literally means "the formation," or "the whole."

Haldol—(See *Psychotherapeutic drugs: antipsychotic drugs.*)

Hypertension—High blood pressure. A person may suffer from hypertension because of a physical disease such as kidney inflammation, or because he has "essential hypertension—hypertension with no other physical cause. The latter is divided into benign and malignant hypertension. The first has fewer, less dramatic symptoms and may be alleviated and controlled; the second is rarer and leads to rapid body deterioration. Stress and anxiety can lead to benign hypertension.

Hyperventilation—An excessive rate and depth of respiration leading to abnormal loss of carbon dioxide from the blood. The condition results from anxiety.

Hypno-drama—Acting out one's fears and fantasies through the use of hypnosis supervised by the therapist.

Hypnotherapy—(See *Hypno-drama.*)

Hypoglycemia—A physical state wherein a person's level of sugar in the blood is too low. The usual cause of hypoglycemia is too much insulin (a hormone formed by the body's pancreas); diabetics, who must take insulin to maintain a normal biochemical balance, are prone to hypoglycemia if they take too much of the insulin. Because blood sugar is used as fuel for the brain, a shortage of blood sugar can result in emotional disturbances: restlessness, depression, and the inability to think clearly.

Insulin therapy—A form of shock treatment, in which the patient is given a large dose of the hormone insulin to produce convulsive shock. Authorities do not know exactly how or why insulin therapy works, but it alleviates the symptoms of schizophrenia, manic-depressive psychosis, and severe depression. (See also *Electroshock therapy* and *Metrazol therapy.*)

Mania—Excitement manifested by mental and physical hyperactivity, disorganization of behavior, and elevation of mood; specifically, the manic phase of manic-depressive psychosis.

Manic-depressive psychosis—Also known as manic-depressive reaction, one of the two serious mental disturbances. (The other is schizophrenia.) Most commonly, the illness has two phases: The depressed phase, during which the patient suffers depression of mood, and a slowing down of thinking and activity; and the manic phase, which is characterized by extreme activity, exaggerated elation, and an extreme speeding up of thinking. (See *Psychotherapeutic drugs: antimanic-depressive drugs.*)

MAO inhibitors—(See *Psychotherapeutic drugs: antidepressant drugs.*)

Megavitamins—Ultra high-potency vitamins given in specified amounts to overcome a patient's deficiency in specific nutrients. Large doses of such vitamins as Niacin, Niacinimide, and other B-vitamins seem to alleviate the symptoms of schizophrenia in many cases, leading megavitamin therapists to suspect that schizophrenics suffer peculiar Niacin deficiencies.

Metabolism—The biochemical process by which food is turned into substances that the various cells of the body can use for growth. In metabolism, the body catabolizes—breaks down food into usable chemicals —and anabolizes—produces new body cells from the usable chemicals.

Metrazol therapy—A drug-induced shock therapy in little use today; formerly used to treat symptoms of severe depression and/or schizophrenia. Metrazol is the trade name for a drug that stimulates the blood circulation and causes shock or convulsion in the patient.

Milieu therapy—Psychotherapy that involves the patient in situations he or she encounters in everyday life: an occupation, household chores, and social activity. Depending upon the facility from which milieu therapy is conducted, the patient's environment can be very controlled and simulated or extend entirely to the "outside" work and social situations; in the latter case, the patient is usually treated as an out-patient.

Minimal brain-damaged child—A child who acts as if he is brain-injured but in whom no evidence of physical damage can be found. A widely used term in the 1960's, it is now frequently considered too vague to be useful.

Misogyny—Having or showing a hatred and distrust of women.

Nardil—(See *Psychotherapeutic Drugs: antidepressant drugs.*)

Neuropathology—The study of abnormal and usually degenerative states of the nerves or nervous system.

Neurosis—A functional nervous disorder based on emotional conflict in which an impulse that has been blocked seeks expression in a disguised response or symptom. (See *Psychoneurosis.*) It is thought that, to some degree, everyone is afflicted with neurosis.

Obsessive-compulsive reaction—An apparently irrational action that is repeated often and that results in anxiety if it is not repeated. The reaction begins with an obsession, a persistent, unwanted idea, and ends in the compulsion, the urge to follow through with the idea, which is often contrary to the person's will and values. Examples: repetitive handwashing, repetitive scratching, repetitive and unsatisfying eating.

Ontological—Relating to or based upon being or existence.

Operant conditioning—In psychotherapy, a form of behavior therapy. Through being given rewards or approval for appropriate behavior the patient is taught to respond to everyday circumstances in a normal way. Used often with children. Effective also in treating phobias, extreme passivity. (See also *Behavior modification.*)

Orthomolecular psychiatry—Literally, psychiatry that practices the correction of a patient's molecules. Orthomolecular psychiatry is commonly used to indicate therapy that involves adjusting one's body chemistry through medications and especially megavitamins to overcome deficiencies that seem to cause certain psychotic illnesses.

Parnate- -(See *Psychotherapeutic drugs: antidepressant drugs.*)

Pathological—Deviating from the normal—diseased.

Phobia—An apparently irrational fear of an object or class of objects. A phobia is considered a neurotic reaction. Phobias can also include fears of types of situations, such as the fear of being in high places (acrophobia), the fear of being in open, large spaces (agoraphobia), or in closed spaces (claustrophobia).

Postpartum depression—A psychoneurotic or emotional disorder occurring after giving birth; the condition is marked by sadness, inactivity, difficulty in thinking or concentrating, and feelings of dejection.

Proprietary homes—Privately owned and managed homes for mental patients.

Psychic states—States of mind or conditions of perception.

Psychoanalysis—A method of treating emotional disorders that emphasizes the importance of the patient's talking freely about himself while under treatment. Dreams and early childhood experiences are considered and analyzed.

Psychoneurosis—Known also as simply neurosis, one of any number of minor emotional disorders which can include simple but minor depressiveness, simple but minor phobias, simple but minor anxiety, nervousness, and compulsiveness. Neurosis is clearly distinct from psychosis in that the patient suffering a neurosis can think and function normally. Most authorities agree that no real line can be drawn between "normal" persons and persons suffering from a neurosis.

Psychopath(ic)—A person whose actions and thoughts are contrary to and unacceptable to the society in which he lives. Officially defined by the Mental Health Act of 1959 in England, a psychopathic disorder "results in abnormally aggressive behavior or seriously irresponsible conduct." It does not necessarily involve below-average or above-average intelligence.

Psychosis—Severe mental illness. Today, two general classes of psychoses are agreed upon: manic-depressive psychosis and schizophrenia. Both require psychiatric treatment and, often, hospitalization. Although there are no proven cures for either psychosis, their symptoms may be alleviated through medications (see *Psychotherapeutic drugs*). Generally, psychosis is distinct from neurosis in that the psychotic patient is out of touch with reality and cannot function normally in everyday life. Ordinary powers of logic and reasoning usually are impaired.

Psychosomatic disorder—Any illness in which the emotions cause (or seem to cause) physical illness. More and more doctors are finding that most physical illnesses that attack the digestive system are related to emotional distress. Some common psychosomatic disorders include: peptic ulcers, ulcerative colitis, duodenal ulcers, and most likely, high blood pressure. Emotional distress can also affect the working of certain of the body's glands, such as the pituitary gland, which secretes hormones that control one's growth.

Psychotherapeutic drugs: antianxiety drugs—Known also as minor tranquilizers, these drugs are commonly prescribed by either psychiatrists or general practitioners to relieve minor symptoms of depression, tension, anxiety, irritability, and emotional distress. Studies by the National Institute of Mental Health and the Veterans Administration show that antianxiety drugs relieve symptoms in at least half the patients receiving them. Most commonly prescribed by trade name (generic name in parentheses): Valium (diazepam); Librium (chlordiazepoxide); Serax (oxazepam); Equanil (meprobamate); Miltown (meprobamate); Solacen (tybamate); Tybatran (tybamate); Atarax (hydroxyzine); and Vistaril (hydroxyzine). Some of the most commonly reported side effects of the various antianxiety drugs include drowsiness, upset stomach, allergic reactions (usually a skin rash), and loss of coordination. Patients taking these drugs are warned not to take sedatives, antihistamines, or drink alcohol while on them; addiction is a possible hazard.

antidepressant drugs—Unlike antianxiety drugs, these are *not* tranquilizers; they are prescribed, primarily by psychiatrists, to depressive patients and although they tend to stimulate the central nervous system, they may have a sedative side effect. Antidepressant drugs are most effective in treating endogenous depression and reactive depression. There are two main types of antidepressant drugs:

(A) THE TRICYCLIC DERIVATIVES: By trade name (with generic name in parentheses): Elavil (amitriptyline); Norpramin (desipramine); Pertofrane (desipramine); Tofranil (imipramine); and Aventyl (nortriptyline) Triavil. Authorities consider these the safest, overall. Some commonly reported side effects include dryness of the mouth and above-normal sweating.

(B) THE MAO INHIBITORS: By trade name (with generic name in parentheses): Marplan (isocarboxazid); Nardil (phenelzine); and Parnate (tranylcypromine). This type of antidepressant drug suppresses the body's production of the MAO (monoamine oxidase) enzyme, a substance which many authorities feel is the cause of depression when there is too much of it. MAO inhibitors are usually prescribed when the tricyclic derivatives do not show results with patients. There are possible adverse side effects such as raised blood pressure if they are taken when the patient is on other drugs.

All antidepressants have side effects, and doctors generally do not prescribe them to people with heart disease, certain types of glaucoma, or prostate gland trouble.

antimanic-depressive drugs: At present there is only one type of drug that is used to control manic-depressive illness—lithium. A lithium carbonate derivative, its trade names are Lithonate, Eskalith, and Lithane. Lithium controls both the depressive and the manic phases of the illness under proper use. Some possible side effects include impaired thyroid gland activity (hypothyroidism), excessive urination, and high blood sugar. Lithium will not produce drowsiness, and is not addictive.

antipsychotic drugs—These include the major tranquilizers and are used to control schizophrenia and any of the major symptoms of schizophrenia: delusions, intense hostility or belligerence, hallucinations, extreme paranoia, emotional withdrawal, and inappropriate emotional responses. None of the antipsychotic drugs cure schizophrenia or its symptoms, but they do control them and have been largely responsible for the decrease in hospitalizations among schizophrenics in the past twenty years. There are three types of antipsychotic drugs: the phenothiazines, the butyrophenones, and the thioxanthenes. By trade name (with generic name in parentheses) the phenothiazines are Thorazine (chloropromazine); Permitil (fluphenazine); Trilafon (perphenazine); and Stelazine (trifluoperazine). The butyrophenone is Haldol (haloperidol). The thioxanthenes are Taractan (chlorprothixene) and Navane (thiothixene). These drugs are not used to alleviate minor anxieties, but prescribed only to psychotic patients. Some of their most prevalent side effects include: slurred speech, drowsiness, trembling of the hands, restlessness, and some of the symptoms of Parkinson's Disease (jerkiness, tremors). Anti-Parkinson's Disease drugs are often prescribed as an adjunct if these side effects occur. Antipsychotic drugs are not addictive.

Psychotherapy—Treatment of mental or emotional disorders (or of related bodily ills) by psychological means.

Recidivism—The tendency to relapse into a previous condition or mode of behavior; in the case of hospitalized mental patients who have been released into society, to fall back into a state that necessities rehospitalization.

Regimen—A set of rules and/or medications established by a doctor for treating an illness.

Reichian analysis—A psychotherapeutic mode based upon the writings and techniques of Wilhelm Reich, which draws upon both Freud's theories of sexuality and the ideals of Karl Marx. Basically, Reichian analysis assumes that the type of society a person lives in affects his sexuality and therefore his emotional problems. An oppressive society is the instrument of repressed, and therefore misused, and misunderstood, sexuality.

Remission—A usually temporary lessening or total lack of one or more symptoms of a mental (or physical) disorder.

Rolfing—A psychotherapeutic method developed by Ida Rolfe. Described generally as a massage technique, Rolfing masseurs use their knuckles and fists in an almost violent massage method to release negative energy that has accumulated in the body's muscles from emotional distress. The Rolfer is specially trained and "Rolfs" all areas of the body. (See also *Bioenergetics*.) Often practiced in groups.

Schizophrenia—One of the two serious mental disturbances. (The other is manic-depressive psychosis.) Literally, the term means "split," but in psychiatry the "split" is a split from reality; schizophrenia is often used popularly to indicate a split personality because of the literal translation of the term. A schizophrenic generally makes no differentiation between fantasy and reality—both are real to him. Delusions, hallucinations, aggressiveness, and hostility are among the major symptoms of this psychosis; other symptoms may be withdrawal and passivity to the point of total inactivity (seeming paralysis, known as catatonia), complete inability to speak clearly, severe depression, and an apparently total return to childhood behavior. Although no cause for schizophrenia has been determined, there is increasing evidence to suggest that it is caused by a lack of specific chemicals in the body (or an overabundance of others). (See also *Psychotherapeutic drugs: antipsychotic drugs*.)

Self-actualization—Formally, the process of getting to know yourself fully, learning and developing your talents and intelligence. Abraham Maslow, the twentieth-century psychologist and philosopher, developed the most commonly used ideas of self-actualization. To become self-actualized, according to his writings, one must get rid of his/her false ideas about him/himself, learn to identify and then do away with defenses, choose experiences that lead to growth rather than those that only seem safe, and learn to be honest with oneself. A self-actualized person is able to become devoted to things other than him/herself and use his-her talents to the fullest. In laymen's terms, a self-actualized person is an unselfishly self-fulfilled person.

Shock treatment/therapy—(See *Insulin therapy; Metrazol therapy; Electroshock treatment.*)

Supportive psychotherapy—A usually short-term psychotherapy in which the therapist supports and advises the patient when the patient is suffering from a distressing event in his/her life or from an acute episode. During supportive psychotherapy, the patient is relieved of his symptoms through the therapists' direct intervention in his/her life; the therapist acts as a protective parent and allows the patient complete dependency for the duration of the therapy. (See also *Directive psychotherapy.*)

Thorazine—(See *Psychotherapeutic drugs: antipsychotic drugs.*)

Tofranil—(See *Psychotherapeutic drugs: antidepressant drugs.*)

Transactional analysis—A therapeutic mode developed by Eric S. Berne that helps people understand and deal with the three basic states of mind: the parent state, the child state, and the adult state. It assumes that each person has these three states and that one's problems are often because the three states are in conflict.

Transcendental meditation—Based on an Eastern religious discipline, it has been discovered that TM can offer relaxation and distance from, or perspective on, psychological problems. As a tool for helping the mildly neurotic, it has had useful applications.

Tricyclic antidepressants—(See *Psychotherapeutic drugs: antidepressant drugs.*)

Trilafon—(See *Psychotherapeutic drugs: antipsychotic drugs.*)

APPENDIX A
Mental health associations

I. The National Institute of Mental Health
For specific information on public and private mental health facilities in your area, you may write or call your regional office of the National Institute of Mental Health (NIMH). The NIMH operates under the auspices of the federal Department of Health, Education and Welfare. In this listing, the states that fall into each region are given first, then the address of the regional office.

Region I

Connecticut
Maine
Massachusetts
New Hampshire
Rhode Island
Vermont

John F. Kennedy Federal Bldg.
Boston, Mass. 02203
(617) 223-6824
Associate Regional Director:
  Anne L. Twomey

Region II

New York
New Jersey
Puerto Rico

26 Federal Plaza
New York, N.Y. 10007
(212) 264-2567
Associate Regional Director:
  Jessie P. Dowling

Region III

Delaware
Maryland
Pennsylvania
Virginia
Washington, D.C.
West Virginia
3521-35 Market Street
Philadelphia, Pa. 19106
(215) 597-6682
Associate Regional Director:
  Richard Sanders, Ph.D

Region IV

Alabama
Florida
Georgia
Kentucky
Mississippi
North Carolina
South Carolina
Tennessee
50 Seventh Street, N.W.
(Rm. 423)
Atlanta, Ga. 30323
(404) 526-5231
Associate Regional Director:
  William D. Wright

Region V

Indiana
Illinois
Michigan
Minnesota
Ohio
Wisconsin
300 Wacker Drive, 33rd Floor
Chicago, Ill. 60606
(312) 353-1700
Associate Regional Director:
  Howard L. Siple, Ph.D.

Region VI

Arkansas
Louisiana
New Mexico
Oklahoma
Texas
1114 Commerce Street
Dallas, Tex. 75202
(214) 749-3426
Associate Regional Director:
  Kathryn M. Fritz

Region VII

Iowa
Kansas
Missouri
Nebraska
601 East 12th Street
Kansas City, Mo. 64106
(816) 374-5291
Acting Associate Regional
Director:
  Elizabeth D. Ossario

Region VIII

Colorado
Montana
North Dakota
South Dakota
Utah
Wyoming
Federal Office Bldg. (Rm. 9017)
1961 Stout Street
Denver, Colo. 80202
(303) 837-3177
Acting Associate Regional
Director:
  Theodore E. Fasso

Region IX	**Region X**
American Samoa	
Arizona	
California	Alaska
Guam	Idaho
Hawaii	Oregon
Nevada	Washington
Wake Island	
Federal Office Bldg.	1321 Second Avenue (Rm. 5082)
50 Fulton Street	Arcade Plaza MS 509
San Francisco, Cal. 94102	Seattle, Wash. 98101
(415) 556-2215	(206) 442-0542
Associate Regional Director:	Associate Regional Director:
Frank M. Ochberg, M.D.	*David N. Hanson*

II. Voluntary Mental Health Organizations
The following listing gives voluntary organizations for mental health as they are listed by the NIMH. These organizations are nongovernmental (private) and may be asked for information about public and private facilities in your state, to supplement information from the NIMH.

National (NAMH)

The National Association for Mental Health
1800 North Kent St.
Rosslyn, Va. 22209

Affiliated state organizations to NAMH

The Alabama Association for Mental Health, Inc.
P.O. Box 3283, 901 Eighteenth St.
South Birmingham, Ala. 35205

Alaska Mental Health Association
1135 W. Eighth St.
Anchorage, Alaska 99501

Arizona Association for Mental Health, Inc.
341 W. McDowell Rd.
Phoenix, Ariz. 85003

The Arkansas Association for Mental Health, Inc.
424 E. Sixth St.
Little Rock, Ark. 72202

California Association for Mental Health
901 "H" Street, Suite 212
Sacramento, Cal. 95814

Colorado Association for Mental Health, Inc.
1375 Delaware St.
Denver, Colo. 80204

Connecticut Association for Mental Health, Inc.
123 Tremont St.
Hartford, Conn. 06105

Mental Health Association of Delaware, Inc.
701 Shipley St.
Wilmington, Del. 19801

District of Columbia Mental Health Association, Inc.
3000 Connecticut Avenue, N.W., Suite 108
Washington, D.C. 20008

Mental Health Association of Florida, Inc.
Suite 207, Myrick Bldg., 132 E. Colonial Dr.
Orlando, Fla. 32801

The Georgia Association for Mental Health, Inc.
230 Peachtree St., N.W., Suite 214
Atlanta, Ga. 30303

The Mental Health Association of Hawaii
200 N. Vineyard Blvd., Suite 101
Honolulu, Hawaii 96817

Idaho Mental Health Association
3105 ½ State St.
Boise, Idaho 83703

Illinois Association for Mental Health, Inc.
710 Reisch Bldg., Lincoln Sq.
Springfield, Ill. 62701

The Mental Health Association in Indiana
1433 N. Meridian St.
Indianapolis, Ind. 46202

The Iowa Association for Mental Health, Inc.
521 14th Street
Des Moines, Iowa 50309

Kansas Association for Mental Health, Inc.
4015 West 21st St.
Topeka, Kan. 66604

The Kentucky Association for Mental Health, Inc.
Suite 104, 310 West Liberty St.
Louisville, Ky. 40202

The Louisiana Association for Mental Health
1528 Jackson Ave.
New Orleans, La. 70130

Maryland Association for Mental Health, Inc.
325 East 25th St.
Baltimore, Md. 21218

The Massachusetts Association for Mental Health, Inc.
38 Chauncy St., Room 801
Boston, Mass. 02111

Michigan Society for Mental Health, Inc.
27208 Southfield Rd.
Lathrup Village, Mich. 48075

Minnesota Association for Mental Health, Inc.
4510 W. 77th St., Room 100
Minneapolis, Minn. 55435

Mississippi Association for Mental Health, Inc.
902-904 Standard Life Bldg., Box 2081
Jackson, Miss. 39205

Missouri Association for Mental Health
411 Madison St.
Jefferson City, Mo. 65101

Montana Association for Mental Health
324 Fuller Ave.
Helena, Mont. 59601

Nebraska Association for Mental Health
c/o Reverend James Green, President
719 Sixth St.
Fairbury, Neb. 68532

Nevada Association for Mental Health
c/o Sister Marie Brigid, President
Rose de Lima Hospital
Lake Mead Dr.
Henderson, Nev. 89015

The New Jersey Association for Mental Health, Inc.
60 South Fullerton Ave.
Montclair, N.J. 07042

Mental Health Association of New Mexico, Inc.
P.O. Drawer R
Sante Fe, N.M. 87501

The New York State Association for Mental Health, Inc.
Executive Park North
Stuyvesent Plaza
Albany, N.Y. 12203

North Carolina Mental Health Association
425 North Boylan Ave.
Raleigh, N.C. 27603

North Dakota Mental Health Association
P.O. Box 160
Bismarck, N.D. 58501

Mental Health Federation, Inc. (Ohio Division)
Neil House-M-59
Columbus, Ohio 43215

Oklahoma Mental Health Association
3113 Classen Blvd.
Oklahoma City, Okla. 73118

Mental Health Association of Oregon
718 W. Burnside St., Room 301
Portland, Ore. 97209

Pennsylvania Mental Health, Inc.
1207 Chestnut St.
Philadelphia, Pa. 19107

Rhode Island Association for Mental Health, Inc.
333 Grotto Ave.
Providence, R.I. 02906

South Carolina Mental Health Association
1823 Gadsden St.
Columbia, S.C. 29201

South Dakota Mental Health Association
101½ S. Pierre St., Box 355
Pierre, S.D. 57501

Tennessee Mental Health Association
1717 West End Bldg., Suite 421
Nashville, Tenn. 37203

The Texas Association for Mental Health
107 Lantern Lane
Austin, Tex. 78731

Utah Association for Mental Health
211 East Third South, Suite 212
Salt Lake City, Utah 84111

The Virginia Association for Mental Health, Inc.
2 North First St.
Richmond, Va. 23219

Washington Association for Mental Health
c/o Mrs. Ruth Coffin, President
1308 S. 72nd Avenue
Yakima, Wash. 98902

The West Virginia Association for Mental Health, Inc.
815 Quarrier St.
418 Morrison Bldg.
Charleston, W. Va. 25301

Wisconsin Association for Mental Health
119 E. Mifflin St.
P.O. Box 1486
Madison, Wis. 53701

Wyoming Association for Mental Health
c/o Mrs. Norman Stark, President
1417 W. Sixth St.
Cheyenne, Wyo. 82001

Unaffiliated State Organization

Vermont Association for Mental Health, Inc.
P.O. Box 165
Montpelier, Vt. 05602

III. Self-Help Organizations for Mental Health

Alcoholics Anonymous
P.O. Box 459
Grand Central Annex
New York, N.Y. 10017

American Schizophrenia Association
Suite 805
56 West 45th St.
New York, N.Y. 10036

Gamblers Anonymous
National Service Office
P.O. Box 17173
Los Angeles, Cal. 90017

Neurotics Anonymous
Colorado Building
1341 G Street, N.W.
Washington, D.C. 20005

Parents Without Partners
International Headquarters
7910 Woodmont Ave.
Bethesda, Md. 20014

Patient Advocacy Legal Service
Washington University Law School
St. Louis, Mo. 63130

Recovery, Inc.
116 South Michigan Ave.
Chicago, Ill. 60603

APPENDIX B
Addresses of facilities and organizations

New York University Medical Center
University Hospital
Department of Psychiatry
560 First Ave.
New York, N.Y. 10016

The Menninger Foundation
P.O. Box 829
Topeka, Kansas 66601

Columbia-Presbyterian Medical Center
Atchley Pavillion
161 Fort Washington Ave.
New York, N.Y. 10032

The Casriel Institute of Group Dynamics
(AREBA)
47 East 51 Street
New York, N.Y. 10022

International Meditation Society (TM)
Wentworth Building
59 W. 46th St.
New York, N.Y. 10036

Karen Horney Clinic
329 East 62nd St.
New York, N.Y. 10021

Fountain House
425 West 47th St.
New York, N.Y. 10036

Institute for Self-Awareness
c/o Father Lloyd
St. Paul the Apostle Church
415 W. 59th St.
New York, N.Y. 10019

Recovery, Inc.
1515 Lexington Ave.
New York, N.Y. 10029

Mental Patients' Liberation
Project (MPLP)
56 East 4th St.
New York, N.Y. 10003

Mental Health Law Project
c/o The American Civil Liberties Union
New York
84 Fifth Ave.
New York, N.Y. 10011

The Psychiatric Institute
Department of Mental Hygiene
(New York State)
722 West 168th St.
New York, N.Y. 10032

INDEX